THE
LAST
WHALERS

THE
LAST
WHALERS

THREE YEARS IN THE FAR PACIFIC
WITH A COURAGEOUS TRIBE
AND A VANISHING WAY OF LIFE

DOUG BOCK CLARK

(L)(B)

Little, Brown and Company
New York   Boston   London

Little, Brown and Company
Hachette Book Group
1290 Avenue of the Americas, New York, NY 10104
littlebrown.com

First Edition: January 2019

Little, Brown and Company is a division of Hachette Book Group, Inc. The Little, Brown name and logo are trademarks of Hachette Book Group, Inc.

The publisher is not responsible for websites (or their content) that are not owned by the publisher.

Map of Lembata by Jeffrey Ward
Map of the Eastern Lesser Sunda Islands copyright © by Jean R. Weiner, originally published in Lundberg (2001), "Being Lost at Sea," and in PhD thesis Lundberg (2000), "Lamaleraland: Tales of Whales and Whale Hunters."

The Hachette Speakers Bureau provides a wide range of authors for speaking events. To find out more, go to hachettespeakersbureau.com or call (866) 376-6591.

ISBN 978-0-316-39062-0
LCCN 2018952824

10 9 8 7 6 5 4 3 2 1

LSC-C

Printed in the United States of America

For all the Lamalerans,
past and present,
especially those who appear in these pages,
and for BKB, R.I.P.

Tenang-tenang mendayung,	Row calmly, row tranquilly,
Didalam ombak selepas pantai.	As the waves are loosed upon the shore.
Tenang-tenang merenung,	Daydream calmly, daydream tranquilly,
Ditengah taufan hidup yang ramai,	In the middle of the typhoon of life,
Ditengah taufan hidup yang ramai.	In the middle of the typhoon of life.

—Hymn sung during Misa Arwah, the Mass for Lost Souls

For by Art is created that great Leviathan called a Common-wealth, or State, (in latine Civitas) which is but an Artificiall Man; though of greater stature and strength than the Naturall.

— Thomas Hobbes, *Leviathan,* 1651

CONTENTS

Contents

Part Three
2016

THE LAMALERANS

The Hariona Family

Yohanes "Jon" Demon Hariona: A young man striving to become a harpooner, custodian of the motorboat *VJO*

Fransiska "Ika" Bribin Hariona: His younger sister

Yosef Boko Hariona: His grandfather

Fransiska "Grandmother" Bribin Hariona: His grandmother

Lusia Sipa Hariona: His mother

Maria "Mari" Hariona: His youngest sister

The Seran Blikololong Family

Ignatius Seran Blikololong: Renowned harpooner and shipwright, trying to teach his sons his trades

Teresea Palang Hariona: His wife

Yosef Tubé Blikololong: His eldest son

Willibrodus "Ondu" Boeang Demon Blikololong III: His middle son

Benyamin "Ben" Kleka Blikololong: His youngest son

Maria "Ela" Hermina Elisabeth Began Blikololong: His youngest daughter

The Mikulangu Bediona Clan

Fransiskus "Frans" Boli Bediona: Head of the Mikulangu lineage of the Bediona clan, shaman, and captain of *Kéna Pukā*

Maria Kleka Blikololong: His wife, younger sister of Ignatius Seran Blikololong

Bernadette "Bena" Bediona: His youngest child

Andreus "Anso" Soge Bediona: His younger relation and Jon Hariona's fishing partner

The Wujon Family

Siprianus "Sipri" Raja Wujon: Head of the Wujon clan, a Lord of the Land

Marsianus Dua Wujon: His son, also a Lord of the Land

Other Lamalerans

Yosef "Ote" Klake Bataona: Friend of Jon Hariona, sometime harpooner of *Kéna Pukā* and *VJO*

Fransiskus Gonsalés "Salés" Usé Bataona: Patron of Jon Hariona, owner of *VJO*, businessman, and former mayor of Lamalera

Aloysius Enga "Alo" Kĕrofa: Boyfriend of Ika Hariona

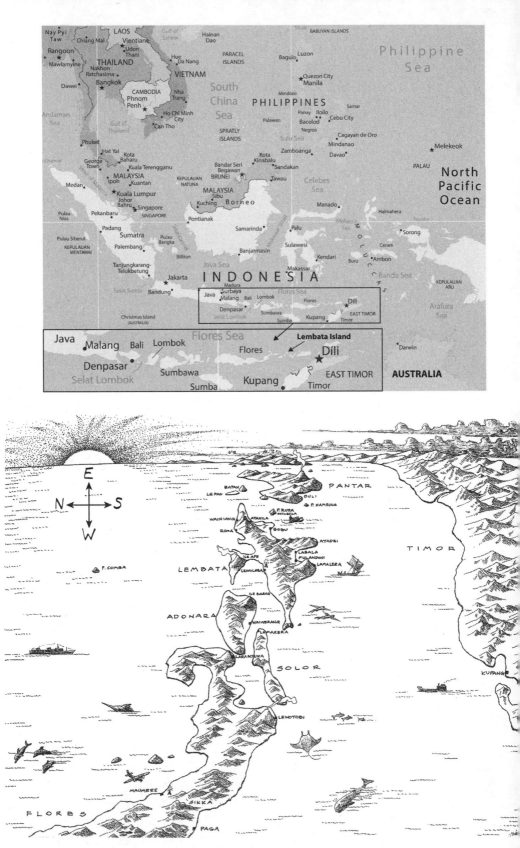

Solor Archipelago

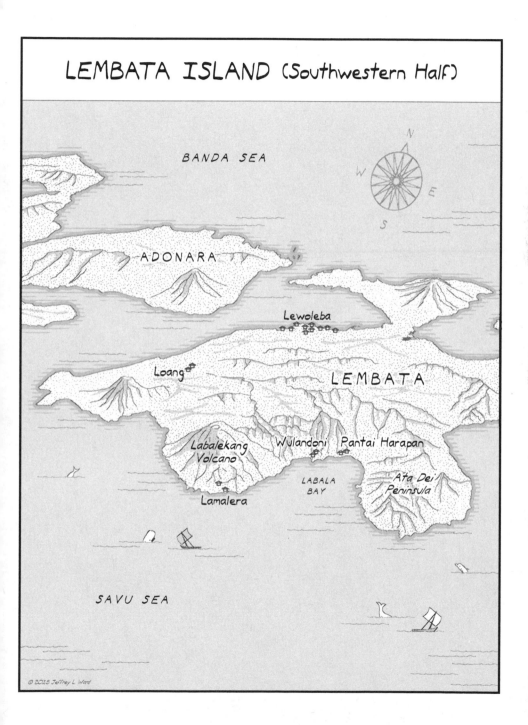

LEMBATA ISLAND (Southwestern Half)

BANDA SEA

ADONARA

Lewoleba

Loang

LEMBATA

Labalekang
Volcano

Wulandoni   Pantai Harapan

LABALA
BAY

Ata Dei
Peninsula

Lamalera

SAVU SEA

© 2018 Jeffrey L. Ward

Lamalera Beach

A Note on the Text

This is a true story. I witnessed many of these events. Scenes that I did not observe were reconstructed from interviews with participants and, when available, historical records. When accounts diverged on minor points, especially regarding hectic events like a hunt, I privileged the view of the person whose perspective frames the passage. When there were major differences of opinion about an occurrence, I made this explicit in the text. Notes to sources can be found at the end of this book. For rendering thoughts, feelings, or spiritual experiences, such as the Lamalerans' communion with their Ancestors, I relied on the testimony of participants. Dialogue in quotation marks represents, most often, words I heard or, occasionally, words that were reconstructed by participants. All other speech is paraphrased. As with hunting a sperm whale, this book is the work of a village.

THE
LAST
WHALERS

THE APPRENTICE'S LESSON

June 27, 2014

Jon

Baleo! Baleo!—"The hunt is on!" The cry resounded through the village. A minute before, a motorboat had raced into the bay, and its crew had screamed the signal to the men on the beach, who themselves had taken up the cry. Now every man, woman, and child who had heard their alarm was adding a voice to the shouted relay, until all fifteen hundred souls in the ramshackle houses and surrounding jungle chorused that the sperm whales had been sighted.

When the clamor reached Yohanes "Jon" Demon Hariona in the decaying home he shared with his grandparents and sisters on the cliffs above Lamalera, he grabbed a baseball cap with frayed threads tasseling its brim, a battered plastic water jug, and a pill bottle stuffed with tobacco confetti and dried palm-leaf rolling papers. Then he dashed down steps chiseled into the stone of this Indonesian island, pushing aside hallooing children as he went.

On the beach, Jon's tribesmen were already shoving the *téna,* their wooden whaling ships, across the sand and into the surf. Captains yelled exhortations at their crews. Jon set his shoulder against a thwart of *Boli Sapang,* the téna belonging to his clan, the Harionas, and strained with a dozen other men to launch it. Once the water unyoked the weight of the boat from him, he leapt aboard.

In the past, he had always manned one of the eight slim common paddles in the center of the téna, but he saw the left *befaje* oar, with its huge circular face, lying unclaimed at the prow, and raced to seize it before anyone else could. Recently engaged to be married, he fancied that he had matured beyond his twenty-two years. As the crew rowed through the breakers, he pulled the befaje oar, showing off his strength to his elders. But he had another reason for claiming the great oar: it was located directly behind the harpooner's platform, so the two befaje oarsmen were sometimes called upon to aid the harpooner. Jon had wanted to be a *lamafa,* a harpooner, all his life. There was no higher honor for a Lamaleran man.

For nearly three hours, the fourteen téna of the Lamaleran fleet chased the spouts of three young bull sperm whales across the Savu Sea, repeatedly closing in only to be saluted by the animals' flukes as they dove. Finally, Ondu Blikololong, the lamafa of Jon's téna, screamed, *Nuro menaluf!* — "Hunger spoon!" or, colloquially, "Row as fast as you'd spoon rice if you were starving!" Or perhaps most accurately, "Row like you want to feed your families!"

Ten hand-carved paddles ripped the sea in professional unison. The thirty-foot sperm whale breached ahead of them, seawater cascading from its flanks. Although the leviathan measured only about the same length as the téna, the beast outweighed their vessel by at least twenty tons.

"Row like you want to feed your families!" Ondu shouted hoarsely, balanced at the front of the téna.

A nasal boom echoed as the whale exhaled. Then droplets showered the hunters: mucous and warm, distinct from the chillier spray off the ocean, as if the whale had blown its nose in their faces. Everyone on the téna knew the animal was filling its colossal lungs for a dive that could last half an hour. Time was short.

Ondu had been holding his sixteen-foot-long bamboo harpoon

horizontally like a tightrope walker to balance himself against the unpredictable pitch, roll, and yaw of the téna. Now he turned the weapon vertical, and aimed the spearhead directly down. "Row like you want to feed your families!" he yelled once again.

Jon braced his feet against the hull and pulled his oar until a headache simmered in his skull and his chest ached. Because the befaje oar faced the stern, while the other paddlers faced forward, he had to keep glancing over his shoulder to track the whale.

Ondu crouched at the tip of the *hâmmâlollo,* the bamboo platform jutting five feet from the prow. His triceps quivered with the effort to poise the harpoon above his head. The platform edged forward, closer and closer, until his shadow dulled the sunlight glittering on the whale's sea-glossed back, until the prow almost nudged the fleeing animal, until it seemed that he would never jump. Then he dove off the hâmmâlollo with kamikaze grace, both hands choking the bamboo shaft, and rammed the weapon into his prey with his entire bodyweight. The harpoon shaft shuddered, bent, and then straightened — but Ondu kept going, rebounding off the flank of the whale and into the sea, his arms and legs flailing. The bamboo remained planted in the animal, quivering.

The sperm whale thunderclapped the ocean with its flukes. A wave swamped the bow of *Boli Sapang.* The harpoon rope zipped so fast across the railing that it smoked, and an oarsman doused it with seawater to prevent it from igniting. The line was tied from the head of the harpoon to the aft of the téna. When it ran out, it jolted the entire ship, almost hurling Jon off his oar. The hawser thinned, with water spitting from its elongating threads, and hummed as it vibrated. The téna lurched forward, plowing through the waves as the whale dragged it like a horse drawing a sleigh.

Jon rushed to stow his oar and help the second harpooner, Fransiskus Boko Hariona, a distant uncle, set the two safety ropes that would prevent the harpoon line from running wild. In the depths, the sperm whale reversed direction, yanking the line against the left safety rope and bending it inward until it creaked. The crew shouted as the boat spun. The whale was striving to get lower, into a deep current that could carry it to freedom.

Then Boko hollered and snatched at two lengths of rope writhing like stepped-on snakes — the left safety rope, three fingers thick, had snapped in two. Boko raced to tie together these broken halves to corral the rogue harpoon line.

In the confusion, the right safety rope had also come undone. Jon stepped over the harpoon line and reached for it. A sudden crushing pain clamped onto his right calf. The harpoon line had broken through Boko's makeshift knot and swung against the left side of the boat, pinning Jon's leg against the hull so that he was bent over the railing, as if vomiting into the sea. He twisted, trying to get a better grip on the rope, but it was as unyielding as an iron bar, drawn taut by the thirty tons straining at the other end.

Jon remained silent as the line sawed across the back of his calf, tearing off skin. He hoped he could extricate himself from this predicament before his elders noticed. Misery elongated the seconds. He lost track of time. He had never considered the old men who hobbled through the village on stump legs with anything more than a teenager's derision, but suddenly he saw that he might join their ranks. A flensing knife lay within reach. He could cut the rope and save his leg. But if the whale escaped, his clan might lack meat for months and his elders would accuse him of valuing his own life over the well-being of the tribe. No, he would have to hope the whale snapped the rope.

Boli Sapang was shaking now. The left railing tipped toward the sea. Though the ocean was calm, the ship rocked as if beset by five-foot waves, more heavily to the left with each heave. The crew mobbed to the right side of the téna to counterbalance it, but they were lofted like eleven men on the losing end of a seesaw. Only Jon remained on the left side, looking up helplessly at his clansmen. When the téna was almost vertical, the crew leapt into the water. Jon alone remained aboard, clawing at the rope, screaming. The boat capsized.

Darkness. A maelstrom of bubbles. Harpoons, ropes, knives, palm-leaf cigarettes, sharpening stones, bamboo hats, ratty T-shirts, and flip-flops — detritus of every kind sank with Jon. Above, silhouetted men kicked through flotsam and away from the overturned téna, which was being dragged beneath the surface. No matter how hard Jon stroked toward the sunlight, he still descended. Pain pulsed in his leg such that his ankle felt as if it were being twisted off. He glanced down through the murk: wound like an ampersand around his foot, tethering him to the whale diving into the abyss, was the harpoon rope. He yanked at it, but it was a rigid line, without so much as a wiggle.

At first, he feared nothing, certain that he had no sins on his heart and so his deliverance was guaranteed by the Ancestors, the spirits of past whalers whom the tribe worshipped. But he soon remembered that his Hariona clansmen had trespassed against the Ancestors and that the spirits required a sacrifice to forgive the wrong. He could feel the ghosts, risen from their seabed graves, thronging around him. He prayed to them and to Jesus that the rope would loosen, that the whale would surface.

He was an orphan, after all, and it was his responsibility to provide for his infirm grandparents and younger sisters, and soon for his fiancée. Who would bring home the whale meat if he did not? Bubbles wobbled above him. Air — *his* air, he realized, escaping his lungs. Only by somehow outpacing the whale would he be able to put enough slack in the line to untangle his foot. As his brain fizzed for lack of oxygen, he inverted himself and swam into the depths.

PART ONE

1994–2014

Chapter One

THE LAMALERAN ODYSSEY

March 10, 1994–April 1994

Frans — Ignatius — Yosef Boko — Fransiska

About five centuries ago, on the western rim of the Pacific Ocean, a tsunami obliterated the village of a band of hunter-gatherers now known as the Lamalerans. After a harrowing odyssey, the survivors built a new home on Lembata, a backwater island so remote that today other Indonesians call that corner of their nation "The Land Left Behind." The shore of Lamalera Bay is too rocky and parched to grow crops, but the newcomers soon discovered that even one of the sperm whales schooling just offshore would provide enough meat to feed everyone for weeks. To survive this harsh environment and the dangerous work, the Lamalerans evolved a unique culture that has been rated by anthropologists as one of the world's most cooperative and generous, a necessity when it comes to coordinating dozens of men to defeat colossal whales and then equitably share the bounty.

Today, the Lamalerans are among the small and ever-dwindling number of hunter-gatherer societies remaining in existence, and the only one to survive by whaling. Although the Lamalerans will harpoon anything from porpoises to orcas, their main prey are sperm whales, the largest toothed carnivore alive. The tribe's three hundred hunters take an average of twenty a year, enough to sustain all fifteen hundred of their people with the jerkied meat through the lean monsoon season, when storms make it difficult to launch their ships. While several Inuit communities also still whale, those arctic seafarers increasingly derive their sustenance from imported packaged food and mechanized fishing methods, making the Lamalerans the world's last true subsistence whalers. Indonesia is not a signatory to the International Convention for the Regulation of Whaling, but even if it were, the agreement still permits aboriginal subsistence hunts like the Lamalerans'. Moreover, several hundred thousand sperm whales survive in the wild, meaning the tribe has little impact on the animal's global population.

For hundreds of years, the hunt has been the foundation of the Lamalerans' nutrition and culture. Even as neighboring tribes have abandoned ancient occupations for modern ones, the Lamalerans have preserved their unique livelihood by limiting foreign influences, worshipping their forebears, and defending the Ways of the Ancestors, a set of whaling and religious practices handed down through the generations. Though outside ideas—Catholicism spread by Jesuit missionaries, for example—have taken root in the tribe, the ancient beliefs remain strong, and the whalers continue to practice shamanism.

But over the last two decades, the Lamalerans, like many other indigenous peoples, have been ever more pressured by the free flow of information, goods, and technology that has transformed even the remotest corners of the earth. Today, the tribe is threatened by its youth abandoning whaling to seek a modern life, by industrial trawlers overfishing its waters, by businessmen and foreign activists attempting to change its livelihood, and by internal battles over how to cope with the conundrums posed by modernity. Unless the Lamalerans can figure out how to navigate these proliferating troubles while remaining true to their identities, they confront their end.

They are not alone in this struggle. Since Europeans began colonizing other continents in the sixteenth century, an accelerating wave of cultural extinction has halved the number of cultures worldwide, with thousands lost in the last century alone and thousands more predicted to be obliterated in the next few decades. In 2009, the United Nations reported that many of humanity's 370 million indigenous people were enduring threats similar to those the Lamalerans face, for though the Lamalerans are almost unique as whalers, numerous groups still survive as herders, swidden agriculturalists, and hunter-gatherers.

The Lamalerans' experience, then, speaks not just to the danger faced by earth's remaining indigenous peoples but to the greater cultural extinction humanity is suffering. Before agriculture was invented, every human was a forager. In the transformation from our first identity to our modern one is the story of how our very nature has changed — for better and for worse. As the number of ways to be human rapidly diminishes, all people, whether in industrialized or traditional societies, must ask: What is being lost as our original modes of life die out? Who are we now? And who will we become?

As RECENTLY AS 1994, most of the outside world's threats to the Lamalerans still lay beyond the horizon. Each morning, the hunters sang prayers to the Ancestors while raising their palm-leaf sails. By early March, the squalls of the winter monsoon, during which whaling mostly pauses, had been replaced by the gray clouds that often lid the sky just before the dry season, when the hunt resumes.

On March 10 of that year, the tribesmen were pile-driving flagstones into the village's dirt road, which had liquefied during the preceding three months of rain, when someone witnessed a sperm whale body slam the Savu Sea. *Baleo! Baleo! Baleo!* echoed. They dropped their shovels and sprinted to the beach. But with so many men working on the road up and down the mountain, there were only enough within earshot to launch six of the twenty-one téna.

Ignatius Blikololong, Ondu Blikololong's father and one of the most renowned harpooners in the tribe despite his slight frame and forty-four years, bid a hasty farewell to Teresea Hariona, his wife. She was due to give birth to their next child at any hour, but a lamafa was responsible for feeding not just his family: he had to spear the prey that would be divided among his whole clan. He felt he could not shirk his duty, especially when the tribe had almost exhausted its food stores during the monsoons, waiting to hunt again. Their parting was notably emotional among the other Lamaleran couples taking their leave without fanfare, for they had endured an epic romance, star-crossed by family feuds, and remained unusually demonstrative afterwards. There was only enough time for him to nod to his seven-year-old son, Ben, before claiming the hâmmâlollo of the ship *Téti Heri*.

Yosef Boko Hariona said goodbye to his two-year-old grandson, Jon, who often howled at leave-takings since his father had abandoned him and his mother. Yosef Boko was entering his sixth decade, but he still whaled, as there was no other man to support his wife, husbandless daughter, and her children. He joined Ignatius and grabbed *Téti Heri*'s tiller oar, for though he could no longer paddle as forcefully as younger men, he could steer with savvy.

Fransiskus "Frans" Boli Bediona, a stocky thirty-six-year-old shaman with an overgrown beard and mane, impatiently took his leave from his wife, who was Ignatius's younger sister, and their three young children, pausing only to kiss the littlest, his infant daughter, Bernadette, whom he called Bena. He burned with an almost religious fervor to get hunting. Whaling connected him to the Ancestors as much as the animal sacrifices and other rituals he helped execute. He served as the backup harpooner on the téna *Kelulus*.

As the six impromptu crews chased after the white spouts contrasting against the dark waves and stormy sky, they sang. At that time, it was still the Age of Song, before outboard engines silenced the hunters. Every man joined in. As they rowed, they chorused:

Kidé ajaka tani-tena	Many widows and orphans cry
Lié doré angina	Requesting for the wind to join us
Hari hélu bo kanato.	And for the fish to come to us.

There were different songs for each kind of prey, songs to celebrate a successful hunt, and songs to mourn returning home empty-handed. On land, there were specific songs for axing trees, building boats, pestling rice into flour, weaving sarongs, rocking babies to sleep, recounting the stories of the Ancestors, and every other aspect of life. The Lamalerans sang in a high nasal pitch, often bridging their choruses with eerie extended notes and ululations.

The songs were more than music — they were prayers. The Lamalerans believe in a kind of animism mixed with Catholicism, with ancestor worship thrown in. For them, everything has a spirit — from their prey to the sun — and it must be honored. The Ancestors might have died, but their ghosts still accompany their descendants. Thus, the songs of the Lamalerans aim to influence both the spiritual and the physical world, entreating the winds to rise, their progenitors to guard them, and the whales to come. For the sperm whales they chase are not just animals but gifts sent by the Ancestors to sustain them as a reward for following their Ways. Maintaining a strong relationship with the spirits is key to a successful life.

As THE GROUP OF TÉNA closed in on its prey, Ignatius tightrope-walked to the tip of the hâmmâlollo. At the tiller, Yosef Boko called out a rhythm, and his men paddled together with seamless coordination. The whole fleet converged with the teamwork of a wolf pack to trap the breeding school of *kotekĕlema,* the fatty-headed whale, the Gift of the Ancestors. To defeat them, the whole tribe would have to unite.

Ignatius's ship approached near enough to the closest fleeing whale that he could read the history of the animal's victories inscribed in its gray hide — ellipses of Os dimpled across its snout, stamped there by the suckers of giant squids it devoured a mile below the surface. He leapt onto the whale's back with a practiced determination, driving his harpoon precisely into the soft flesh two feet below the dorsal hump, before swimming back to his téna.

The Lamalerans' strategy was to land as many harpoons as possible, and soon other téna had added their weapons. Now, pulling the accumulating weight of multiple ships, the whale would exhaust itself, and the hunters could harry it from all sides. While one téna was significantly outmatched, a team could overwhelm it.

At first, the battle was close enough to shore that the wives of the whalers spectated as if the headlands were bleachers and the sea a stadium. While Fransiska Hariona, Yosef Boko's wife, was normally a fretful person, the frothy explosions raised by the thrashing whales concerned her less than keeping an eye on the toddler Jon. Whaling was always risky, with injuries or even, occasionally, deaths resulting, but it was also routine enough that any sense of danger was dulled. Besides, Lamaleran women had their own work to occupy them, from shelling rice, to curing whale steaks, to bartering with the mountain tribes, to weaving sarongs from jungle cotton and then dyeing them with colors crushed from roots.

Two téna quickly overcame a thirty-ton female and a toothless ten-foot-long infant, which probably belonged to a fleeing whale, and then paddled them to shore, their crews singing gratefully to honor the Gifts of the Ancestors. But *Téti Heri* and *Kelulus,* as well as two other téna, were dragged by a pair of different whales over the horizon.

The wives returned to work, keeping one eye on the sea. But in the late afternoon instead of sails appearing, a storm front arose. Although the Ancestors forbade the use of engines in the hunt, the tribe did have two skiffs equipped with outboard motors, which they dispatched to find the missing hunters. But strafing precipitation turned the search party around.

At evening, the downpour broke, and the tribe lit signal fires on the beach. Fresh rain soon extinguished them, however. When Fransiska and the other wives tried hanging gas pressure lanterns under the awnings of the boat sheds, the deluge blotted out their light. The weather made them nervous, but hunts normally lasted hours and once or twice a year extended overnight. There was no cause for great concern yet.

Except for Teresea Hariona, Ignatius's wife and Yosef Boko's close relative, who crouched in her bamboo hut and cradled her pregnant stomach. Her youngest son, Ben, slept nearby on a mattress stitched out of old rice sacks and stuffed with corn husks, having tried to maintain a vigil for his father and comfort his nervous mother, before eventually succumbing to exhaustion. Every so often she would rise and peer out the door through the storm toward the thrashing ocean, wondering if the baby, which was due at any moment, or Ignatius would arrive home first.

As THE PAIR OF WHALES had towed Ignatius, Frans, and Yosef Boko east, with two téna attached to each whale, the hunters had rested for five hours, confident that the combination of blood loss and the drogue of the téna would exhaust their prey. But while Labalekang, the volcano behind Lamalera village, diminished from a mile-high peak to a thimble of dirt, the cetaceans never faltered. When a tempest swept onto the horizon in the late afternoon, the Lamalerans realized they would soon have to finish off the whales or brave the storm.

Frans and his lamafa managed to lance their whale again, but in response it uppercut the prow of *Kelulus* with its tail. The crew fled to the back of the téna as the whale brutalized the front with its flukes. Frantically, they rowed in reverse, letting out rope so they remained attached to the whale. Once safe, they stuffed the two cracks zigzagging through the hull with their sarongs, but the sea kept bubbling in.

The whale that Ignatius on *Téti Heri* and the lamafa of another téna, *Kéna Pukā,* had been needling tore through their harpoon ropes at last and dove. With only one chance left to return to Lamalera with a catch, the two téna turned to chase the whale that had just disabled *Kelulus.* The animal was being kept from escaping by the harpoon ropes attaching it to *Kelulus* and *Kebako Pukā,* the flagship vessel of the fleet.

As Ignatius embedded a harpoon in the whale, he glimpsed through the froth of battle a grotesque beast: its head and belly were streaked with white, as if it were partially albino, and its lower jaw had been snapped in half during some ancient battle. In response to this new harpoon, the whale began lobtailing—inverting itself so that its tail stood out of the water and its nose pointed at the seafloor, and then sledgehammering its flukes into the waves. Ignatius ordered a retreat, spooling out rope.

To cover *Téti Heri*'s flight, *Kebako Pukā* landed a tenth harpoon, but in retaliation the whale stove in the ship's bow strake. Half the crew stripped to plug the puncture with their shirts, while the rest bailed and back-paddled.

Stymied, the fleet let their opponent take several hundred feet of rope, rowed close together, and conferenced. Some of the men said they had seen a baby suckling the whale when they first attacked— the baby the other téna had killed. They guessed that the mother was strengthened by a desire for revenge. Ignatius feared that she was not an animal but an unholy monster—though she was only about forty-five feet long, already she had done more damage to the fleet than bull whales twenty feet longer.

The sun crisped to an ember on the western horizon, and then its last rays were blotted out by thickening clouds. As the whale drew them toward the onrushing storm, Ignatius realized that the whale was not trapped by them: they were trapped by the whale. From the hâmmâlollo, he waved a two-foot-long flensing knife and addressed his fellows: "The time has come for us to cut our harpoon rope and go home!"

But the whalers responded, "Don't let it go! We'll take it tomorrow!" And so, they kept on.

Night soiled the evening. The men hammered sprung boards tight with whetstones, roped the shattered strakes back into place, and stuffed pith caulking into the cracks. The stars turned off as a blacker darkness conquered the sky. Lightning flared. Thunder drummed.

Rain began to pellet the Lamalerans. Waves tackled the téna. The men became so exhausted bailing with halved coconut shells that they had to work in shifts. Ignatius labored stoically, not resting like many of the others, trying to ignore his yearning for his wife, his worry about if their child had yet been born, and his guilt for not being with them.

Around midnight, the storm subsided. From his knotty beard and mane of hair, Frans wrung water into his mouth; the fleet had rushed into battle so suddenly that they carried almost no food or drink. Though he missed his children and wife, he remained enthusiastic for the hunt: he was sure the Ancestors were testing the mettle of their descendants, and he meant to pass that challenge. And his clan's storehouse, like many others, was running perilously low on whale jerky.

The men bedded down atop wound ropes and the furled sail. Yosef Boko stowed his steering oar, which was useless against the whale's overwhelming strength, but remained awake, tracking her movements telegraphed through the harpoon rope. It was his job to guide the men home, and even if he could not steer them to safety, he still felt the responsibility to watch over them. But he also trembled with the premonition that this whale would defeat them. When Ignatius had offered to cut the rope, he had silently urged him on. If he was lost, who would care for his wife and grandchildren, including Jon?

By the time dawn pearled, the broken-jawed whale was hauling them through sea beyond the sight of land. She showed no signs of wearing out.

Ignatius called the téna together and announced, "We must have offended the Ancestors yesterday for the whale to be so fierce. We must all clean our mouths, so God will entrust this whale to us and the village can eat." The hunters prayed.

Soon after, at last the whale's strength began to wane. She no longer porpoised, but paddled tiredly along the surface. Instead of fountaining, she spouted a light mist, as if hyperventilating. Believing her weakened, Ignatius did not select a harpoon from the weapons rack. Instead, he tied a rusty boat hook to a bamboo pole and ordered his men to row quietly forward. He slid the hook into the whale's blow-hole and yanked back. The colossal head turned. A massive eye judged him.

The whale geysered, dislodging the hook. Then she head-butted *Téti Heri* so hard that the caulking popped out from between its boards and the Savu Sea began trickling in.

A terrifying possibility dawned on Ignatius: perhaps the whale had just been playing dead, trying to draw in the fleet. No blood reddened her spouting, which meant that the dozen or so harpoon strikes had failed to penetrate her vital organs. Her wounds were only skin-deep.

The whale battered *Téti Heri* with its tail, until the listing téna retreated. Next it broke off the hâmmâlollo of *Kéna Pukā*, and the already hobbled *Kelulus* had its bow rammed open after it tried to cover for its escaping fellows.

But still, many men, including Frans, wanted to finish the battle and claim the whale, which could feed the tribe until the hunting season began in two months. The lamafa of all four ships gathered in a phalanx on the prow of *Kebako Pukā*, the lone undamaged ship, wielding lances made of *duri*, flensing knives as long as a man's forearm, lashed to harpoon shafts. The téna attacked the whale perpendicularly, maneuvering to keep out of range of her tail. But no matter how much pink blood poured from her lacerated hide, her spouting remained pure.

Ignatius was honing his duri with a whetstone when the hull leapt beneath his feet, almost catapulting him, as the whale's flukes tore open the bow of the téna, so that the halves only connected like a clamshell at the keel.

The men fled the wreckage, swimming to *Téti Heri,* the only remaining seaworthy téna. The whale lobtailed, as if challenging the Lamalerans to return to the ring. Ignatius, Yosef Boko, and many of the other men had become convinced that their opponent was not a real whale but a "Satan-like" evil spirit. The hunters finally agreed among themselves to cut the ropes that bound them to the devil whale.

But the harpoon lines were not disposable factory-made ropes: they were the *leo,* the Spirit Ropes of the téna, whose souls were twinned with the souls of each clan's Spirit House, the locus of their powers. And the leo were woven from jungle cotton, as well as the bark of gebang palms and hibiscus trees, so practically, they represented weeks of work for the community. They could not be carelessly trashed. It was decided that someone would swim through the shark fins razoring the bloody ocean and cut the lines near the harpoon heads to save as much of their length as possible.

Frans volunteered for the mission. As he pulled himself along a harpoon rope with one hand and clutched a duri in the other, he did not fear the hammerhead, white pointer, and tiger sharks ghosting below him through the red mist. When a few zipped in and nosed him like dogs, he kicked the nerve bundles in their snouts. The Lamalerans believe that a shark will not hurt a man with a pure heart, and he knew himself to be righteous. While hunting, he would regularly manhandle sharks into his téna and knife them open. (An anthropologist living with the tribe in the 1980s described seeing men wade into the breakers of Lamalera Bay, pull tiger sharks ashore by their tails, and club them to death.) As he drew closer to the slowly swimming whale, the sharks peeled off to avoid the reach of its tail. But he approached within a few feet of the flukes, then hacked through the four harpoon lines that had endured — at least six others had torn. The ropes were reeled in, and he hitched a ride on the last one.

The whale stroked away, shadowed by dorsal fins. Then she spouted and raised her flukes — either in threat or leave-taking — and dove. She did not resurface.

The Lamalerans set about improvising what repairs they could. The crew of *Kéna Puḳā* winched ropes around its prow, squeezing the boards tight enough to prevent it from taking on more water. It could support a skeleton crew. But even though *Kebaḳo Puḳā* and *Kelulus* were similarly salvaged, they were only able to buoy Frans and a few other diehards to bail them. Those ships' crews mostly loaded into

Kéna Pukā, though one man joined *Téti Heri.* Then the whalers lashed the fleet into a line, with *Téti Heri* followed by *Kéna Pukā,* both towing the foundering *Kelulus* and *Kebako Pukā.* Abandoning the damaged téna was never discussed, for the Lamalerans believe the whaling ships have spirits just as men do. Frans felt that *Kelulus* and *Kéna Pukā,* on both of which he often served, had mothered him through trials "like a hen protecting her chick," and he had to protect them.

With clouds smothering the sun and land hidden by the horizon, the Lamalerans were unable to track north. To save their flagging strength, for they had not eaten and had only drunk rainwater since embarking, they decided to play the lottery of the wind. The crew of *Téti Heri* stood up a twenty-foot bamboo bipod mast. From it, they unscrolled a sail that looked like a giant sheet of papyrus. It was made of dozens of eight-by-ten-inch squares woven from strips of dried palm leaf that were quilted together across a grid of ropes. Few if any other such sails remained outside of Lamalera, though once whole fleets had sailed the Pacific using them. The whalers rotated the sail around the mast to confront the zephyr, and the téna skidded over the waves.

In the midafternoon, palm-fringed hills edged above the southeastern horizon like a cloud bank. It was Semau Island. But although the Lamalerans had located themselves, the discovery was not a happy one: Semau lay more than one hundred miles from home.

As evening neared, another typhoon swaggered toward them. By then, it had become apparent that the more badly damaged boats were slowing them down, and the men of *Téti Heri* ordered Ignatius to ask the other crews to let them go ahead. Ignatius strained his sandpapered throat to make himself heard over the groaning squall. "May we go ahead? The wind is strong. We will tell the village what has happened and where you are."

Frans was enraged. It was unthinkable that the crew of *Téti Heri* would even consider leaving them: that was not the spirit of the Lamalerans. The most important directive of the Ways of the Ancestors was that the unity of the tribe was paramount, as expressed in the saying that all fathers taught their sons: *Talé tou, kemui tou, onã tou, mata tou* — One family, one heart, one action, one goal.

"We live and die together!" the men in the damaged téna answered. "You can't go ahead!"

Waves were sharpening into whitecaps. The crew of *Téti Heri* urged Ignatius to try again.

Contradictory feelings roiled Ignatius's heart: He would never abandon his tribesmen, but would not they all have a better chance of survival if *Téti Heri* raced ahead to summon help? There was no use dying in solidarity with his tribesmen if that meant his children, including his unborn baby, would lose a father. And ultimately, it was not a request. Even if he wanted to remain with the fleet, he could not overrule his crew.

"May we go first so the village knows we are not all dead and can send help?" Ignatius shouted.

Again, he was rebuffed. Only this time, as he was calling to his brethren, the crew untied the linking rope. Unburdened, *Téti Heri* shot ahead on the turbulence pushed before the storm. The other téna shrank to three nodding sails. Then the lowering heavens curtained them off.

Ignatius could not control his tears. It felt as if he had been forced to forsake the Ancestors and his tribesmen. And he knew that the spirits always exacted revenge for such failures, on individuals and on the tribe as a whole.

As evening thickened, the gale threatened to use their sail as a lever to flip *Téti Heri*. It took Ignatius and two other men to dismantle the mast, though usually one man could handle it. Buckshot raindrops bulleted them. The tempest doubled the darkness of the night and whirled them willy-nilly, heaving the sea over the outriggers. The rowers slumped against the thwarts, bailing desultorily. Those too exhausted to work crawled under the sail. Five times Ignatius gathered the crew and led them in prayer until the accumulating water forced them to return to bailing.

We are all brothers, Ignatius thought. *It would have been better if we had died together. Lord, at least bring us to shore, so our families can find our bodies and give us proper funerals, and we can join the Ancestors.*

THAT FRIDAY NIGHT, AS THE STORM pummeled the sea, the eighth child of Ignatius and Teresea came crying into the world. Even though she was a girl, she was named Ignatius Seran Blikololong Jr., for the family was convinced her father was dead. Christening her with his name was a way of summoning home his lost soul.

Saturday morning, dawn flickered behind the wet clouds like the flame of a whale oil lantern sputtering to life behind its woven bamboo lampshade. Grandmother Fransiska, who had slept on the beach to tend the signal fires, woke with sand in her hair. She had refused to eat the previous day, since it became clear Yosef Boko's disappearance was serious, and ignored her grandson Jon, who cried and pawed at her for attention. Nearby, Maria Kleka Blikololong, Frans's wife and Ignatius's sister, also maintained a vigil while relatives mothered her toddlers.

Nearly half a hundred wives embalmed in grieving hope watched as the remaining fleet, perhaps seventeen boats in all, dispersed toward every point on the compass in search of their missing husbands, bearing fresh coconuts, water, and rice wrapped in banana leaves. The male bloodlines of several of the tribe's twenty-one clans now lay over the horizon.

Back on that first night of the whalers' absence, anxieties had been controlled. But a second day without sighting the boats was troubling. The Savu Sea is not wide — on a clear morning, it is possible to glimpse the peaks of Timor Island on the other side from Lamalera's cliffs. Even if the téna had been dragged south out of the Savu Sea into the Indian Ocean, they should have been able to navigate back to where search parties could spot their sails.

As the third day shortened, everyone knew the likelihood of a safe return was swiftly diminishing. Two brutish storms had scoured the sea, and even if the lost crews had survived those and the whale, they had taken no provisions with them. Whalers died with heartbreaking regularity: the town's Catholic priest inaugurated every hunting season by reading off the dozens of names of men lost at sea in the last century.

The elders gathered under the banyan tree in the village square to ferret out and rectify the crime the Ancestors must be punishing them for. A runner was dispatched to the island's capital, a thirty-mile marathon over the mountains, so that the authorities would broadcast a radio message to alert ships in transit. As the sun declined behind Labalekang, the tribe gathered on the beach for a service led by the priest.

Shortly thereafter, as if by the will of God, someone spotted a diamond sail decorating the horizon. A motorboat was dispatched to rush supplies to the téna. A man with binoculars announced to a gathering crowd that *Téti Heri* was being towed in. A rumor circulated that a corpse was aboard. The whalers had been nearly three days at sea without water, after all. Grandmother Fransiska wept, knowing that Yosef Boko crewed *Téti Heri*. Maria wondered: Where were the other ships and her husband?

The sun had almost smoldered out when men dragged the téna ashore and exhumed a group of still-living sunburned skeletons. Skin from their chests and thighs had peeled away for they had used their shirts and pants to stuff the holes in the ship. Their lips were puffed, blistered, and chapped. Bloodshot, their eyes glowed. Even supported by a man on either side, the returned could barely walk.

Tribesmen had to coax Yosef Boko into letting go of the tiller oar before they could get him to step down from the boat: he had barely slept the entire journey, believing that as long as he held the tiller oar, it was his responsibility to watch his men. Grandmother Fransiska had grown almost as haggard as he was during her fast. The emaciated couple clung to each other, wracked with sobs, though both normally prided themselves on their reserve. Lusia Hariona, Yosef Boko's daughter and Jon's mother, supported him up the cliff, while Jon toddled after them, crying. At their house, Yosef Boko washed off the salt water with a bucket shower, devoured a plate of plain rice, and then fell into a sleep that would last nearly a full day.

While the rest of the men were surrounded by their families, Ignatius wandered the beach alone. Fear unmanned him. Where was his wife? Had something gone wrong with the pregnancy? A female relative approached and slapped him on the shoulder. She cried, "Where is my husband? Where is my husband?"

His throat was so painfully dry, he could not speak, for he had been unable to stomach the water and mushed bananas given to him by the crew of the motorboat. Besides, how could he explain that they had left her husband?

But then his eldest daughter pushed out of the crowd and embraced him. "You have a daughter!" she said. "We would have called her by your name even though she was a girl. But you're home!"

Ignatius croaked an apology for not being there, but his daughter laughed. "The important thing is that you're home!"

At his hut, the first time Ignatius held his new child, he cradled possibility so pure it did not even have a name, and he almost wept trying to decide what to call her, for his daughter no longer needed to bear his masculine cognomen. Meanwhile, his son Ben clutched his leg as if he would never let go.

Once the happy families had returned home, only the desolate wives were left to build a bonfire of their hopes on the headlands. Maria threw deadwood onto the flames as if it were an offering, as if the desperate light could summon her lost husband. She was grateful that her brother Ignatius had been returned, but the fact that so many men besides Frans had been saved only highlighted her grief. She was sure she was a widow—a status every Lamaleran woman feared not only because of their loss but also because their Catholic faith permitted no possibility of remarriage. If Frans did not return, she and her three children would have to subsist on charity.

Every few minutes, eerie trumpeting echoed from the darkness. After the captain of *Téti Heri* had admitted to abandoning the rest of the fleet, the motorboats had been sent forth bearing conch shells. Between notes, Maria and the other yearning wives listened for an answering call from the lost téna. Around midnight, the motorboats puttered home alone. The wailing of the women woke the village.

Still, for days afterwards, Maria waited on the beach for sails that never came. Eventually, when hope was lost, the clans sent divers to retrieve nautilus shells, those bones bent into the shape of eternity, which they buried in place of the bodies.

ON THE FRIDAY AFTERNOON WHEN *Téti Heri* left, it had seemed to Frans that the betrayers took a long time to abandon the fleet. Each time the distant téna would sink into the trough between waves, as though finally vanishing, after a moment the tip of its sail would once more appear when the ship was lofted by a roller.

As Frans watched his brother-in-law forsake him, he thought of his three children, especially of Bena, only nine months old, with her sweet bubbling laugh. The Ancestors had granted him barely any time to get to know her. He tried not to brood on the hardships his children would endure without a father to protect them. He hoped Ignatius would do so, for almost all of their male relatives in the Mikulangu Bediona clan, who could have provided for them in his stead, clung to the wrecks of the three téna along with Frans. If they did not make it home, the clan would be decimated.

Eventually, *Téti Heri*'s sail did not rise again.

Frans and his men were in desperate condition. They had already eaten the few bananas that had been aboard and drunk their clay water pot dry. Frans had caulked a breach in *Kelulus* with his shirt, leaving him wearing only shorts; already his chest and shoulders blazed and prickled with sunburn. Thirty-four men had been crammed onto *Kéna Pukā,* which normally held no more than fourteen, and it rode so low that waves constantly spilled over its railings.

Still, Frans would not have sailed away with *Téti Heri*. *Kéna Pukā* was the téna of his branch of the Bediona clan, the Mikulangus, while *Kelulus* served the other branch. He would have no more abandoned them than left a wounded cousin on the battlefield. Each clan has one téna, which is considered a living being, with its soul linked to the bloodline's Spirit House, the family's temple. It is this spiritual invest- ment in the téna that has kept the tribe building the ships exactly according to ancient methods, so that they are the last lashed-lug ships in the world, though once the seas of Southeast Asia and even Europe were full of them. Screws, nails, or other modern tools are banned in their construction, and all their materials are sourced from the jungle, for each copies the design of the original téna the Ancestors sailed on to Lamalera, *Kebako Pukā*. The whalers could have lightened the load of their gradually swamping ships by discarding equipment, but they believed that the sails were the ships' sarongs, and the boats would be naked without them.

The gale swept them east until they caught a glimpse of the bent tip of Labalekang. The mile-high volcano topping their island was a mere anthill in the distance, but it provided a small hope. They began to paddle weakly, taking a few strokes then resting. Black clouds ava- lanched toward their backs. Soon night hid Labalekang. Then the storm pounced. Despite the waves the men had to furiously bail, Frans was thankful for relief from the torturing sun. The rain also proved a blessing: he wrung water from his thick Melanesian curls into his mouth while other men used the sail to funnel water down their parched throats.

Dawn emerged bluebird-clear, hazeless. But Labalekang had van- ished. The crew had lost all sense of position in the night as the tem- pest whirligigged them around. No one had possessed the strength to lift a paddle, so they had let the wind have its way with them. Every few hours, the men had prayed communally for their salvation.

The sun reflected off the ocean, irradiating them from below and above. Frans's throat hurt to talk. His lips had dried until riven. The

28

speech of his fellows slurred, becoming nearly incomprehensible. He estimated that he had only a 25 percent chance of surviving now. The thought of his family pricked his eyes with tears, but he told himself he must not cry: he needed the moisture.

In the late afternoon, not long before Ignatius and the crew of *Téti Heri* would arrive home, the whalers spotted a pair of cinder-cone volcanoes to the east—but rather than comforting Frans, the sight crushed him: it was Flores, two islands to the west of Lembata. They had been swept by the second storm seventy-five miles from home and outside the area that any Lamaleran ship would search for them. They tried to maneuver north and east, but the wind was against them, driving them farther from the Savu Sea and into the wilderness of the Indian Ocean. Some men tied themselves to the ship, so that their bodies could be returned to Lamalera if it was found. Frans was not yet ready to do that, but he decided that the next day he would. He prayed, knowing he was powerless to save himself.

That night, a forgiving rain—without a storm, for once. The men suckled from their shirts, their beards, and the sail. Once they had rehydrated, some began chewing their clothes. One thin hunter gorged himself on the dried tree pith they used to stem leaks between the boards. Except for a few noodles of seaweed plucked from the ocean, they had eaten nothing. With too many men for everyone to lie down in the hull, they slumped over the thwarts or sprawled on the hâmmâlollo, nodding against the ropes tied around them that kept them from falling off.

Frans fever-dreamed about God, heaven, hell, and his family. At a vague hour, the cloud cover momentarily parted to reveal the star-encrusted sky. The Southern Cross was staked into the horizon. Frans knew this constellation by the name the "Pointer," since from the Savu Sea it always aimed toward Lamalera, and for a moment the way home was revealed. If they could just follow that course, he might survive and once more balance Bena atop his head, his two hands upraised to keep her safe, and marvel at how light and fragile she was, and yet how vital, as she screamed laughter and pulled at the hair of her perch. But then the clouds returned and stole his knowledge of even what direction his wife and children were in.

By morning, though *Kéna Pukā* and *Kelulus* remained seaworthy, *Kebako Pukā* had begun to take on water, for no one had enough strength to keep bailing it. The ur-téna, the téna of téna, would have to be abandoned. Even Fransiskus "Sisu" Bataona, the captain of *Kebako Pukā* and the head of the Ola Langu lineage of the Bataona clan, which owned the téna, agreed. He volunteered to go down with his ship, before others convinced him that was unnecessary.

Sisu climbed atop the hâmmâlollo jutting above the waterline. His throat was so dry and he was so exhausted that he felt like a leaf at the end of the dry season, withered and about to fall. He addressed the spirit of the téna. "We now have no more strength. It is better that you go before us and wait for us onshore." He was invoking the Molo Ge Tede Kame re Mara, a ceremonial leave-taking sometimes used to say goodbye to the dead.

Behind him, the other Lamalerans wept. They knew everyone shared responsibility for abandoning the sacred téna. The disappointed Ancestors would exact their vengeance.

By the time Sisu climbed aboard *Kéna Pukā,* the currents had started to take *Kebako Pukā*. It swiveled, its hâmmâlollo grazing the harpooning platforms of its two fellows, as if in farewell. Already, the waves edged up the prow. Soon the ocean swallowed it. A hoarse wail burst from the Lamalerans.

They raised *Kéna Pukā*'s sail. Before long, Frans and his tribesmen hallucinated that they could see Lamalera just a few miles away, with signal fires burning bright as if it were dark, though it was full daylight. With what little strength they had, they rowed, but throughout the day, their home always remained just out of reach.

WHEN EVENING COAGULATED, THE VISION vanished and the Lamalerans lay still as corpses in the ships. Frans thought some of his fellows had already died. Still, he did not lash himself to the thwarts. He could endure a little more. If morning dawned hopelessly, he would tie himself to the téna. It would be as God willed it. He dreamed of his wife cradling his newborn.

A little before midnight, Frans stirred from his fugue to the sound of one of his shipmates croaking. The man was pointing into the darkness. Then he saw a row of halogen-lit windows floating above the Savu Sea, framing fancily clothed men and women with pale skin. A thick beam of light roved across the waves, blinding him when it settled on the téna. He suddenly understood why the Ancestors had teased the whalers with the phantasm of their home: they had been encouraging them to cling to life for just a few more hours.

A metal ship four times as long as the téna, with the words *Spice Islander* painted across its hull, chugged toward the Lamalerans. Frans had glimpsed modern ships while hunting but rarely seen one this close. When a metal arm lowered a speedboat into the water, he thought he was delirious. The speedboat zoomed up to them, lashed the téna to itself, and dragged the whalers to the *Spice Islander*. Promises of food and water enticed the hunters to untie themselves from *Kéna Pukā* and furl the sail.

As the Lamalerans stepped onto metal stairs lowered from the bow, forty or so foreigners lined the railing, aiming strange metal boxes, which blinded them with white flashes. The hunters leaned against Indonesian sailors, infantile with weakness. The white-skinned men and women shook their hands and gave them plastic water bottles they struggled to open until someone showed them how to unscrew the caps. The tourists made them pose and held up the metal boxes once more. Frans was too tired and thankful to care.

Then the captain of the ship, a man named Sebastianus Rosari, led them to the mess hall. There they were served coffee sugared with condensed milk, along with crumbly slices of white cake, which tasted bitter to Frans, and which Sebastianus told them was called bread. He was from Larantuka, the largest city in the Solor Archipelago, and had met Lamalerans who made supply runs there. His eastern Indonesian accent and familiarity with their culture put them at ease. He explained that the *Spice Islander* had been cruising from the Komodo Islands, home of the legendary dragons, to Timor, from where the tourists would fly home, when he heard a radio bulletin about their lost ships. His marine radar pinged two unidentified vessels adrift off normal shipping lanes, and he had set out to investigate.

At the end of the meal, Sebastianus apologized that the two surviving téna would have to be scuttled. Frans and the other Lamalerans begged him to save the téna, explaining that the boats had souls like humans. He agreed to try. Using the onboard crane, the crew winched *Kéna Pukã* onto the deck, where its ravaged hull was bared for all to see. But when they tried to lift *Kelulus,* the damaged ship began to break apart.

The Lamalerans beseeched Sebastianus to drag the téna to the nearest island, where they could stash the wreck until they could return. But he explained that it would be more than seventy-five miles out of their way and he had to get the passengers to Kupang the next day for their flight. "The law of the sea is to save people, not boats."

Until then, a Lamaleran had remained aboard *Kelulus* to bail, eating and drinking there, but the man was recalled. He brought with him the leo rope, but left the ship's sail and harpoons for the Ancestors who would row it in the watery underworld.

The floodlights of the *Spice Islander* illuminated *Kelulus.* Already, without someone to bail it, it was sinking.

"You go ahead and wait for us onshore," the owner of *Kelulus* cried to the téna. "Soon we will join you!"

The rope between *Kelulus* and the *Spice Islander* was unknotted.

A whaler declared, "It's better that I go with my téna!" He tried to climb over the railing, but other men restrained him.

Many Lamalerans wept hysterically. Others covered their eyes, unable to watch the sinking of the second ship they had lost in one hunt. Frans tried to face the leave-taking unblinkingly, but he grieved as if he were watching the drowning of a family member.

Every téna has a pair of eyes painted on either side of its bow. As the *Spice Islander* motored away, its wake spun *Kelulus* to face the departing Lamalerans. As the two vessels separated, *Kelulus* never broke eye contact. Frans was sure that its spirit was bidding him a personal farewell. At last, he cried. Years later, telling the story to Lamaleran youth would still unman him with tears.

The tourists photographed the spectacle.

The Lamalerans slept that night on a nest of blankets and pillows piled on the viewing deck. Many of the tourists had donated clothes. Frans was pajamaed in a long-sleeve dress shirt, the cuffs of which covered his hands and the tails of which tangled around his knees. Most Lamalerans felt similarly ridiculous, as the Westerners seemed gigantic and obese to the small, ectomorphic whalers.

Frans was so exhausted he could not help but sleep, but he kept waking abruptly to unquiet thoughts. What would have happened if the *Spice Islander* had not discovered them? And how would the Ancestors judge them for losing the téna?

The next morning, Frans was thrilled and unnerved by the cruise ship. He had never been on a vessel that did not rock in the waves before. The air-conditioning baffled him. He was amazed by the miniature waterfall that poured from the bathroom ceiling to clean him. He was amused that tourists pooped in a chair—Lamalerans use squat toilets. When he glimpsed the queen-sized beds and ceiling lights of one of the tourist's cabins, he could not help wistfully comparing it to his mattress stuffed with corn husks and his tiny brick house with no electricity.

Sebastianus had radioed ahead, and a crowd of government officials, journalists, and expat Lamalerans thronged the wharf of Kupang Harbor. Behind them, sunlight glittered on thousands of corrugated tin roofs, TV aerials, and radio antennas.

Frans had never visited Timor before, having traveled only to the rural islands neighboring Lembata to fish. His first instinct was to hide, but he had no choice except to confront this brave new world. During the next week, as he and the rest of the Lamalerans waited for a ferry to take them back to Lembata, he wandered Kupang's dusty lanes. The provincial capital was a backwater compared to the rest of Indonesia, a place where people still wore traditional handwoven sarongs to church on Sundays and some rode horses, but it was enough to reveal to Frans the impending future: multistory concrete buildings; TVs blabbing about Indonesia's president, and radios playing Ace of Base; a few motorbikes zooming across the newly built asphalt roads; more than 100,000 people who had forgotten their Ancestors.

Kéna Pukā was loaded into the cavernous metallic hold of the ferry, and the Lamalerans escorted it home. Before Frans and the other hunters could reenter the village, they had to pause for several days at a neighboring town while the tribe dug up the nautilus shells buried in their places and performed a shamanistic ceremony to reverse their funerals. Later, Frans helped lead a separate rite to recall the souls of the sunken téna to their clans' Spirit Houses.

But even once the fleet was rebuilt, Frans worried that everything was not the way it had been before. The betrayal by *Téti Heri*'s crew of the unity prescribed by the Ancestors was never fully resolved — it was so unprecedented that there was no ritual for healing it — and even decades later, Ignatius, Frans, and Yosef Boko would find it difficult to discuss. When Frans stared at the western horizon, he remembered the alien world beyond it, and he could only wonder when it would arrive.

Chapter Two

AT PLAY IN THE GRAVEYARD
OF WHALES

February 10, 1992–August 2013

Jon

Frans's prophecy proved correct: the outside world did steadily encroach on Lamalera. Through the 1990s, its progress was slow enough that it seemed as if the Lamalerans could still duck foreign influences, but by the early 2000s, it had become clear that globalization could not be resisted. Outboard engines, electricity, cell phones, Hollywood, and governmental oversight challenged the Ways of the Ancestors. By 2013, it was uncertain if the whalers' unique way of life would survive. The youth of the tribe straddled two worlds. In their decision to follow or abandon the Ways of the Ancestors lay the future of Lamalera.

When Jon—who would later suffer his leg being crushed by the rogue harpoon rope—woke in the witching hours one August night, his heart smoldered with the desire to become a lamafa. Never mind the cell phone in his pocket or the Indonesian pop songs in his head. When he arrived at the beach under a sky still salted with stars, he settled his throwing harpoon in the prow of his sampan. Then he and Yohanes Narek Hariona, a clansman and mentor a decade older, pushed the two-person boat laden with gill nets into the moonlit surf. The ten-foot-long boat was so stuffed with gear that they had to sit atop the piled nets as they rowed through the breakers. Past the cliffs of Lamalera Bay, they raised a sail stitched from the campaign banner of an Indonesian congressional candidate, the politician's mustachioed smile stretching as the winds blowing off Labalekang volcano bellied the sail and pushed them out to sea.

The gears of the heavenly bodies spun. The constellations were primeval, the kind that city dwellers have forgotten. When dawn shellacked the sky in mother-of-pearl, they were already reeling in the first gill net of the day.

Jon was twenty-one but, despite his desire to become a lamafa, had not yet harpooned much of anything. To rise to the position of a lamafa, a man had to be called by a ship's captain to wield its harpoons. Every time a téna put to sea, Jon hoped that the captain would select him. Lately, though, he had realized he was waiting in vain: Who would honor him when he had not proven himself by spearing anything? And yet how could he harpoon anything if he was never given the chance? This paradox frustrated him.

Before the start of the whaling season, he had labored as a construction worker in Lewoleba, the capital of the island of Lembata, which though it lay less than fifteen miles away might as well have been a different world. The Lamalerans' corner of Lembata's lightly populated southern coast was filled with tribes that mostly kept the Old Ways. Yet on the other side of 4,500-foot jungled mountains, also inhabited by traditional tribes, the island's northern shore supported 30,000 or so modernized Indonesian citizens. With this mecca of TVs and motorbikes just a half-day's journey away in the bed of a dump truck, it was hard for tribal youth not to get distracted. Impatience had lately turned Jon's thoughts toward laying brick in Lewoleba again or even finding a factory job in Jakarta, Indonesia's capital, an up-to-the-minute metropolis with around thirty million inhabitants. But as he fed out the monofilament gill nets, he kept an eye on the throwing harpoon lying in the fore of the sampan.

By eight o'clock the dawn's gleam had intensified into an interrogator's searchlight, scorching away all shadows. An hour later, the white-hot bulb of the sun glinted off the tinfoil ocean. Flying fish shoaled into the mesh all morning, and Jon and Narek reeled them in quickly to prevent dolphins from shredding the plastic webbing with their needle teeth and pirating the fish. As they pulled the catch out through the tight weave, glittering scales flipped into the air, as if rainbow snow was falling, and pasted to their skin. By early afternoon they had filled three buckets with about two hundred fifty Exocoetidae.

They were unfurling the mug of the congressional hopeful to sail home when suddenly Narek yelled from the back of the sampan, *"Bōu!"*

"Where? Where?" Jon answered, scrutinizing the waves.

"In front!"

Narek, already a lamafa, had known the moment his practiced eyes glimpsed the tip of a golden-brown wing scalping a wave that it was a short-fin devil ray. Meanwhile, Jon struggled to even see the animal. Narek demanded that the younger man vacate the prow. Jon answered that the ray might be lost if they took the time to switch positions, though what he really wanted, of course, was to wield the harpoon himself.

"Do you see it now?" Narek asked.

"Yes."

"Fine, I'll row."

Jon screwed the spearhead of the throwing harpoon tighter into the bamboo shaft while Narek paddled them closer to a shadow skimming along beneath the surface. He braced his front foot atop the tip of the sampan and his back foot against a thwart, like a sprinter settling into the blocks, and lifted the harpoon.

The bōu circled ahead of them. It was a mature devil ray, weighing a hundred pounds, its five-foot wingspan regally spread. The sampan rocked as Jon tensed. The ray looped toward him, its wings undulating rather than flapping stiffly like a bird's.

Jon flung himself off the sampan and toward his prey, hurling the harpoon like a javelin. It was lighter and longer than the ballista bolt used for whales, and it traveled with an arrow's flight. The ray accelerated, twisting so it aimed straight down, revealing the white diamond of its underbelly.

At the moment the weapon left Jon's hand, everything became predetermined. Physics and fate were crunching the equation of the harpoon's and the ray's velocities and the answer was already set, if not yet known. During a lecture in his childhood, Lamaleran elders had once told him that men were like harpoons thrown by the Ancestors or by God: they were all traveling toward a target that would remain unknown until they hit it. For his whole life, Jon had aimed himself toward becoming a lamafa, but it remained uncertain whether he would hit his mark.

Jon had grown up playing in the boneyard of whales on Lamalera's beach. He crawled over sperm whale skeletons as if they were jungle gyms. He stacked giant vertebrae like building blocks, and hammered tall rib bones into the black volcanic sand to mark the goals of soccer fields.

When he was four, some afternoons he borrowed his grandfather's machete and felled a bamboo culm in the jungle, after which he sharpened one end with the blade. Then he carried this improvised harpoon to the beach, where the colossal skulls awaited. Having been stripped of their jaws, the skulls were all forehead now, massive shields of bone guarding nothing. He lifted his spear and imagined that he stood on a hâmmâlollo. Then he lanced his target repeatedly, until the tip of his weapon splintered and he collapsed, sweating, on the sand, his tiny belly ballooning with each gasp. The skull, not even dented, looked past him at the waves trying to reclaim it.

By the time Jon was five, he had learned that not even the strongest lamafa could drive an iron spearhead through the spermaccti helmet of a sperm whale. Instead of attacking the skulls, he and the other children sculpted their prey out of sand beside the dry-docked téna, making sure it was anatomically perfect from flukes to blowhole. When the adults were not watching, they stole real harpoons from the weapons racks, balanced atop the unstable planks of the hâmmâlollo, and then stabbed the beached whale below the dorsal fin. The most fun was after a garden was cleared, and the trunk of a banana tree was floated into Lamalera Bay. The current drew it beneath the eastern headlands, where it bobbed. Then the children hurled themselves off the stone ramparts and pierced the log until it unraveled like a giant green onion, and its layers sank.

In 1998, when Jon was six, every afternoon he watched the fleet of his grandfather, uncles, and cousins—but not his father, whom he had never met—sail home. As the sun rolled behind Labalekang volcano, which towered over the village, he tracked the palm-leaf sails as they expanded from tiny black diamonds to billowing sheets glowing in the honeyed afternoon light. When the téna were close enough that he could hear the chants of the rowers, he squinted to discover what prize they had brought home: a wing drooping over the lugs signaled a manta ray and a fin poking above the thwarts a shark. Best of all was when a sperm whale was lashed alongside the téna, dwarfing the boat itself, so heavy the craft listed toward it.

The children played with the corpse until dark. Jon loved King of the Whale, a no-holds-barred melee to be the last child standing atop the blowhole. It did not matter that he was smaller than his peers; his balance and speed helped him keep his feet atop the rubbery, seawater-slicked skin. Almost as fun was taking a running start from on top of the whale's head, diving face-first onto the slope of its back, and zipping down its slippery body.

Lamaleran children play on a slain whale.

If it was Hariona, Jon's clan, that had taken the whale, he feigned sleep on his bamboo pallet until his grandmother snored. Then he snuck down to the beach, where his grandfather, Yosef Boko, who had steered *Téti Heri* during the catastrophic hunt of the devil whale, and his clansmen huddled around a fire, drinking *tuak,* palm wine. Eventually, his grandfather noticed him crouching in the shadows and called out, "Is there a little gecko hiding in the night?" Then Jon laid his head on his grandfather's lap and listened to the men replay the hunt like sportscasters, analyzing every strike of the lamafa and every blow of the whale's flukes. Soon enough, the men fell asleep on the sand, but every few hours they woke to drag the whale higher as the rising tide buoyed it, and to check the fishing lines set to hook scavenging sharks.

Jon woke at first light to the rasp of knives being sharpened on boulders as the Lamalerans prepared their duri for sawing through foot-thick blubber. Yosef Boko assigned Jon a simple task, like peeling the rubbery casings off entrails or digging through the putrid stomach sack, sifting through thousands of squid beaks and occasional shark bones in search of nuggets of ambergris.

But soon Jon ran to watch a team of a hundred men tug-of-war the corpse, whose upper side had been filleted to the ribs, to flip it and expose the meat remaining on its bottom. Or he scampered to the women boiling python-like innards in cauldrons and sampled the pungent, chunky, yellow stew. Often one of the older children got his hands on an enormous severed penis and chased his friends around, wielding it like a baseball bat. Jon and the other kids climbed naked into the whale's chest cavity and waded through blood past their ankles to explore the fantastic cave, until they emerged sputtering with laughter and dripping gore. Yosef Boko would exasperatedly remind Jon that he should have been helping, but the old man rarely struck him as Lamaleran fathers often did their disobedient sons. Some patriarchs even kept the severed tails of whiptail stingrays braceleted around their wrists for this purpose, a punishment that hurt all the worse owing to the toxins in the tail's barbs.

Once the tons of meat had been divided among the dozens of hunters, Jon and his grandfather loaded their share of the huge purple steaks onto sea turtle shells. Then they balanced them like trays on their heads, as blood dripped through the punctures in the bone where the fatal blows had entered, and slogged up the mountain. At their home atop the cliffs, they sliced the meat into strips, which they hung on bamboo racks to leather in the tropical sun and desert-dry air. The jerky would sustain them for the weeks or months it took them to land their next whale, or until they could barter it for vegetables grown by neighboring mountain tribes, who farmed rather than fished. Meanwhile, Jon's grandmother Fransiska stuffed soft organs into coconut shells, topping the natural bowls off with whale blood, seaweed harvested from the tidal pools, and lime leaves plucked from the orchards. She roasted the coconuts until the mixture became goulashy. Then Jon slurped down the salty sour broth while it was still hot enough to sear his palate.

Two years before the turning of the millennium—and four years after Frans's encounter with the cruise ship—Jon and his family still

41

lived much as their forebears had, hunting for their sustenance, weaving sails out of threads of palm leaf, and participating in a barter economy with neighboring mountain tribes, who, like the Lamalerans, rarely used Indonesian cash. Even when the Southeast Asian financial crisis ravaged the region's economies that year, wiping out more than 80 percent of the value of the Indonesian rupiah in six months, the Lamalerans barely noticed. Why should they have? After all, there was no change in the price of *faré kotekělema,* the six-inch strips of sperm whale jerky that were the standard unit of currency in the Lamaleran barter economy, convertible for a dozen bananas or a kilo of unhusked rice from the agricultural mountain tribes.

Lamalera was insulated from the world's turmoil by its position at the far eastern tip of the Indonesian Archipelago, two thousand miles from mainland Asia and six hundred miles northwest of Australia. The jungly mountains walled it off, and the dangerous currents swirling the nearby straits had kept boats away for centuries. The tribe's dedication to the Ways of the Ancestors meant they were content to live in their own self-sufficient universe rather than seek to join the outside world.

To most Lamaleran elders, like Yosef Boko, it seemed that Lamalera would never change. Each wave looked identical to the last as they battered the same shore they had eroded for thousands of years. Tomorrow was yesterday. But, especially after Frans's visit to Kupang and the homecoming of tribesmen who had spent years working overseas, the most prescient Lamalerans could glimpse the impending upheavals that were already decimating other indigenous societies across the globe. In fact, Jon's birth had been a product of one of those first changes.

When Jon enrolled in first grade at Lamalera's elementary school on July 20, 1998, one of the first things he learned, along with the Indonesian pledge of allegiance, was that his father had never married his mother. Even more, the other children teased Jon that his two younger sisters had a different dad, whom his mom had also failed to marry, a situation that was almost unheard of in Lamaleran society. He endured

taunts that he was not a true Lamaleran, that he was a *kefela,* a mountain dweller, because his father was from the upland tribes. His school-
mates mocked him that he would have to stay ashore and tend the pigs
with the women, as he was not a natural seaman. That he would never
become a lamafa was a given, as the position was reserved by tribal law
for the children of lamafa, though occasionally exceptions were made
for prodigiously talented whalers.

Jon tried to calmly explain that he did have a father who wanted to
take care of him, but his grandfather hated his father and would not
allow it. He declared that he was not illegitimate because he and his
mother knew who his father was. But inevitably the taunters would
push Jon too far, and knees would be skinned and hair torn.

Jon's mother, Lusia Sipa Hariona, had always been forthright with
Jon that his father had been the driver of the biweekly longboat that
ran from Wulandoni, a market village seven miles up the coast, to
Lewoleba, taking all day to circumnavigate Labalekang and Mingar
volcanoes and get to the other side of the island. They had fallen in
love while she was traveling to Lewoleba's market to buy goods the
Lamalerans could not make from the jungle or the sea, like soap or
steel pots. The boat's load of candlenuts, cashews, whale jerky, and
goats usually forced the passengers to sit thigh to thigh, and she spent
every ride lounging in the back of the boat, near Jon's father.

Lusia was already pregnant with Jon when his father climbed the
stacked-stone staircase to the last house on the cliffs to ask Yosef Boko's
permission to marry his daughter. The fact that a kefela was even asking for a Lamaleran woman's hand was itself a sign of the changing
times, as Lembatan youth increasingly crossed the cultural boundaries that had separated tribes and tried to choose their own spouses.
For centuries, marriages in Lamalera had been arranged according to
an intricate triangular system among the clans that had been decreed
by the Ancestors. In it, the twenty-one clans constituting the Lamaleran tribe were divided into three groups, each of which received
brides exclusively from one group but not the other — thus, A from B,

B from C, and C from A. Yosef Boko refused Jon's father. He felt the proposal was not even a possibility within the Ways of the Ancestors, and that it was better she never marry at all than be bound to a kefela ferryman.

Jon was born on February 10, 1992, and almost immediately fell seriously ill. Jon's father kept climbing the precarious stairs, begging to see his sick child, whom he could sometimes hear crying behind the door, but each time, Yosef Boko rebuffed him. For a month, he diligently appeared. Then he started coming less. Eventually, he stopped appearing at all. Rumor had it that he had moved to Larantuka, the only true city in the region, three islands away, to start a new life. All through Jon's youth, his mother would say, "Remember, you're not a Lamaleran. You're a man from Botoh," the mountain village of his father. "If your father and your mother get married, then we can move to Larantuka." When Jon accompanied his mother to Lewoleba as an elementary-school-aged boy, he would cram into the post office phone booth with her and watch her face as she spoke with his father.

In the classroom, Jon was distinguished mostly for his inability to sit still and obey his teachers. Often he could not have done his work anyway, as he frequently lacked paper or a pencil, items his family could not afford. His belligerence resulted in him spending many mornings fetching water from a well half a mile away to fill the concrete basin behind the schoolhouse. He hated portering. *Do I go to school to study how to carry things?* he thought. He developed a reputation for scrapping with the other children and arguing with adults, which was taboo in the stringent age-based hierarchy of Lamalera. He alternately clung to his mother and fought with her. He was similarly bewildering with his grandparents, sweetly beseeching at times, and throwing tantrums at others.

As Jon's childhood became more chaotic, it seemed as if the world was falling to pieces too. On May 21, 1998, Major General Suharto, the dictator who had ruled Indonesia for thirty-one years, announced that he was resigning. He had been brought down by violent protests across

Indonesia's major cities, sparked by the Southeast Asian financial crisis, which had left Jakarta a scorched husk with hundreds dead.

Under Suharto's military rule, the Lamalerans' participation in government had been limited, but a year after his ouster, they built voting booths of downed saplings and blankets in the square where they had argued village matters for centuries. Yosef Boko, Fransiska, and Lusia used nails to poke a hole through paper ballots in Indonesia's first genuinely democratic election in four decades. Their preferred candidate became the president of Indonesia, and one of his first initiatives was to decentralize power, a countrywide reshuffling of borders and hierarchies that saw Lembata form its own administrative district. Lewoleba became the capital of the island, and a native son of Lamalera, Petrus Keraf, who had been living there, was elected governor.

In 2000—as the one hundredth space shuttle mission was flown and George Walker Bush was elected the forty-third president of the United States—one of the first major public works of Petrus's administration was to build a proper road to Lamalera, a project the Lamalerans had desired for decades. At the time, a cobbled road constructed in colonial times stretched from Lewoleba into the interior of the island, but it broke down on the upper slopes of Labalekang, and the occasional vehicles that continued had to off-road across a hellacious dirt track. To reach Lewoleba, most Lamalerans sailed around the coast or walked through the mountains. But on May 6, a backhoe clanked into Lamalera, after having plowed a path through the jungle to the village. To protect its rusted metal treads, it had traveled the whole way on a carpet of halved, used motorcycle tires, which a line of workers had created by continually putting tires that had been run over back in front of the machine so they could be crushed again. The heavy machine's final task was to carve a path across the face of the cliffs connecting Lower Lamalera, the portion of the village centered around the beach, with Upper Lamalera, the plateau where most of the tribe lived.

By the time the metal behemoth had turned back toward Lewoleba, the world had finally made inroads into Lamalera. It was not much of a road, unpaved and barely passable in the dry season and a quagmire once the monsoons arrived. But one could now bus to Lewoleba on it, and from Lewoleba board a boat to Larantuka, and from Larantuka continue to the regional capitals of Maumere or Kupang, and from there ferry more than a thousand miles to Jakarta, and from the capital fly anywhere on the globe. Soon after the road was complete, an *auto,* a dump truck converted into a bus that was half a day faster than the Lamalera-Lewoleba ferry service, put the boats out of business, and the last reminder of Jon's father in Lamalera vanished. Within a year, Jon was seeing many amazing goods — drop-cast steel axes, outboard motors, an electric generator for the town — arrive in Lamalera on the back of the dump truck. But what mattered most to him was that around 2001, when he was nine, his mother, Lusia, took those roads into the outside world herself, leaving her children behind.

Jon would later tell two versions of this story: that his mother informed him of her departure ahead of time in tears, or alternately that after several weeks his grandparents had been forced to break the news to him that she was not on a bartering expedition but had left for good. Either way, Jon's mother was done bearing the scarlet letter in Lamalera, where she never escaped the stigma of her indiscretions, both with Jon's father and with her daughters' father. She decided to relocate to Kupang, the capital of the province — the same city where the *Spice Islander* had brought Frans and the other whalers after discovering them adrift — to live with her brother, who worked as a carpenter there.

While most Lamalerans spend their whole lives on the few square miles of coast the tribe claims, a significant minority have sought their fortunes elsewhere. Starting in the 1920s, when missionaries converted the tribe, a few Lamalerans left to attend seminary or work for the church elsewhere in Indonesia, forming microcommunities where they landed. In the 1970s, using these established expat networks, a small number of Lamalerans began settling abroad for nonreligious reasons. Many had clashed with their families, as Lusia's brother did with the domineering Yosef Boko, or had violated societal norms, like Lusia, but some were also chasing rumors of a richer life as the tribe bumped up against the limit of the population its territory could support. By the late 1990s almost every inch of flat land had been built on and there was nowhere to put new houses. Over the decades, as more Lamalerans settled abroad and the allurements of the outside world sparkled brighter, this outflow increased, taking off in the early 2000s.

Lusia was supposed to find work and send money for her children's school fees, one of the few expenses that existed outside the Lamaleran barter economy, and which families often struggled to find the cash to pay. But the next news Jon had of her came more than two years later, in a letter. As his younger sister Fransiska "Ika" Hariona read it aloud — her grandparents were illiterate — the family discovered that Jon's uncle had died falling off a roof while building a home. There was another revelation: not long after arriving in Kupang, Lusia had been training to become a nurse, planning to use her stipend to pay for her children's school, when a rice farmer twenty years her senior had greeted her as she strolled past his paddy. They had talked all afternoon, and he had proposed before evening. Jon and his sisters already had two new half-siblings.

After informing the family of her brother's death, Lusia did not contact them for another four years. She returned to Lamalera only twice in the next decade and a half. Jon never traveled to Kupang or met his new brothers and sisters. The letter meant that his family had shrunk to his grandparents and his two younger sisters, Ika and Maria "Mari" Hariona. Even as a nine-year-old, he knew that he would have to be the man of the house. Jon stayed officially enrolled in school through fourth grade, but any pretense of his attending classes was dropped. Yosef Boko, who himself had not finished elementary school, encouraged Jon's absenteeism, and his grandson began trying to earn food for the family instead. He fished off the headlands with a handline, pried giant barnacles from rocks at low tide, stalked jungle birds using a slingshot made of dozens of rubber bands braided together, and spearfished, his favorite activity. Now his dream of becoming a lamafa gained extra importance beyond proving himself a Lamaleran — the harpooners were awarded extra meat, which they could share with their families.

Released to gather food on his own recognizance, Jon became, as an older Lamaleran would later describe it, "as wild as a dog whose owner had died." After a triumphant hunt, his older friend Narek would sometimes buy a bamboo tube filled with tuak, and they would get so drunk they threw up. He often scrapped with his former classmates if they taunted him for being unlearned. Eventually, his older clansmen gave up trying to govern him, saying, "He needs a father to control him." At the age of ten, he received his first Communion and — his soul now safe should he die — he went to sea.

Had Jon been born five years earlier, he would have apprenticed aboard his clan's téna, *Boli Sapang:* bailing, coiling harpoon lines, mastering the many ropes of the palm-leaf sail, before eventually earning his own paddle. But instead he apprenticed on *Felana,* a new kind of boat the Lamalerans began building in the 1990s, about half the size of a téna and powered by a fifteen-horsepower outboard motor. These boats were christened with the name of the first such motors the tribe had encountered: American-made Johnson engines, or *jonson,* as the word was adapted in Lamaleran. They proved popular among younger tribesmen because they allowed hunters to chase down prey like dolphins and swordfish, which had previously been too agile for them. While many older whalers distrusted the motorboats and enforced a rule that only the téna could hunt kotekĕlema, the efficiency of the jonson rapidly converted liberal whalers to their use. In the early 2000s, a governmental loan program and donations from Lamalerans living outside the village allowed a burgeoning number of clans to purchase outboard motors, and soon both téna and jonson were launching each morning. Jon's second uncle, Gregorious Dengekae Kĕrofa, was one of the early adopters of the jonson, and Jon was recruited to crew his vessel.

On Jon's first day of hunting, a storm roughened the seas. He did not prove himself a natural. That day, and in the following weeks, he often became seasick, the ultimate humiliation for a Lamaleran. To cure him, Gregorious made him drink seawater after each time he vomited. The taunts that he was a kefela intensified. For many months, forbidden to touch the ropes or harpoons, Jon bailed and rolled cigarettes for the older men until his fingers were yellowed by tobacco. He started to smoke about this time too. But eventually, he graduated to preparing harpoons, assembling different combinations of the seven harpoon heads, six bamboo shafts, and half-dozen ropes, depending on the type of prey, and then handing them up to the lamafa. He mastered dozens of knots. He learned to read the face of the ocean so well that he could spot a ray by the wake it created swimming under the surface, a current often countering the natural direction of the waves. He no longer threw up.

Jon's early training on a jonson rather than a téna began to look like a stroke of fortune. In 2004, when he was twelve, the twenty-first jonson was added to the Lamaleran fleet. Just several years earlier, there had been only half a dozen, but now the number of jonson surpassed the number of téna, which had declined to about fourteen, as clans found it harder to assemble a full crew, with many of their youth preferring the motorboats. Die-hard old-timers still rowed out every dawn, but *Felana* would land its first manta while the téna were still trying to escape the coastal currents. The tribe's youth were enamored of the engines, which allowed them to cover great distances quickly without the hard labor of paddling, but their elders began to worry that the machines were causing the loss of traditional knowledge, like the whaling songs and sailing, which were being obviated. They also fretted that the outboard motors undermined the unity of crews and the tribe because hunters no longer had to coordinate to paddle and sail but just relaxed while one man worked the engine.

Some elders even argued that jonson were actually causing the tribe to bring home less meat in the long run, as the motorboats could not handle the huge orcas or sperm whales that the téna caught and that fed everyone for months. In this, they were not wrong, for anthropologists have estimated that back then Lamalerans who hunted communally in téna earned more calories over the long run than those who fished from sampans or jonson, though they had to wait longer between landing prey. What motivated the youth, though, were short-term returns, and even the elders had to concede that jonson were more likely to bring home minor prey on any given day. Even more important, because téna were co-owned by everyone in a clan, the animals caught by a téna hunt had to be widely shared. Jonson, on the other hand, were often run by small private groups, meaning that their crews got to keep more meat for themselves, which appealed to younger hunters.

As the millennium approached, several youthful Lamalerans came up with a revolutionary technique to use the jonson for hunting sperm whales, though until then the motorboats had been kept away from the colossi, as their engines were too expensive and their hulls too slight to risk in combat. By roping the jonson to téna and then towing the traditional boats to within a few hundred feet of the whales before detaching, the innovators claimed that they were making the hunt more efficient even while not changing its fundamental nature or offending the Ancestors — for in the end, it was just the téna paddling after the whales, as it had always been. In 2001, in a momentous moment in Lamaleran history, a group of conservative elders tried to ban this practice at the Council on the Beach, an annual meeting of all the hunters at which rules are made. The Council, however, ended up ratifying the towing method, as moderate elders and liberal youth out-shouted the conservatives. By the late aughts, the jonson were ascendant: most Lamalerans started each day hunting with the motorboats, then rushed back to shore and towed the téna to sea if sperm whales were sighted, and only a handful of clans still launched their téna each dawn.

The village, meanwhile, was transforming as well. In the 1980s, the last bamboo and grass-thatched houses were replaced with brick structures roofed with corrugated tin, though many people retained the artfully arranged whale bones in their yards. In 2005, the Indonesian government set up a diesel generator on the slopes of Labalekang and electrified Lamalera from six every evening to six the following morning. The tribe's whale oil lamps began to rust. In 2007, when Jon was fifteen, a technical high school opened in Lamalera, the first such institution in southern Lembata, teaching how to preserve fish and farm cassava, as well as chemistry and Indonesian history. But Jon never thought of returning to the classroom: no degree would qualify him to become a lamafa. He had left *Felana* for another jonson named *VJO,* whose owner taught him to handle its Yamaha Enduro outboard motor and charged Jon with taking care of the boat while he was away on long business trips. On days *VJO* did not launch, Jon was in demand as a driver throughout the fleet. Sometimes, after the lamafa landed the first harpoon, Jon would get to try "doubling," adding a second barb to secure the prey. When *Boli Sapang* launched, he pulled his own paddle.

By now, the stick-figure child had developed the lithe proportioned muscles of a gymnast. But he remained short even for a Lamaleran, standing not much over five feet, while most Lamalerans had another few inches. He weighed barely in excess of a hundred pounds. He had sprouted a beard early, a knotty black ruff to match the bearish tangle atop his head. His facial features were big — pouty lips, a broad nose with bull nostrils, and wide feminine eyes rimmed with mascara-commercial eyelashes — as if proportioned to billboard his outsized emotions, which he was usually too sensitive and impulsive to hide. He believed himself to be a Lamaleran man.

One particular event that had cemented this feeling in him was reckoning with his kefela father. Two years earlier, when he was thirteen, a cell phone tower had been built about ten miles away. The Lamalerans could snag a signal by climbing a hill to the soccer pitch outside of town. The handful of cell phones in the village were used communally, and during daylight hours a child was posted with a phone by the dusty field. One day, as Jon was trying to score, bystanders informed him he had a call. He thought it might be his mother, but it was his father. He was shocked, but he clamped down on the tumult in his heart so tightly that he seemed disinterested when he said, "What do you want, sir?"

Jon's father, like most adults indulging an unfamiliar boy, asked him the usual bland questions: what was his favorite pastime, soccer team, etc. At length, when his father could see that Jon was going to give him only one-word answers, he desperately explained to Jon that he had wanted to marry Lusia, but Yosef Boko would not let him. "You're not a Lamaleran, Jon, you're a man of the mountains," he declared.

After a lifetime of anticipating talking to his father, Jon found only fury for him. Here his father was unwittingly visiting upon him the same taunt he had been trying to escape ever since he could remember. Jon canceled the call. Every few days, his father kept telephoning, but he refused to answer. Eventually, his father did not call again. Having at last banished his lingering desire for a father, Jon felt that he had finally put his kefela past behind him.

Every year since the beginning of the millennium, fewer men had gathered on the beach to launch the téna as the sky blushed with dawn. In 2000, about twenty téna had sailed forth each morning, but as the decade closed, only a few sallied out as jonson zipped past them. In 2009, the chants of the *materos,* the téna's rowers, beseeching the Ancestors for wind or prey mostly fell silent. The mechanical roar of the motors echoed across the water. When the téna unfurled their sails to chase sperm whales, they revealed palm leaf stained with mold.

As the téna were retired from everyday use, Yosef Boko stopped regularly descending to the beach by waning starlight as he had for at least five decades. No one knew exactly how old he was, but they were certain he had been born before World War II. Cataracts fogged his eyes, his beard had molted until it was just individual hairs tasseling his chin, and his once muscular arms had withered to baggy sleeves of skin draped from bones. He had worked long past when most men would have quit, trying to ease the burden on his grandson of bringing home all the food. But Jon, at seventeen — though he told everyone he was nineteen — believed himself a skilled enough hunter to provide for his family and encouraged Yosef Boko to retire. Besides, he worried that other Lamalerans were gossiping that he forced his grandfather to work because he could not feed his dependents by himself.

Partnered with Jon in taking care of their family was Ika, his sister two years his junior. Several years earlier, Grandmother Fransiska had broken her femur when she fell carrying meat through the jungle to barter with the mountain tribes. Ika had quit sixth grade to assume her duties: tending house, cooking, and trading the fish Jon caught for rice and corn. Mari they kept in school, at Ika's insistence, since she did not want her little sister cooking over a wood fire her whole life.

But though Jon had become bound to the hunt by his responsibility for his family, and though he still dreamed of becoming a lamafa, by the time he turned twenty he had become fascinated with life outside the tribe. TV had been present in Lamalera since around 1983, when the government donated a fritzy machine along with a portable diesel generator to the mayor. But it was not until around 2010 that many households began owning TVs, often purchased for them by relatives living off-island. After a friend erected a satellite dish, Jon started staying up all night watching shows about Jakarta and America and then sleeping through the day. His reputation as a tireless worker suffered. He began to consider some traditions of the Ancestors fusty, like sprinkling holy water on his boat before launching it, though he swore by others, such as keeping the dried wing tip of a manta ray nailed to his sampan for good luck.

Another lure tempted him toward the outside world: money. While the barter economy continued to dominate southern Lembata, Lamalerans had begun to covet the medicine, TVs, and modern tools like gill nets that could be obtained only with tissue-like Indonesian rupiah bills and bendable coins cut from a cheap aluminum alloy. As the years passed, more and more men left the tribe when the annual monsoon beached the téna, and labored in faraway towns to earn the cash they could not get in Lamalera. Jon's neighbor led a construction crew in Loang, a village on the opposite side of the mountains, and Jon agreed to help build an elementary school there during the 2012 rainy season. At first, Jon was bitterly disappointed: Loang was a backwater village little more modernized than Lamalera. As the youngest crew member, he had to do "wife work" for the other men, like rising early to boil coffee and cooking dinner after a day of laying brick. He earned the equivalent of only about a hundred U.S. dollars a month, much of which he had to spend on necessities like soap and cigarettes, so he saved little money.

But soon his desire to explore the outside world was rewarded: Loang was only a short ride in the bed of a pickup from Lewoleba. There he encountered people from Indonesia's distant metropolitan islands, as well as technology, like computers and smartphones, he had only heard about. And he was relieved to find that his elders' warnings about violent clashes between the island's Christian and Muslim tribes seemed mostly scare tactics to keep him home. With much of his wages, he bought a fifth-hand keypad Nokia cell phone. It gave him an opportunity to flirt with the Loang girls, who would stop by the half-built elementary school to charge their phones because only government buildings had electricity in the otherwise unwired town. He got them to show him how to text, play songs, and use a simplified, pictureless version of Facebook. At about that time, Telkomsel, the Indonesian cell phone company, was erecting a red-and-white-striped tower on the cliffs above Lamalera.

Jon stayed in Loang six months. Having seen Lewoleba, he fantasized about joining the small community of Lamalerans living in the futurescape of Jakarta. But he worried about who would take care of his grandparents and sisters, as well as about disappointing the Ancestors and being taken advantage of by notoriously sly city dwellers. And the old dream of becoming a lamafa still pinched his heart.

Most of the earth's indigenous people, more than a third of a billion in all, face the same quandary as Jon: adopt an industrialized life-style or remain loyal to their traditions and be disadvantaged in the contemporary world. Globalization has brought undeniable improvements in health, education, and wealth to certain swaths of the human population. But by joining the modern world, aboriginal people often trade livelihoods that are harmonized to their ecosystems for ones that destroy it, bespoke mythologies for impersonal Hollywood or Bolly-wood or Nollywood legends, and a tight-knit tribal identity for an indifferent national one, which usually aims to subordinate their tribal bonds so that they will melt into the wider population.

This challenging choice is a daily struggle for Jon and his fellow Lamalerans. Labor as a whaler or a construction worker. Participate in a barter or a cash economy. Believe in the stories of the Ancestors or the ones being told on TV. The sum of their decisions and those of other indigenous peoples will ultimately determine if humanity can sustain its myriad identities, or if, in the end, these ways of being human will be extinguished and we will become a homogenized mass, with all cultures diluted into an industrial monoculture.

Before the hunting season opened in May 2013, Jon decided to return to Lamalera. The modern world drew him, but, for the moment, the Ways of the Ancestors still exerted more gravity. While hunting, he would stand atop the thwarts of his jonson or téna and survey the horizon for sperm whale spouts and the splash of belly-flopping manta, trying to embody the Lamaleran saying: *What is most important is not the strength of the lamafa's arm: it is the strength of his physical and spiritual balance.* Even when the wind and the waves rose and the ship's lamafa sat down, Jon would adjust to the bucking seas without ever showing the pale soles of his otherwise sun-blackened feet, all in an effort to will the crew to imagine him on the hâmmâlollo.

Fortunately, one modernization meant that Jon's goal was achievable: the position of lamafa had become a meritocracy, the tradition of it being passed from father to son having been phased out except for in a handful of exceptional families, like that of Ignatius Blikololong, after too many heirs to the hâmmâlollo had gone abroad for school. This year, Jon promised himself, he would become a lamafa. That was one desire the modern world could not fulfill.

AFTER LEAPING FROM THE SAMPAN and hurling the harpoon at the devil ray, Jon tracked the missile's path as he fell toward the water, but by the time he hit, he was sure he had missed. Froth blinded him. He kicked back to the surface to see the harpoon line skidding over the railing, spitting splinters as it chewed into the wood.

Narek, fighting to wrangle the coils, yelled at him, "Get in!"

Jon had harpooned his first prey.

He hauled himself aboard, grabbed the slithering rope, and braced his feet against the hull, using his whole body as a chock. Still, the nylon tore calluses off his palms. On a jonson or a téna, five or six men would usually handle prey of this size rather than two. But at last the whizzing rope slowed. It jerked right, left, up, down, instead of sliding straight out. Then it slackened — not the abrupt limpness of the line breaking or the harpoon head jerking forth, but the droop of the ray turning back toward the boat to relieve the pain. Left hand over right hand, Jon and Narek reeled the rope in, feeding it out whenever the boʉu dove so as not to risk the harpoon flange ripping free or the line snapping, and then stealthily stealing line again whenever the fish circled closer. The sun blazed. The sail flapped in a rising wind, its congressman smiling down on them. The rope had scraped Jon's palms to a hamburgery mush. His fingers, forearms, and shoulders were cramping, and his feet, braced against the hull, had ached until they numbed. But he knew the ray was hurting more: ribbons of blood had drifted to the surface, slicking it.

You are sent by the Ancestors, Jon prayed. *Give yourself to me.* He asked the Ancestors to prevent any sharks from stealing the ray off his line.

Soon the ray was close enough that he could see curlicues of blood burping from around the harpoon shaft embedded in its pale belly. It swam in a wide corkscrew toward the surface, like a reverse death spiral. The hunters did not even have to fight it anymore, but Narek screwed a harpoon into a bamboo shaft while Jon took up the slack in the rope. Soon its wing tips almost brushed the boat and Jon could see remoras hitchhiking on its belly. Narek poised himself just behind the prow, so his shadow did not fall on the water, and then drove the harpoon down with both hands. Wings buffeted the hull. Once the ray's thrashing eased, Narek embedded a gaff hook into its gasping, sucker mouth and dragged its head above the water. They did not want to mangle the meat further by stabbing the body again, so Jon drove a duri into the skull until he had opened a hole. Then he sank three fingers into the cavity up to their knuckles. Inside was clammy, cavernlike. He stirred the slippery gob of the brain until it broke into nuggets. The gray matter stuck like cold grease beneath his fingernails.

Throughout the battle, he had been autopiloted by adrenaline, but as the sampan rocked beneath the baking sun and the wind sighed, he realized he had taken his first prize as a hunter. Triumphantly, he began imagining how he would divide the manta steaks among his family and clan.

As the two were preparing to haul the catch aboard, a jonson charged up to them. The crew had seen the struggle from afar and had come to investigate on the chance that more bōu were schooling nearby. Jon's grandfather was aboard, as he still occasionally went to sea on days he felt strong enough to do light work, like bailing. Yosef Boko yelled, "Narek, did you kill it already? Are there others?"

"Jon got it!" Narek answered.

"I don't believe it!" Yosef Boko shouted, squinting, trying to descry the evidence through his cataracts. Before Jon could answer, the jonson's driver restarted the engine and piloted the craft toward the splashing of distant dolphins.

Jon and Narek finished dragging the ray atop the mound of nets, where it would be clearly visible when they sailed into Lamalera Bay. With its weight, the sampan rode considerably lower in the water. Jon fetched the plastic container that still held leftovers of his breakfast, *fata biti,* popcorn smashed flat by his grandmother between two rocks, and scooped the ray's brains into it. His love of ray brains was famous in Lamalera, and friends who were less enthusiastic about the delicacy brought him the gray matter of any rays they caught. As they sailed home, Jon splashed seawater on the meat to keep it from overheating. Labalekang volcano rose before them like a colossal sperm whale, petrified mid-arc as it prepared to dive, its rounded sides rising nearly a mile from sea to summit until peaking in a dorsal hump-like fragment of cone. Five more distant stratovolcanoes interrupted the horizon, links in the more than 13,000 islands that make up Indonesia. But the mountains were anthills compared to the seemingly boundless Savu Sea.

Soon Jon could discern individual trees balanced on the precipitous ridges of Labalekang, riven with flumes and gorges. The top half of the volcano was cloaked with old-growth jungle, but the bottom half was a patchwork of cashew orchards, cassava gardens, and maize fields. It was August, halfway through the dry season, and the leaves that had shone an almost iridescent green just a month earlier had desiccated to a shade of tinder. The coast was a mariner's nightmare: gnarled headlands of petrified lava against which the waves shredded themselves. From the ocean, Lamalera's placement seemed inevitable, above the only beach for miles. The houses were stacked on drywall terraces balanced against the steep slope of the volcano, with fairytale staircases chiseled into the cliffs connecting the landings. The paint of the houses, regardless of whether it had started as green or blue or purple, had been bleached a uniform white by the sun. In the scouring afternoon light, the town seemed lifeless, except for the geckos wiggling over the cracked concrete walls. Despite a patina of rust on many of the corrugated tin roofs, the sun reflected off the metal, such that a halo seemed to crown the village.

As Jon glided over a coral garden and sunken whale ribs, he sniffed the funk of the dolphin steaks and manta wings jerkying on bamboo racks, as well as hundreds of flying fish baking on sun-heated roofing. He and Narek back-paddled at the edge of the breakers, waiting for a lull, and then surfed a small wave onto the black sand beach, littered with gigantic discarded rib bones and vertebrae. The skulls of whales and porpoises were arranged totemically on the boulders framing each end. Three shoeless men hotfooted it across the scorching sand and helped them drag the laden sampan to the boat sheds.

Because Lamalera Bay is just a nook in the coastline and provides little protection from waves, the Lamalerans do not anchor their vessels there but store them in boat sheds lining the back of the beach. Beneath the palm-leaf thatch of a shelter, it was as cool as a seaside forest, and the five men leaned against pillars made of unplaned tree trunks as they rolled cigarettes.

One eyed the devil ray and asked Narek, "You get it with a harpoon or the nets?"

"Jon got it," Narek answered.

The man looked at Jon. "No way!"

"You think I'm a kefela?" Jon said. "That I can't harpoon a ray? I'm a Lamaleran, and that's mine."

Meanwhile, children raided the buckets of catch. They popped the eyes out of the fishes' sockets with their uncut fingernails, slurped the orbs into their mouths, crushing the treats between their tongues and their palates, savoring the bursts of salty sweet fluid. Afterwards, they spit out only the wadded indigestible lenses as if they were exhausted gum. Jon made a show of grumpily shooing the children away, though really he was pleased because he remembered how much he had once enjoyed the morsels. He even snuck a few whole fish to the kids he knew were from especially poor families.

Narek divided up the fish while Jon managed the ray. As Jon had never butchered one before, he summoned Vinsent "Senti" Sulaona, the head of the Sulaona clan, to show him how. It was important that the catch be divided according to the Ways of the Ancestors. First, the largest portion was set aside for Jon, for spearing the animal. Then three shares, about half the size of Jon's, were portioned out: one for Narek, one for the owner of the sampan, and one for Senti, as homage for the butchering and the lesson. Each man would then give several portions of his meat to his family or the needy in his clan, like widows. (For larger types of prey, like a whale, Jon would have received a third lamafa's portion, which he was then supposed to bestow on his family, though he could not eat a morsel of it himself, on danger of a curse that would enfeeble him.) Of course, there was another reason to have Senti there. Jon had also calculated that the chief might someday need a new lamafa to work his jonson or téna, and he would see how deep the harpoon had penetrated and how perfectly centered the wound was in the ray's chest. The accumulation of trophies such as this gave a man the chance to step to the front of the hâmmâlollo.

Senti was knifing the wings of the ray into even strips when Jon heard a raspy laugh — Ika, his younger sister. "Jon! You caught this!" She had seen him sail into the bay from their home on the cliffs above. Jon loved Ika's laugh, hoarse as if she had been chain-smoking all her eighteen years, though she had never touched a cigarette. It was a laugh that hijacked her body no matter how inconsequential the happiness was. She clutched her sides now as if invisible hands were tickling her, giggling over the sheer size of the ray. Jon tried to play it cool in front of Senti, but he could not help grinning when Ika exclaimed, "How am I going to be able to carry this? It's such a big one!"

Jon and Ika washed beach grit off their meat in the ocean and then piled the slabs into a plastic tub. Ika wrapped a towel around the top of her head, then squatted down, and Jon settled the container on top of the cushion. Because the load was so heavy, he helped her stand. Jon lifted two buckets crammed with hundreds of flying fish. As they climbed the stacked-stone stairs up the cliffs, Ika hymned in her smoky alto about unexpected blessings. She was renowned as one of the best soloists in the Lamaleran choir.

Jon and Ika's house was the very last one before the volcano became too steep to finagle any more land out of the slope. Beyond, the jungle rioted. The house was perched on a quadruple terrace of dry stack, forty feet high, so that the branches of the ancient tamarind tree rooted at the base of the terraces tapped against the dwelling's roof.

Jon and Ika's house

Even by Lamaleran standards, Jon's house was a poor dwelling, its pasteboard walls rotting, its yellow paint flaking away. Rocks had been stacked on its roof to keep the corrugated tin from flapping up in a strong wind, and rust had chewed the edges to lace. Its three rooms encompassed about two hundred fifty square feet. But it had a millionaire's view: the tousled palm trees, the beach, the bay, the endless Savu Sea, the sunset horizon. The rocky yard was filled with broken fishing floats used to pot thorny flowers and bamboo racks draped with jerkying flesh.

Grandmother Fransiska appeared in the doorway, beneath the desiccated toothy maw of a shark lashed to the crossbeam, as Jon set down his buckets. Her hands shook as she presented him a mug of coffee. Her skin was shrink-wrapped to her bones, her hair a dirty white, her joints knobby with arthritis, and her back hunched like a question mark. She showed off her three remaining teeth when she smiled.

Jon savored the sugary jolt of the condensed milk sweetening the drink — a special treat his grandmother must have added to celebrate the occasion.

Yosef Boko edged out of the house, his eyes like cracked marbles, his hands extended like a mummy's. The jonson he had crewed, with its engine, had beat the sampan home. He did not speak quite in the direction of his grandchildren. "Did you get it with a harpoon or the net?" he asked.

"Harpoon," Jon answered.

"Good," Yosef Boko said. "When you said that at sea, I wasn't sure I'd heard right."

"You think I'm a kefela too?"

"I'm not calling you a liar. I just can't see far, and you do like telling stories. But I'm proud of you." In the future, Yosef Boko said, Jon could become a lamafa.

Jon sipped his coffee, letting gratitude suffuse him. He waved flies away from the meat, enough for at least two weeks, so they would not have to subsist on only rice and smashed corn. There would even be surplus for Ika to sell outside the tribe to earn a little money for Mari's school fees, as they hoped to send her to high school in Lewoleba next year.

At that moment, the family's assets were meager: about a week's worth of fresh flying fish and twice that in dried flying fish; twenty pounds of devil ray meat, half of which Ika would transform into four sacks of corn from the mountain tribes; an emergency store of sperm whale jerky and rice mixed with ash to keep the weevils off; a few hens tied to the table in the kitchen with fishing line to keep them and their chicks from wandering into the jungle and getting eaten by wildcats; two mature pigs and their piglets in wallows out back; a dozen or so hooks and lures; two knives forged in the village; a one-thirteenth share of any catches from the clan's téna, for Jon's work as a paddler; a few dollars in Indonesian rupiah they kept on their persons; and the crumbling house itself.

In addition, Jon personally owned two pairs of torn, imitation Levi's jeans that had been too long for him until he cut off their cuffs; a few factory-made sarongs; a treasured Real Madrid knockoff soccer jersey; a cell phone that had some of its missing keys replaced by glued-on rubber tabs, and that often lacked enough credits to make a call; a Justin Bieber poster with Ika's name tattooed in pen on the heartthrob's neck; a few magazine advertisements featuring South Korean supermodels that he had carefully ripped from their bindings; a repurposed pill bottle stuffed with tobacco confetti and *lontar*-leaf rolling papers; a few lighters almost empty of fluid; and a pair of sandals he had stitched together himself with fishing line, though he usually went barefoot.

But today Jon felt rich.

He kicked the tub of devil ray meat to scare off the flies, then opened his breakfast container, which had once contained smashed popcorn, to show off the mess inside. Ika cackled, Grandmother Fransiska clapped her hands softly so as not to aggravate her arthritis, and Yosef Boko squinted in perplexity until he caught a pungent whiff, and then he laughed too.

Jon had a ritual for cooking ray brains. First, he would fetch a bamboo staff stored beside the house for just this purpose, carefully lean over the edge of the terrace with it, and knock a tamarind pod off the uppermost branches of the *tobi* tree. Then he would boil the pod in a wok over a wood fire in a soot-encrusted kitchen shack until the velvety casing spit out the lacquered pebble-like seeds inside. Once the seeds had colored the water maroon, he would dump in the brains. The flesh was gray, threaded with blue and purple veins, but it would quickly blanch in the heat, then take on the tamarind's reddish tinge. As it cooked down, its oil would grease the water. Every thirty seconds, he would poke the brains with a spoon. When they no longer recoiled like jelly but remained firm, he would add the waxed sparks of bird's-eye chilies — but only three, as they were expensive and had to be bought from Lewoleba. Once the water was reduced to a hissing puddle beneath the brain meatballs, he would drop in diminutive shallots coaxed from the rocky hills out back. Then he would spoon one lobe directly into his mouth and savor the salty, fiery, lemony fishiness.

But that afternoon Labalekang was already hiding the sun, and Jon could fillet flying fish faster than Ika, so he asked her to cook the brains. Soon she presented four plates stacked with the steaming gray matter and its gravy piled atop a mound of rice mixed with milled corn. The family gathered on a wooden bench next to the bamboo platform covered with fish innards. Jon thanked God and the Ancestors, then blessed his family and the food. He felt like a true Lamaleran man. Before long, his preoccupation with the world beyond the horizon was bound to return, but at times like this, he believed there could be no better way to live.

Chapter Three

THE CHILD-EATING EEL AND THE CURSE OF THE BLACK GOAT

Time Immemorial–May 1, 2014

Sipri — Frans

S o say the stories of the Ancestors: Before the past ossified into history, before time was straitjacketed in a calendar, at the very moment memory began, a typhoon engulfed Lembata and Labalekang volcano. When the storm finally lifted, it revealed a naked man spirit astride the peak: Sipri Raja Rimo. From that vantage, he surveyed unruly jungle, footprintless beaches — and a woman spirit, Jawa Lepang Ina, who had just crawled forth from a cave to the soft music of rain dripping off pine boughs. They had seven sons and became the Wujon clan, the Lords of the Land.

After many years, a new animal arrived in their realm. The Wujons spied on it from the forest. It looked like them, but it lacked their ability to fly and to communicate with other spirits. And unlike the Wujons, who wove their clothes from tree bark and ate raw grubs, these new animals had clothes spun from jungle cotton, fishing hooks and harpoons carved from sappanwood, and crops they coaxed from the iron-red earth. This was man, the clan of Tapoonā.

One day when the Wujons were shadowing a woodcutting party, the humans' dogs barked, bounded into the underbrush, and sniffed out the spies. When the humans saw the Lords of the Land, they realized at once that they were in the presence of the mountain's native spirits. They offered tribute to the Wujons and promised to teach them their arts in exchange for the right to remain. Years passed. The more time the Wujons spent with the Tapoonãs, the more human they became, dyeing cotton sarongs with roots and squid ink, cutting their dreadlocks, sowing cassava, and fishing the coastal reefs—though neither the Wujons nor the Tapoonãs dared to challenge the whales that breached in the nearby sea.

But eventually a wooden boat with eyes carved in its prow and a furled palm-leaf sail plowed onto their beach. A dozen men swapped their paddles for machetes and leapt out. These were the Lamalerans. Despite their fierce appearance, they were refugees, having fled to the rim of the Indonesian Archipelago, searching for a new home after a tragedy.

Although the Lamalerans could not have known this, they had reached what would become their home just as Europe launched its colonial conquest of Asia, heralding the onset of globalization, which would move unprecedented numbers of people, ideas, and goods across the earth, and forever transform humanity. The Lamalerans had no calendar yet, but the date would probably have been not long after January 1522, when during the first circumnavigation of the earth the Portuguese explorer Ferdinand Magellan passed within sight of the tribe's original home, the island of Lepan Batan, off the eastern coast of Lembata, and noted it was inhabited. However, within a few years it would be desolate.

For centuries, the Lamalerans had lived prosperously on Lepan Batan, hunting manta rays and whales with harpoon heads made of sappan heartwood. But one afternoon, while gathering shellfish, a childless crone discovered an eel and brought it home. She reared the eel until it reached python-esque proportions. Then it disappeared.

She circled the village, calling its name as if it were a lost dog, weeping. The next day, when the men returned from fishing and the women from their gardens, a child was missing. Another vanished the day after. The young survivors told of a grotesque beast slithering among the shadows as soon as the adults left.

When the Lamalerans tracked the eel to a hollow tree in the jungle, the animal hissed at them from inside the trunk. But the men heated an iron rod over a fire until it glowed. The crone pleaded with them to spare her eel, warning that they would be cursed if they killed it, for the eel was beloved of the sea, but they jammed the weapon into a hole in the tree.

A rancid green smoke poured forth. A roar echoed through the jungle. The Lamalerans rushed home just in time to meet a tsunami. A wall of ocean engulfed them, splintering their boats and bamboo huts, and drowning most of them. When the waters receded, their leader, Tana Kĕrofa, decided that a new home would have to be found. The survivors were so few and their possessions so meager that everything and everyone fit into the single remaining téna, *Kebako Pukā*. When they raised their sails, they left only one thing behind: the crone.

Thus began the Lamalerans' odyssey, which in the coming years carried them across the Alor Strait and down the eastern coast of Lembata. Along the way, they weathered storms, the wrath of powerful territorial spirits, and conflicts with other tribes. The Lamalerans did not immediately settle in present-day Lamalera but in the hills above a nearby paradisiacal bay. There they taught locals how to make pottery in return for the knowledge of how to forge iron harpoon heads.

However, their idyll was shattered when a son of Tana Kĕrofa slept with the unmarried daughter of the region's chieftain. Tana Kĕrofa was then deposed by a Lamaleran named Korohama, who set forth to find the Lamalerans a new home to avoid war with the offended father. While hunting, Korohama had noticed that the winds and currents often nudged the téna to a shallow bay bracketed by steep cliffs.

The black sand beach at that time was uninhabited because the Wujons and the Tapoonās lived on the volcanic ridges above, like most of the island's denizens, to protect themselves from raiding slavers and headhunting, which was common practice then among most tribes, including the Lamalerans.

When Korohama climbed the cliffs above the bay, the Wujons confronted him. Immediately, he recognized that they were native spirits. He asked if the Lamalerans could settle there and pay tribute. At first, Gési Raja, who had succeeded his father, Sipri Raja, rejected him. But each morning, Korohama returned, increasing his offer: first promising five brass bracelets, then adding a golden chain, and finally including an elephant tusk the length of one *dpa,* a Lamaleran measurement that extends from the center of the speaker's chest to the tip of his finger when his arm is outstretched. It was only when Korohama agreed to render the eyes, a portion of the head flesh, and the skull of every slain whale to the Wujons that Gési said, "Bring your wives and children! You will live here like we are your older brothers."

The formulation of "older brother" had a very specific meaning in a culture of strict family hierarchies: younger siblings obeyed older ones, and so the Lamalerans were promising to follow the Wujons. Under the banyan tree in what is today the center of Upper Lamalera, in the presence of the Nuba Nara, the sacred stones that were the locus of the Wujons' power, the Wujons received the Lamalerans' oath.

The Lamalerans relocated to modern-day Upper Lamalera, built a téna fleet, and planted the tree trunk pillars of their boathouses. In the back of those sheds, they piled the skulls of the forebears and rubbed them with coconut oil and fed them chicken blood. They erected wooden houses with thatched roofs pointed like buffalo horns and planted cacti around the village to form a fence of natural barbed wire. As the years passed, the Wujons piled their cachalot skulls in the center of the beach, so soon it was called Ikā Kotā, the place of fish heads.

Korohama waxed old. When he felt he would soon join the Ances-

tors, he summoned his three sons. The eldest he charged with maintaining the sacred rituals and the village temple — from him would
spring the Blikololong clan. His middle son he gave a magical *kris* dag-
ger and ordered him to guard the tribe — from his children would rise
the Bataona clan and its various offshoots, including the Bediona clan.
His youngest son he tasked with administrating the village — from
him descended the Lefõ Tukang clan. Together, these three clans
would become known as the Lika Telo, or the Big Three, a reference
to the three hearthstones that support a rice pot above a cooking fire.
They are the aristocracy of Lamalera and continue to influence village
matters more strongly than other clans to the present day.

The Wujons never lost their unique place in Lamaleran society,
but eventually their prestige slipped. The more time the supernatural
Lords of the Land spent around the Lamalerans, the more they lived
like them. They became part of the tribe, intermarrying and sharing
their daily life, eventually even hunting in their own téna, and yet
always holding themselves aloof. As the centuries passed, they lost
many of their powers, such as the ability to fly, but nevertheless, they
continued practicing shamanistic ceremonies, which could curse their
enemies or conjure the Ancestors. Their most important ritual was Ige
Gerek, the Calling of the Whales, which they performed annually to
summon the Lamalerans' prey on the last day of April, as the monsoons ended and the Hunger Season turned to Léfa, the Season of the
Open Sea — the hunting season.

But before the Lords of the Land would enact Ige Gerek, the Lika
Telo had to climb the cliffs to pay homage to them as Korohama had
to Gési Raja.

ON APRIL 28, 2014, the Lamalerans were aflutter: men whispered on
the beach and women visited one another's kitchens to spread the news
that Ige Gerek would not be performed that year. The Wujons were
offended because the Lika Telo had failed to make their annual pilgrimage bearing gifts, including an all-important sacrificial chicken.

In the past, the Calling of the Whales had occasionally been skipped, usually when the Wujons were angry at the Lamalerans for failing to properly honor them as "older brothers." The Wujons were proud and took offense at many slights, from individuals transgressing the Ways of the Ancestors to clans failing to pay them tribute, such as the eyes of the sperm whales that had been caught, which the shamans liked to dry until the spheres imploded like rotten gourds and then boil for soup. The consequence of infuriating the Wujons had often been famine—or worse.

The hunting season two years before had provided a stark reminder of what happened when the Wujons were displeased. As Siprianus "Sipri" Raja Wujon, the current head of the clan, had descended to the beach to complete Ige Gerek at the end of April 2012, a gang of youth sitting under a tamarind tree had drunkenly waved their jerrican of tuak at him and shouted, *Baleo! Baleo!* While most of the older generation venerated the Lords of the Land, the youth were more skeptical.

Thereafter, that whaling season, the Lamalerans had chased spouts futilely, until after several months, a lamafa named Gregorious Klake Sulaona finally harpooned a monstrous seventy-foot-long schoolmaster sperm whale. But rather than capitulating like a gift sent by the Ancestors, the old bull turned on them, battering its way through the fleet so that many of the ships would need to spend the next few weeks drydocked for repairs. Seeking an opportunity to land another harpoon, Gregorious bravely stayed above deck while the rest of the crew huddled below the thwarts. But he failed to glimpse the flukes sweeping up from behind him and was swatted into the ocean. Another téna dragged him aboard and rushed him to shore, while his comrades stayed to revenge themselves on the whale.

Gregorious, however, would never taste its meat. He lasted two days, vomiting and pissing blood. He had lived by the Old Ways and he died by the Old Ways, refusing to go to a hospital, putting his faith in a compress of turmeric and candlenut leaves, as well as sprinklings of holy water from shamans.

Not that modern medicine could have solved what afflicted him. Many Lamalerans believed Gregorious had been punished for the sins of the whole tribe, since they had angered the Lords of the Land. (Some of his tribespeople also whispered that his end had been poetic justice written by the Ancestors: it was rumored he had been beating his wife and so the whale beat him.) For the rest of 2012, the Lamalerans did not catch a single whale, and while the gigantic bull tided the whole tribe over for several months, it could not replace the other nineteen usually caught, and soon many men had exhausted their stores of jerky and were forced to journey over the mountains to find work to send food back to their families.

In 2014, the Lamaleran rumormongers blamed one man in particular for the displeasure of the Lords of the Land: Gregorious "Kupa" Bataona, the head of the Bataona clan, who did not believe in the Ancestors and had traveled to a nearby island to avoid what he felt was a humiliating obligation. Many younger Lamalerans publicly pointed out that sometimes when the Wujons called down their curses, the whales arrived anyway, but it was an unprecedented crisis to have a faithless man in such an important position.

Kupa had spent most of his life abroad, working as a tailor and managing a coconut plantation, only returning to guard his clan's Spirit House when his older brother passed, and during his time away his beliefs had modernized. When a rare visitor would join him on his porch, he would complain about how the tribe still bartered and suggest that the government needed to build an icebox so they could freeze their catch to export it for cash. The rest of the time, he sat alone, toeing a pedal-powered sewing machine and letting shreds of cloth blow across the village square while children sent by their mothers scavenged the scraps. The gong with which his progenitors had assembled the tribe hung on a hook beside him, rusted and cracked.

The other two clan leaders of the Lika Telo were embarrassed to face the Wujons without Kupa. But they knew just whom to deputize: Frans.

Since Frans had survived his odyssey to Kupang, he had ascended to become the captain of the téna *Kéna Pukā* and acting leader of the Mikulangu Bediona clan. Though not of the aristocratic bloodline, he had been uplifted when his clansmen decided the hereditary head was unfit. He was also a respected shaman whose healing prayers were so renowned that expat Lamalerans telephoned from Jakarta asking him to bless their broken bones remotely. Additionally, he had become a renowned *ata mola*—a shipwright—and ironworker. His harpoon heads were considered the best in the tribe.

Frans was nearing sixty these days, and his once leonine mane and beard had withered until tufts of white hair sprouted only above his ears. But he still had the arms of a blacksmith, with topographical triceps and deltoids. His right forearm was now as crooked as a boomerang: several years earlier, he had been swimming alongside a floundering sperm whale, sawing at it with his duri, when its flailing flukes shattered the bones in his forearm. On returning to shore, he refused to go to the hospital in Lewoleba. Fearing that the doctors would only amputate his limb, he preferred his own holy-water cures. Two days later, he was once again hauling boats and rowing. The bone healed crooked and his right thumb stiffened and became permanently unresponsive. But the disfigurement was not totally useless: if he wanted to intimidate a wayward clansman, he would drape his twisted arm over the man's shoulder while he whispered into his ear.

The Lika Telo chose Frans as their emissary to the Wujon leader, Sipri, because of the Bediona shaman's conservative and serious reputation: he avoided Lamaleran parties, considering them drunken and frivolous; his favorite food was cucumber with salt; and the compliment that most pleased him was to be called "humble." (In private, though, he was slyly funny, making ironic observations about his tribespeople, and he loved to sing old whaling songs while rocking his grandnieces and grandnephew to sleep.) But there was another reason Frans was deputized: as the old Lamaleran saying goes, *Leka puo iri efel,* which roughly translates as: Wujons and Bedionas divide the

Frans

heart, the liver, and the tongue of their catches. A story of the Ancestors related how the Bedionas had once drawn their swords to protect the ambushed Wujons from an assassination attempt by the enemy Lefō Leìn clan. From that day forth, the Wujons and the Mikulangu Bediona clan have been as one, even sharing feasts of whale organs. As for the Lefō Leìn, one night the Wujons sacrificed a black goat and asked the Ancestors to curse their enemies. Sickness and accidents stalked the clan until they went extinct.

And so, early on the morning of April 30, Frans climbed onto the back of a motorcycle driven by another Lamaleran elder, headed for Lewoleba, where Sipri lived. Then they began the long climb up the potholed, muddy road twisting around Labalekang, which had long ago been stripped of most of its asphalt. At first, they drove through mountain hamlets, humble brick and bamboo houses backed by groves of banana plants with prehistoric-sized leaves and cashew trees hung with unripe fruits like green bells. Women swept their ferrous dirt yards with hand brooms made of dried and knotted grass, as though they were Zen monks patterning sand. Barefoot men led goats to pasture, their machetes slapping against their thighs with each step. Girls balanced bundles of vine-bound firewood on their heads, waving at the passersby without turning to look for fear of dislodging their burdens. Mangy dogs barked and chased them. The Lamalerans cruised past a graveyard where bowls and spoons lay on the concrete slabs like table settings for the Ancestors.

These were the mountain tribes, who for centuries had traded corn for whale jerky with the Lamalerans. For while the Savu Sea provided ample protein to the Lamalerans, it was almost impossible to grow vegetables on the arid coast, and the mountain tribes had bountiful crops in their lush valleys but few ways to get protein. Because the kefela were of a Melanesian stock distinct from the Lamalerans' Asiatic roots, and had been pushed inland by the whalers and other Austronesian newcomers migrating to their home, they had separate cultures and dialects. Yet the two groups had managed to overcome their differences through the mutual reliance of the barter economy. The Lamalerans were further bound to their trading partners by religion, for though some of the other coastal fishing tribes were Islamic, the mountain tribes had also converted to Christianity.

As the motorbike ground up Labalekang, the air cooled and the trees flanking opposite sides of the road linked branches to form a tunnel. Roadkill snakes shone like rumpled, still-glossy ribbons. Near the rim of Labalekang, they coasted through a cathedral of candlenut trees whose trunks were like the pillars of a great temple, their vault of foliage so dense that the sunlight filtering through was tinged green and no underbrush grew there.

As they slalomed down the back side of the volcano toward Lewoleba, the towns increased and the spaces between them shortened. Stalks of mountain rice so green that they seemed to glow poked up through ashes in swidden clearings. Strands of teak trees, planted for lumber, replaced native jungle, with leaves the size of dinner plates clapping in the wind. The Lamalerans squeezed the motorcycle onto the shoulder of the road whenever a dump truck trundled past, masking their faces with their shirts against the sand billowing off the back. As they approached Lewoleba, they passed Timorese construction workers laying new asphalt, and the road suddenly smoothed to a raceway. Finally, they glided with herds of other motorbikes past concrete houses and a garage-like store displaying shrink-wrapped TVs and refrigerators — Lewoleba.

As the crow flies, the journey was only about fifteen miles, but it was like they had passed into a different world. Any visitor from Jakarta or Bali would have sneered at the goats roaming the streets and the population of about 25,000 people. To Frans and the rest of Lembata's inhabitants, however, it was the Big City. Soon, caught in its maze, he was struggling to remember the directions to Sipri's home.

Although Frans had been to Lewoleba dozens of times, he still always got lost in its grid of brick houses and palm-tree-lined streets — a fact that Bena, his favorite daughter, teased him about when he picked her up from its port on her biannual trips home from a faraway university. His confusion stemmed from the fact that the Lamaleran system of orientation draws its locus from the Blikololong Spirit Houses, as they are the spiritual center of the tribe. Accordingly, a direction might be literally translated from Lamaleran as "east of Teti Nama Papã Spirit House," an instruction that becomes progressively less helpful the farther away one is from the wellspring of the Ancestors. Even more, the Lamalerans are so intimate with their geography that the proper names of their landmarks incorporate this knowledge — Labalekang, for instance, means "The Volcano Behind Us"— and they use special verbs to describe their movement in relation to them. Outside of southern Lembata, of course, those terms are useless. Frans could guide *Kéna Pukā* home through soupy fog, but beyond Lamalera he quickly lost his bearings.

Eventually, the elder driving the motorbike asked directions, and the two men soon pulled up to a newly plastered brick house with a shiny metal roof, tucked away on a dirt backstreet. A hand-painted whalebone sign announced WHALE OIL SOLD HERE, for about two dollars a bottle. A man who looked too old to still be alive met them at the door. Already frail, Sipri had been starved thinner by age, his skin wrapped so tightly around his skull that the pulsing of the veins crossing his temples was clearly visible. The Lord of the Land lived outside his land because for decades he had worked as a tax collector in Lewoleba, earning money for his clan while his older brother ruled at home, though Sipri had always returned to Lamalera to attend important rituals, such as the Calling of the Whales. When his brother died several years earlier, Sipri had inherited his leadership and the responsibility to perform Ige Gerek. But he had continued dwelling in the city so that he could be near medical care for his wife, who had recently become bedridden from a stroke.

Two days earlier, Sipri had traveled to Lamalera to receive the Lika Telo in the grass-thatched Wujon Spirit House—the last structure in Lamalera built in the old style, for the shamans believed the Ancestors would not visit a newfangled brick house—but left aggrieved when the trio did not show. For years he had been brooding that the Lamalerans were abandoning the Ways of the Ancestors, and the recent trespass confirmed this. Even more, he felt it was his responsibility to do something about this falling off, for though the Lords of the Land were nominally Catholic, like all their tribesmen, they were also the guardians of the ancient and undercover religion the Lamalerans had once followed.

Before Christianity arrived in Lembata, its inhabitants, along with the people of the rest of the Solor Archipelago, had worshipped Lera Wulan, the Sun-Moon God, and the Ancestors. They had communicated with them through the Nuba Nara, the sacred stones, with one representing each clan, which were assembled in a ring around the banyan tree in the center of Lamalera. Lera Wulan was a double-faced god who divided men into factions, the "Demon" and the "Paji," according to each of his sides, and set them at eternal war so that he would always have blood offerings. (The Lamalerans were Demon, as evidenced by the middle name of Yohanes "Jon" Demon Hariona. For the most part, the Demon tribes lived in the mountains and farmed, while the Paji groups occupied the coast and fished, with the Lamalerans being an exception to that rule.) Droughts signaled that Lera Wulan was thirsty, and often precipitated fighting between Demon and Paji groups as each side sought blood to drizzle on their Nuba Nara to summon rain.

Although Jesuit missionaries first visited Lamalera in the late nineteenth century, it was not until the arrival of German missionary Bernardus Bode, in 1920, that Christianity — and, by extension, the outside world for the first time — really made inroads into Lamalera. Undaunted by the totemic pile of whale bones and the tribe's occasional cannibalism, he learned the Lamaleran tongue and preached. (In his letters, he described hearing that Lamaleran warriors had killed twelve Paji men, cut off their hands and feet, sun-dried the appendages, and then ground them with stones to dust, which they mixed with palm wine and drank the next time they went into battle to strengthen their own limbs.)

At first, thirty sorcerers — as Bode called them — led a stiff resistance. But not long into his tenure he wrote home describing how "remarkably, almost all of [the sorcerers] died within a very short time." In three years, he expanded his ministry to neighboring villages and quadrupled the number of baptized Christians on the island from three hundred to twelve hundred. As his influence grew, he banned human sacrifice, though animal sacrifice continued behind his back, and supervised Christian burials for the skulls enshrined in the boat sheds. He also burned the mountain of skulls at Ikā Kotā and erected on the ashes a chapel to Saint Peter, the fisher of souls, who would become the patron saint of Lamalera. When he announced plans to dig up the Nuba Nara and use the stones as the foundation for a church, threats were made against his life. But in the hunt the next day every single téna in the village landed prey, which the Lamalerans took as a sign of the power of the Catholic God, perhaps saving Bode. The Wujons spirited their Nuba Nara into the jungle, but the other clans let theirs be subsumed into the new house of worship. The following year was particularly good for hunting, cementing the tribe's faith. When Bode summoned all the men to the church altar to swear away their heathenism, none refused, even the Wujons. At the same time the Demon tribes of Lembata were converting to Christianity — including the Lamalerans and their mountain tribe trading partners — the coastal fishing Paji tribes were mostly joining Islam, meaning that the old conflicts would continue under new religions to the modern day.

By 1925, Bode wrote that there was only one heathen left in Lamalera. But he did not know that every year, on the final day of April, the Wujons stole from the village in the witching hours, bearing sacrifices to the Nuba Nara and ancient Spirit Houses hidden atop Labalekang. Beneath the Catholic façade, the Wujons kept the old beliefs thriving among their tribesmen.

As the decades passed, and the Lamalerans took Christian names, the religions fused so that the Lamalerans came to view their Christian and animist traditions as one. Bode had eased the Lamalerans into Catholicism by arguing that Lera Wulan was actually God and that the Ancestors were saints, essentially overlaying Christianity onto the indigenous religion, so the synthesis was no great leap. Today, a statue of Bode rides the hâmmâlollo of a concrete téna in front of the church, the tribe regards itself as fervently Catholic, and many Lamalerans do not remember there was ever an un-Christianized version of Lera Wulan. Only a handful of Lamalerans — mainly the Wujons — distinguish between the two religions, though even Sipri had described them as parts of a whole, sincerely believing himself Christian even while sacrificing animals as the Lord of the Land. Several pagan ceremonies have been openly incorporated into Catholic worship, such as Misa Arwah, the Mass for Lost Souls that follows Ige Gerek.

Thus, Ige Gerek remains one of the few authentic bridges to the old religion that used to define Lamalera. As such, Sipri felt, its survival or erasure would define the tribe's future.

THE BEST PART OF SIPRI'S YEAR had always been communing with the Ancestors and Lera Wulan at Ige Gerek. In 2013, the year before the Lika Telo failed him, Sipri had leaned on the Spear of the Dragon as he crutched up Labalekang in the predawn darkness, the rusted heirloom that guaranteed the Lords of the Land victory in any battle now reduced to a walking stick. His knees popped every few steps. It was only the anticipation of meeting the Ancestors that energized him up the steep mountainside. His son, his grandsons, and his nephews all followed him, carrying the Gong of Calling, the Sword of the Ancestors, and other heirlooms, as well as offerings: bamboo tubes filled with tuak and a trussed and clucking chicken. He dressed in the old habit—black robes and a conical bamboo hat—but despite his disapproval, the younger Wujons wore cutoff jean shorts and T-shirts, or went bare-chested.

As they crossed the cashew orchards of the mountain tribes, it was still early enough that stars bejeweled the sky. Then the jungle dwarfed them. Colossal banyan trees unfurled like forests unto themselves, with ferns and other epiphytes sprouting from their branches. Rattan vines tangled their feet. The foliage was so dense that it still seemed night under the canopy even after dawn lit the tops of the trees.

In the late morning, they at last reached Itok Kefélong Fata, the First Spirit House of the Ancestors, a huge boulder in the shape of a whale nose, complete with a blowhole, near the precipice where Sipri Raja Rimo, the spirit from whom they had descended, had materialized. In the sacral clearing, the Wujons mitered themselves with crowns woven from tree branches. Then Sipri smushed a hen egg against the stone, and smeared the yolk in swirls speckled with shell. Next, he laid the chicken on the rock. Metal rang on stone as he knifed through lungs and vertebrae. Gripping the corpse by the spurs, he upended it, letting its blood spray until the concave nostril overflowed. Then he finger-painted red into the yellow.

Sipri's grandsons roasted the corpse over a coconut-husk fire, then the Wujons plucked apart the charred mess, licking their singed fingers as they ate and snapping bones to suck the marrow. But most of the meat they arranged atop the bloody boulder as a meal for the Ancestors, garnishing the gory mess with tobacco rolled in dried palm leaves. As the roasted flesh perfumed the wilderness, Sipri knew the spirits were assembling, enticed by the scent.

With crimson hands, Sipri raised the Spear of the Dragon and shouted: "From the peak of the mountain where our father appeared, from the cave in the mountain where our mother appeared, from the Spirit House of Itok Kefélong Fata, from the Spirit Houses at every point, we call the Ancestors to come in their hundreds and thousands, to bring the food for the widows and the children of the Two Villages because they are hungry and thirsty, and they cry day and night for your arrival."

Sipri could not see the Ancestors, but he felt their presence like body heat emanating from skin centimeters away from his own. He thanked them for coming. The day before, at the Tobo Nama Fata, the Council on the Beach, his tribesmen had entrusted him with their cares — fears that the catch of manta rays was declining, as well as anger about outsiders dynamite-fishing their reefs — and he unburdened himself of those to the Ancestors. He also apologized that the tribe had strayed from the Old Ways, as outboard motors had replaced sails and the young hunters failed to attend the ceremonies honoring their progenitors. He complained about the suggestion from some of his young tribesmen, which he had ignored, that he should not sit at the head of the Tobo Nama Fata but in the crowd, so the ritual would be more democratic.

But despite his frustrations, this communion with the Ancestors was when Sipri felt purest. He had the sense of being part of not just a contemporary tribe but an ancient one. A younger Wujon began pounding the Gong of Calling. Then the Lords of the Land filed down the trail, their forebears, from oldest to youngest, marching behind them, so it seemed to Sipri as if he was but the present link in an infinite chain, extending from the beginning of human time to that very moment.

The *bong, bong, bong* of the metal instrument echoed in the mountain alley, intimidating the normally raucous jungle birds into silence, and one of the young Wujons chanted without stop a sorcerous incantation, entreating the spirits onward. Sipri was careful never to look back, but he heard the Ancestors chattering behind him, as sibilant as a shushing breeze. Normally, Labalekang was busy with the kefela men working their gardens, but everyone knew the spirits were out that day, and the footpaths were empty. The jungle steamed. Butterflies flitted across their path like windblown scraps of rainbow.

About three kilometers downslope, Sipri stopped at the next Spirit House, Pau Lera, another petrified whale, and threaded a rope woven of jungle grass through a nostril-like hole, as if inserting a lead through the nose ring of an ox, before yanking the animal toward the sea. Farther downhill, the Wujons stopped at Enaj Senoa, the Nuba Nara stone Sipri's grandfather had hidden after Christian missionaries tried to destroy it, and with magic divided the evil spirits from the good spirits. Sipri's last stop was at the most important Spirit House: Fato Kotekĕlema, the Whale Stone, a spine of rock breaching through red clay like a bull whale swimming through an ocean of earth.

Sipri climbed the boulder and traded the Spear of the Dragon for a leafy bough lopped from a nearby tree. The good Ancestors and the Wujons stood at attention. The only specters missing were the Seven Whale Spirits. Through gaps in the surrounding palm trees, he could glimpse the rising horizon of the ocean. He swept the bough to the east. "Come from the East!" He swung the bough to the opposite horizon. "Come from the West! Do not roil the ocean! Swim close to the land!

Be calm so the lamafa may take you with half a rope and one harpoon! Come so that the widows and the orphans of Lamalera do not starve!" He repeated the summons three times, ending each verse by squawking like a chicken, grunting like a water buffalo, and then bleating like a goat. It was for this practice that the ceremony was named: in Lamaleran, *Ige* means "to beckon" and *Gerek* means "to call using animal sounds," like how a Lamaleran owner will bark at a dog to summon it.

The Seven Whale Spirits joined the procession. Many miles later, Sipri led the multitudes down the cliffs to the beach, through the breakers, and into the peace of the bay, where they melted into the Savu Sea like water into water, and he was left puddled in his black robes. From the shade of the boat sheds, old whalers watched with their grandsons, whom they had conscripted to join them.

Ige Gerek always made Sipri feel vindicated. It was a demonstration of how crucial he and the Ancestors were to the tribe's survival. Floating in the bay, buoyed by the afterglow of communing with the spirits, he blazed with the conviction that the appearance of the whales that year would persuade his tribesmen to give up their modern affectations. He knew he would pass soon, but he was comforted by the fact that when he became an Ancestor, he would annually answer his descendants' summons and retrace the pilgrimage from the volcano's peak to the ocean, the way that the stars revolved to the same positions on that day every year. The hunt, he believed, would never cease.

Of course, Sipri realized the outside world was relentlessly encroaching on Lembata. During his years in Lewoleba, he had watched it transform from a village of thatched huts to a large town with brick homes, a port, concrete government buildings, and several tens of thousands of inhabitants. Now the island was spiked with TV and cell phone towers to service it. And he had heard rumors that a port would soon be constructed in Wulandoni, a village neighboring Lamalera where the weekly market was held. Once the port was functional, all of southern Lembata would be exposed to the outside world.

Sipri had even seen evidence of the powers of the Ancestors waning.

The Wujons perform Ige Gerek in 2015. Sipri stands with hands folded while his son, Marsianus, holds the gong, and his grandsons look on.

He remembered that when he was a child, thousands of grasshoppers had hummed orchestrally around the Wujons during Ige Gerek and followed them in a biblical storm to the beach — a sign that the Ancestors were pleased. But the grasshoppers no longer appeared. Still, he had believed that while the world might change in less important ways, the Lamalerans' covenant with their Ancestors would endure.

It was not until the evening of April 28, 2014, after Sipri had waited all day for the Lika Telo to visit him in the Wujon Spirit House, that he accepted the Lamalerans might truly forget who they were. If the bloodlines of Korohama could stray, then any betrayal was possible. Unlike the spats between the tribe and the Wujons in the past, this rupture felt potentially permanent to Sipri. The Ancestors had always taught that the unity of the tribe was paramount: *Talé tou, kemui tou, onā tou, mata tou.* But the Big Three chieftains were no longer of one family or action with him. There would be no Ige Gerek. The Ancestors would exact revenge. No whales would surrender themselves to the Lamalerans' harpoons. A year of starvation threatened. He mourned for his people, but they had brought it on themselves. Maybe only a truly severe punishment could save them by reminding them of the potency of the Ancestors.

Until Frans arrived at Sipri's house, the Lord of the Land had darkly wondered: Could the Lamalerans and their culture survive in the modern world?

SIPRI WAS POSING HIS QUESTION about the possibility of the Lamalerans' survival at the tail end of almost 14,000 years of accelerating cultural extinction. In the twelfth century BCE, when all of humanity still lived in hunter-gatherer bands, there were about 100,000 languages worldwide, each representing its own culture, which can thus serve as a way to roughly tally how many existed—and their eventual decline. At that time, the linguistic diversity of the earth probably most resembled the contemporary nations of Indonesia and its neighbor Papua New Guinea, which are home to more than fifteen hundred living languages, and where mountainous islands can shelter tongues as different as English and Mandarin Chinese in valleys only ten miles apart. Living in small bands widely spaced to support a foraging lifestyle, these isolated groups evolved their own unique tongues and ways of life.

As agriculture developed in several places across the continents, people started to stay put and form larger groups to better process the land. These growing farming populations competed with hunter-gatherers for prime territory. They had several advantages in these conflicts, including being more numerous, and having food surpluses to support full-time soldiers and individuals in specialized trades who created advanced technologies. Over thousands of years, agricultural societies grew from villages, to city-states, to kingdoms, to empires. Empires needed a single culture to unite their ever more diverse peoples, and divergent ways of life were sometimes plowed under by official decree.

Even when minorities escaped overt persecution, they often assimilated, abandoning their traditions to gain the advantages of being part of the majority. As foragers either joined civilizations or were wiped out by them, the number of languages and cultures shrank.

Still, at the launch of European colonialism five hundred years ago, there were about 15,000 languages worldwide, more than twice as many as there are today, and hunter-gatherers still occupied a third of the world. Improvements in maritime technology and weaponry, however, allowed European countries to rapidly conquer the globe, intensifying linguistic and cultural extinction. American settlers decimated Native American populations; Australian colonizers executed a policy of genocide against aboriginals; Belgians in the Congo murdered and worked to death around ten million of their African subjects. Whole civilizations were erased by the spread of European diseases such as smallpox, which the immune systems of indigenous peoples had not evolved to handle. In the Americas alone, it is estimated that Europeans were responsible for the deaths of 95 percent of the population in just a few generations. The colonizers imposed their languages, cultures, and religions on the defeated populations, further erasing aboriginal lifestyles. In the 1920s, the British Empire ruled over 20 percent of the world's population and nearly a quarter of the earth, the largest empire in history, while the French controlled a tenth of the earth's landmass.

The Lamalerans were spared the worst brutalities of colonialism by the remoteness of Lembata and its lack of enticing resources. Europeans had little permanent presence in the Solor Archipelago once a fort built by the Portuguese to protect the sandalwood trade was abandoned in the mid-1600s after proving too difficult to provision. Transiting sailors who put ashore searching for fresh water were attacked by men wearing bark and firing arrows tipped with sharpened goat bones, and Westerners began to avoid the islands, fearing their people as cannibals. Around 1850, when the Netherlands bought the Solor Archipelago from the Portuguese, a Dutch administrator wrote that the only facts known about the Lamalerans were that they whaled, were heathens, and pledged allegiance to neither the Dutch nor the Portuguese. In the late nineteenth century, a Dutch official noted that the interior of Lembata had still not been visited by Europeans.

But as the Dutch solidified their control over western Indonesia, they turned their attention east. In 1910, a company of Dutch soldiers visited Lembata to register the population and disarm them of crude rifles acquired through trade. Not long after, Father Bode arrived. But when the Dutch surrendered their claims to Indonesia after World War II, it barely registered with the Lamalerans, for the colonizers had paid almost no attention to the tribe beyond occasionally taxing them for cocoa and coconuts.

Even as colonialism collapsed, however, industrialization was over-taking the earth. Rising living standards enticed foragers into cities. Phones, radios, TVs, and eventually the internet beamed Hollywood movies and British rock songs into previously unreachable places. Cars, trains, and planes overcame once buffering distances. Countries such as Australia and Russia forced aboriginal children into boarding schools, banned their languages, and denied the existence of their tribes to enforce a singular national identity. Amazonians and other indigenous peoples who claim ownership of lucrative natural resources, like untouched forests and oil, are still massacred by those wanting to usurp the riches. Though five centuries earlier hunter-gatherers had occupied the entirety of Australia, most of North America, and much of South America, Africa, and Asia, by the dawn of the second millennium they had been almost wiped out.

In 2016, only around 7,100 languages remained, about 7 percent of peak linguistic diversity. And the pace of language loss was accelerating. Of the surviving tongues, 1,500 or so had fewer than a thousand living speakers, most of them elderly, without a critical mass of fluent youth to ensure their survival. One scholarly estimate suggests that by 2100, as many as 90 percent of the world's extant languages will be dead — leaving just 700 — and that the global population will communicate mostly in English, Mandarin Chinese, and Spanish. What this means is that right now, on average, two entire languages and their accompanying cultures—the millennial accretions of history, philosophy, livelihood, religion, and tradition that express the total character of those peoples—die every month. Of course, languages and cultures have always risen and vanished throughout time, but what humanity is living through now is no more natural than the massive global die-offs of plant and animal species the world is suffering. While it's true that smaller cultural extinctions have happened before, the current wave is happening at an unprecedented speed and scope.

WHEN FRANS AND THE OTHER Lamaleran deputy arrived at Sipri's house to apologize about the debacle surrounding Ige Gerek, the Lord of the Land welcomed them with a traditional sign of hospitality in eastern Indonesia, a plate of *sirih pinang,* a combination of betel nut mixed with peppers and crushed dried coral, which provides a mild buzz when chewed. They sat on lawn chairs in a room that held little more than a humidity-warped Bible and a boxy TV perched on a cabinet. In that bureau's locked wooden drawers were hidden the Heirlooms of the Ancestors: five crocodilian scales white and brittle with age, which Sipri believed to be the last remaining dragon scales in the world; a polished ovoid chunk of elephant tusk, like an ivory egg; and four walnut-sized stones, one gray, one red, and two white, unremarkable to others but which Sipri believed contained the power of his Ancestors, like the Nuba Nara of old. Though most Lamalerans just feasted their progenitors on holy days, and many not even then, he regularly fed these talismans egg yolks and tuak in coconut-shell bowls.

Frans opened his embassy by asking not why Sipri had failed to perform Ige Gerek but why the ceremony had failed to happen. In Lamaleran society, where politeness is of the utmost importance, it is essential to avoid assigning blame so that no one loses face. This is so crucial that Bahasa Indonesian and Lamaleran both construct sentences in the passive voice whenever sensitive topics are discussed, to circumvent faulting anyone directly.

Sipri complained that the Lika Telo had not come to pay him proper homage.

Frans apologized for their transgression, and asked for Sipri to perform the ceremony anyway, or at least to give his blessing for one of his younger relatives to do it.

"The ritual will return," Sipri announced, "but we need to have a full understanding. This year there is no sympathy between the Wujons and the tribe."

Lamaleran discussions are very formal, and the four men took turns speechifying for over an hour. Increasingly, Sipri became agitated and cleaned tears from his red-rimmed eyes with bony fingers. Salt water often dripped down his long nose because of an undiagnosed condition, but that afternoon it was unclear if it was from his pupils burning or sadness.

"The Ways of the Ancestors are being lost," he warned. He catalogued the many offenses the Lamalerans had offered his clan: from bulldozing a road through the jungle near a sacred stone to failing to properly render him whale eyes. He threatened that the Lamalerans would face starvation without his intercession to summon the whales.

Underlying Sipri's frustration was the fact that the Wujons' importance had been slipping recently. In the old days, they had been spiritual leaders, but by 2014, some Lamalerans whispered that they were charlatans. Advantages they once had enjoyed had transformed into disadvantages: before, their clifftop houses had kept them safe from raiders, but now that remove separated them from village life; in the past their intense conservatism had placed them at the pinnacle of Lamaleran society, but in recent decades it had prevented them from adopting innovations enjoyed by other clans. Their only material advantage was the extra meat they received from the head of the whale, a benefit some clans bilked from them. Increasingly, the Lords of the Land had little that made them lordly at all.

In Lamaleran culture, emotions are supposed to be tightly controlled, but because frustration is so often tamped down, when it is finally expressed it often erupts. Sipri's rage escalated until he threatened that if the Lamalerans did not recommit to the Ways of the Ancestors by the next year, the Wujons would execute the Curse of the Black Goat. (This, of course, was the same curse that had caused the Lefŏ Leìn clan to go extinct.) Instead of performing Ige Gerek, Sipri would lead a black goat into the jungle as afternoon swooned into evening. He would dig a pit and perch the bleating goat on its edge. Then he would jam a knife into its lungs and throw the animal into the unmarked grave, where it would asphyxiate before it could bleed to death. The animal would act like a voodoo doll, and the Ancestors would wrack the Lamalerans with diseases and waylay the fleet with accidents. Even more, in the Wujons' shamanistic hierarchy of sacrificial animals—including chickens, water buffalo, and sheep—a black goat was one of the most potent sorcerous fuels. It was the nuclear option of Lamaleran witchery. Throughout, Sipri spoke in an eldritch brand of Lamaleran full of ancient phrases that the younger generation had not heard for years, which gave his oratory a prophetic resonance.

Then Sipri explained what the Lamalerans needed to do to save themselves: abandon their outboard motors and return to solely paddling and sailing; do a better job of ritually honoring the Ancestors; and respect the Wujons as their older brothers, as Korohama had promised.

Frans weathered the outburst in chagrined silence, then he swore to bring the Lika Telo to the Lord of the Land soon. But he feared Kupa would scoff at apologizing. Even more, he knew the Lamalerans would never give up their outboard motors or bow before the Wujons as they once had—the world had changed too much.

When Frans returned to Lamalera, he told everyone but the most trustworthy elders that their mission had gone well—that is, he answered the villagers who bothered to ask. Many younger whalers no longer paid attention to the Wujon ceremonies at all. Frans sympathized with Sipri. Personally, he was a staunch defender of the Ways of the Ancestors, such that he had kept *Kéna Pukā* sailing long after most clans had switched to jonson, until his clansmen had demanded to use an outboard motor or they would crew other boats. But he also recognized that the Lamalerans had to adapt to the changing times or perish, and that even if he preferred the Old Ways, he had to respect the wishes of the majority of his clansmen. It was possible, he fervently believed, that the tribe could preserve its culture while joining the modern world if it was careful and intentional — otherwise he never would have let his beloved daughter Bena go off to university, even though she had promised to come back.

For years he had tried to steer the tribe along this middle path, judiciously melding past and future. In 2001, when the Council on the Beach had debated banning the jonson, he had helped broker the compromise that kept the sperm whale hunt reserved for the téna while legalizing the motorboats to pursue other prey. What was inviolable to Frans was that the Lamalerans must always engage with the whales as the Ancestors had, so that even if the jonson towed the téna to their prey, the ancient ships then unleashed themselves and paddled the last gap alone. Ultimately, he feared that if the tribe lacked his moderating influence, the partisans — both progressives and conservatives — might permanently rend the unity of their people with fighting and the tribe might not survive.

LATE IN THE AFTERNOON OF April 30, Jon, Ika, Frans, and the rest of the Lamalerans descended to the beach for Misa Arwah. The silvery afternoon sunlight refracted off the ocean beyond the shadow of the volcano, softly illuminating the crowd. Everyone wore church dress, the men in button-down shirts above traditional checkered sarongs, and the women in blouses pulled over sarongs decorated with motifs of whales, manta rays, and téna. But they moved with the stiffness of people unused to and afraid of ruining expensive clothes. Despite the formality of the occasion, many went barefoot, hopscotching across sand still radiating pent-up heat from the sun, pressing their toes together to protect the delicate webbing between them.

They massed in front of the neat blue chapel at the center of the beach. Ferns potted in halved buoys surrounded an altar robed in white sheets and topped with candles whose flames were barely visible in the daylight. An altar boy tapped a microphone with a fingernail and static susurrated over the swishing of the waves. Father Romo opened the ceremony with a short prayer.

Then Ika Hariona contributed her voice to the choir. Their hymns transformed the cove into a natural cathedral, and her voice soared out of the chorus like a dove from a flock of pigeons. What distinguished her smoky alto was not just its diva power but the pleasant roughness at its bottom, as if she had just gotten over a cough. She kept her chin tilted up, her shoulders squared, her hands clasped in front of her, her body rigid except for the flexing muscles inside her stalk-thin neck. For once, the adult worry that normally shadowed her face evanesced, her often agitated expression purified by joy, and she looked only her nineteen years.

Tenang-tenang mendayung,	Row calmly, row tranquilly,
Didalam ombak selepas pantai.	As the waves are loosed upon the shore.
Tenang-tenang merenung,	Daydream calmly, daydream tranquilly,
Ditengah taufan hidup yang ramai,	In the middle of the typhoon of life,
Ditengah taufan hidup yang ramai.	In the middle of the typhoon of life.
Bila terbawa arus didalam doa.	If you are swept away by the currents: Pray.
Laut terenang.	You can swim this ocean.
Sabda penguat doa.	Let the Word brace you.
Resapkanlah didasar hatimu	Let it soak into the depths of your heart
Sedalam laut medan hidupmu.	And your life will be as deep and wide as the ocean.

Father Romo, in a white vestment draped with a purple stole, read a list of the names of the whalers who had been lost at sea, thirty-nine since the parish had begun recording such deaths in October 1916. Then he continued into the deeper past, identifying the nameless dead only as the great-grandfather, etc., of someone living. By the time he reached the era of the Ancestors, he no longer catalogued individual crew members but whole crews lost to storms or ferocious whales. The roll call extended until it seemed that all Lamalerans past and present had assembled.

The sun guttered, and evening invaded the beach. As Father Romo preached about God and heaven and hell, sea eagles beat toward their mountain roosts like restless souls returning to their graves. The candles on the altar brightened as their backdrop blackened. Bats, invisible in the gloom, roiled the air like restless ghosts. Sea and sky merged into universal darkness. Then the Lamalerans queued to eat the body and drink the blood of the Lord.

Once the villagers had swallowed their Communion wafers and wine, Father Romo lit a trio of candles in a miniature téna, complete with a tiny sail, laureled with pink orchids and white frangipani flowers. He bore the vessel through the crowd to the waterline. The debris of shells rattled inside the shorebreak as the expectant silent congregation bowed their heads. Father Romo deposited the ship on the backwash so that it rode the foam down the slope, bumped over the hump of a forming wave, and lodged in a rip current. Fifteen hundred pairs of eyes followed the sailing candles. The beach strobed with mechanical lightning as expat Lamalerans, visiting for the holy day, triggered the flashes on their cell phone cameras.

Then constellations of candles kindled onshore. Fathers drizzled melting wax from tapers onto the decks of dwarf téna and cemented their bases in the cooling wax. Their children waded out and released the boats. Less traditional families used slabs of packing foam as their vessels. Soon, drawn into the same current, the tiny téna had formed an armada lit by match-like torches. By custom, only families who had

Launching the miniature téna

lost relatives at sea launched a boat, though because of the close-knit structure of the tribe, this was about half. The rest of the Lamalerans set their candles in holes dug in the sand, bunkering them against the breeze twirling off the ocean. A few Lamalerans strewed the troughs with frangipani petals, whole orchids, or handfuls of glitter that shimmered in the firelight.

When all the boats had been released, Father Romo led the tribe through an Our Father. Then, in the ensuing silence, each Lamaleran was left to internally voice his or her personal desire. Fifteen hundred candles, each representing a personal universe and its dreams, shook in the wind rising off the Savu Sea.

Jon wished to become a lamafa and provide well for his family. But never far behind these wishes lurked fantasies about moving to Jakarta, taking hot girls to malls on dates, and becoming rich enough to buy a racing motorcycle.

Misa Arwah

Ika dreamed of going to middle school, then high school, and maybe even college, though she tried to save herself from disappointment by mocking her desires, reminding herself of her advanced age.

Frans prayed to the Ancestors that his clan would prosper, that his téna would take many whales, that the rift with the Wujons would heal, and that he would see another Misa Arwah. For hunters, it was never certain. Nearby, his brother-in-law, Ignatius, was preparing a boat with Maria, Frans's wife and Ignatius's younger sister. If the *Spice Islander* had not discovered him adrift two decades earlier, they would have been dispatching that candle to him. But Frans had long since accepted Ignatius's apologies for abandoning him, remembering *Talé tou, ĸemui tou, onã tou, mata tou:* the unity of the tribe was paramount.

Ignatius's family launched a foam box lid with four candles balanced on it, one each for the father and his three sons. Though the ceremony officially honored only fallen whalers, all four were mourning Teresea, wife and mother, whom malaria had snatched away nearly a year before. For Ignatius, the loss had been so severe that sometimes he wished he could join her. He still believed himself an excellent lamafa despite entering the back half of his seventh decade, but he had decided to prepare his offspring for the day he was no longer with them. Recently, he had turned over the hâmmâlollo of his téna to his eldest son, Yosef. Both Yosef and Ondu, his middle son, had long ago become lamafa, but his youngest son, Ben, had not yet. Ignatius hoped this year he would tidy up that final loose end.

Ben, meanwhile, prayed that his secret plan to move to the tourist island of Bali would come to fruition—and that instead of being heartbroken at his departure, his father would understand that if he stayed in Lamalera he would go crazy yearning to lead a modern life.

After all the candles had been lit, the Lamalerans sang: "Hallelujah! Hallelujah!" The current reeled the burning fleet into the darkness. As the ships were pulled farther away, it became impossible to tell whose spark was whose. Were the boats explorers or refugees? What messages did they carry to the outside world? Some of the candles never made it out of the bay. Every minute or so one of the miniature téna would list, unbalanced by pooling wax, and then flip. Other vessels took on water and sank with a hiss and a burst of smoke. But some flames burned on until they vanished past the cliffs. In the end, it was impossible to tell whose prayers foundered in the bay, whose capsized on the ensuing journey, and whose reached the Ancestors or the outside world waiting beyond the horizon.

Chapter Four

THE CLEANSING OF HARMFUL LANGUAGE

June 27, 2014–late July 2014

Jon

Despite Sipri's threats that the Ancestors would starve the tribe, by late June the Lamalerans had already taken eight sperm whales — a slightly above-average harvest for the first two months of the hunting season. Some rumormongers whispered that the village elders had convinced one of Sipri's relatives to perform a miniature Ige Gerek in his stead. Sipri would subsequently claim that despite the disrespect of the Lamalerans, he had allowed the whales to come so the tribe would not starve before they could change their ways.

But on June 27, the Ancestors claimed their revenge — though they did not retaliate against the whole tribe. Instead, they chose Jon Hariona. Or at least that is what people later speculated, after Jon answered the baleo and claimed the great befaje oar at the front of *Boli Sapang*. For how else could they interpret what had happened to him? How the safety rope had snapped and Jon had become entangled in the harpoon line, how the téna had flipped and he had been dragged beneath the waves by a kotekělema, the very embodiment of the Ancestors.

While Jon was drowning that day, one of his fondest memories arose: spearfishing with his boyhood friends. Sometimes when the moon was fat, they would crouch on the petrified lava headlands flanking Lamalera and sharpen iron dowels on the stone that had once been fire. The moon silvered the tidal pools into pans of mercury and drew tinsel boas across the shoulders of charging waves, transmogrifying their frothy explosions into waterfalls of diamonds. In the lull between sets, the boys leapt into the liquid darkness below.

Bellies puffed with breath, the young hunters schooled in pairs along the grottoed sea cliffs and coral gardens of Lamalera Bay. The lead diver shined a waterproof flashlight into crannies. Jon followed with a hand-adzed wooden spear gun whose projectile, a honed dowel, was held taut by the giant rubber band of a tread cut off an old motorbike tire. They watched for squid sucking their tentacles into their shells like chrysanthemums unblooming, or the melting color of a camouflaging octopus. Jon hovered his weapon's muzzle inches from sleeping fish hammocked in the current. The arrow rammed through their dreams. Once the cloud of blood had dispersed and the fish's scales had settled on the seafloor, he slid a rope, which was knotted at one end around his hips, through the punctured animal. As the hunt continued, his belt began to glitter with piscine gemstones: parrot fish like chunks of beryl aquamarine, electric-blue tang fish like skipping stones of lapis lazuli, angelfish like sapphire shards wrapped in gold wire.

While spearfishing Jon could stay underwater more than two minutes at a stretch. Now, tangled in the harpoon rope with the whale diving, he conserved oxygen by going limp. A burn started in the pit of his stomach. It blazed upward like the urge to vomit, consuming his thoughts one by one until even his worry for his grandparents and siblings vanished and all that endured was the directive *Don't open your mouth*. He promised himself he would not pass. With the necessary faith of those who have no other recourse, he prayed.

Then he rose. The rope pulled straight by the whale had slackened into arcs. The cuff around his ankle loosened. He slipped his fingers beneath it and drew the rope off as easily as a sock. Somewhere in the darkness below, the sperm whale had run out of air before him, and was returning to the surface. As he struggled upward, he found he had not been drawn as deep as he had feared. Panic and pain had squeezed breath and reason from him.

When he broke the skin of the ocean, the first breath stuffed his head with sensation, his hearing rebooted like the world's speakers had been turned up to deafening volume. Shrill shouting. Paddles clapping the water. Boat engines grinding. Then the whale surfaced with a boom like a storm burst. He tried to kick toward the overturned *Boli Sapang,* but the anesthesia of adrenaline was fading. Pain clamped onto his right leg like a bear trap. He struggled to stay afloat.

The whir of an engine faded as the throttle was cut. A small foam buoy tied to a rope splashed beside him. He grabbed it, and the crew of the jonson *Ala Jati* reeled him boatside.

An impatient voice said, "Jon, get in."

"I can't," he answered.

There was no way to hide his mistake anymore. The men exclaimed as they noticed his leg. Many hands hauled him over the bow. Tears dripped off his chin, and he hoped they were indistinguishable from beads of seawater. The men of *Ala Jati* gathered over him, speculating about whether his leg was broken.

"Lolo—," someone said. It was his childhood nickname, given to him because his mother had often been too distracted to cuddle him, and so he had been known for toddling around the village crying, "Lolo," the sobriquet of Frans's wife, who would always hold him. "Does it hurt?"

He would have lied if he could have, but the pain was too true.

"Can you be patient?"

"No," he choked. Indignity after indignity: being coddled, being called by his childhood nickname, depriving his fellow whalers of the hunt.

Even with the throttle fully cranked, the journey home seemed like hours of juddering over whitecaps. His leg ignited in anguish with every bump. After confirming that he was not in immediate danger, the crew of *Ala Jati* turned to watch the hunt play out behind them. Jon hid his crying as best he could. Questions garroted him: Would he ever hunt again? Who would feed his grandparents and Ika? Would his fiancée still marry him?

A crowd of women, children, and old men — everyone who could not hunt — awaited them on the beach. From the cliffs, they had seen the lone jonson sprinting into the bay and known something was wrong. Wails met the crew of *Ala Jati* at the breakers, as the onlookers tried to determine what had happened.

The jonson's hull scraped against rocks, and one of the men aboard shouted, "A rope hurt Jon!"

Jon tried to suppress groans while he was manhandled out of the boat and borne through his tribespeople. Aunts and uncles, nephews and nieces, cousins and second and third cousins, for almost everyone was related to him in some way, they all pityingly stroked him with their fingertips. But people also exhaled that it was not their son, brother, father, or some other provider for their clan.

In the crowd, Jon noticed an old man whom he had overlooked almost every day of his life: Sebastianus Batafor, a gaunt grandfather whose overgrown eyebrows and nose hairs, and cheeks sagging without teeth to prop them up, made him appear more ancient than his seventy years. The old man's empty right shirtsleeve waved like a flag of surrender.

On Wednesday, August 3, 1983, a date that Sebastianus can still instantly recall, he leapt off the hâmmâlollo of his téna and lanced a manta ray that outsized him. As he swam back to the ship, a searing pain collared his arm, and he was yanked underwater — the manta had doubled back, looping the rope around his biceps. He tried to untangle himself, but the manta fled one way while his clansmen pulled in the opposite direction. The rope sawed his arm to the bone as they tug-of-warred.

With the line tensioned, Sebastianus was trapped beneath the waves. He could see the wavering outlines of his fellows above the surface. If they let the animal take more line, he would surely drown. He stomped on the manta's head. The armlet loosened, and he slipped his bleeding limb out. Then he used his uninjured arm to climb the rope. He clawed over the side of the boat, grabbed another harpoon, and killed the beast with his off hand.

Back in the village, his wife and mother treated the flayed arm for a week with a compress of jungle roots and leaves, but his coffee-colored skin blanched and then rot blackened it. When they ferried him to the hospital in Lewoleba, it took all his strength not to dishonor himself as a seaman by throwing up. At noon the next day, the doctor, as if disavowing responsibility, announced that Sebastianus would have only a 10 percent chance of survival even if the arm was amputated. Sebastianus told his family that he put his faith in God. The doctor finished what the manta had begun, excavating the humerus from the scapula and scalpeling out the corruption.

As he sailed home two weeks later, he instructually scanned for prey, but he would never hunt again. In the following decades, he was relegated to rushing to the beach whenever a téna arrived or departed, to lend his remaining arm. Though most Lamaleran men often went shirtless, he always wore one.

Jon had never known Sebastianus as a lamafa, only as an old man who took twice as many trips as normal to carry slop buckets to his pigs and who sold his wife's penny cakes outside the elementary school. He had smirked when he saw the former harpooner wrapping his legs around his toddler granddaughter to keep her from squirming away while using his remaining hand to spoon mushy rice into her mouth.

Had Jon asked Sebastianus's opinion of life as an amputee, the old man would have said that what one arm had lost in its power to kill, the other had gained in the opportunity to love. Yes, he regretted never being able to go to sea again. The plunge from being one of the most respected men in Lamalera to the most pitied was painful. But he was thankful that when his granddaughter grew up, she would remember it was his weak hand that had cradled her through infancy, that had steadied her as she learned to walk, and that had pointed out manta rays leaping offshore, silhouetted against the sunset. "God works in mysterious ways," he would often say, and from him it sounded not like a platitude but like earned wisdom. For Jon, though, the thought that Sebastianus prophesied his future filled him with horror.

The men carrying Jon were huffing by the time they reached the stairs climbing the cliffs, so he was deposited on a bamboo pallet in a nearby house, and his pants, along with his underwear, were scissored off. Rubberneckers packed the tiny room, but Jon was too exhausted to complain about his exposure. Eventually, he was blanketed with a sarong—which he was thankful for when he heard his sister's raspy voice: "Jon, what happened?"

Yosef Boko followed behind, spit bubbling as he babbled in grief, supporting the mewling Grandmother Fransiska. Jon's family bent over him, their tears spattering his forehead like the first raindrops of a developing storm, and he wept with them, certain his dream of becoming a lamafa was ruined. But more important than that, he had failed his family. Once their store of jerkied whale ran out, they would have to beg when the boats came in. And he did not know what his fiancée, who was off working as a housekeeper on a different island, would think of him if he were crippled. The old taunt—kefela— resonated in his mind. He had been his family's hope. What would happen to them now?

A group of women pushed through the crowd, carrying a steaming wooden bowl. They rolled up the sarong and lathered Jon's leg in a paste made of turmeric, candlenuts, and candlenut leaves. The glop scalded his calf, multiplying his pain, and turned his skin yellow. *You have to endure if you want to get healthy,* he told himself. Then the women bandaged his newly jaundiced leg in a rag.

Father Romo had been waiting in the wings. He blessed Jon and draped a plastic rosary over his head, insisting that Jon use it, as he had noticed the young man was often absent from services. Then Jon devoured a bowl of rice porridge mixed with tea instead of water, his hunger surprising him.

His respite was short. In came the town nurse, a pretty, unmarried woman with whom he had traded flirting glances. Once Jon turned over and peeled back the sarong to reveal his bare buttocks, the nurse syringed him with an antibiotic. The shot stung, but what hurt worse was this attractive woman witnessing his weakness.

She asked how his leg felt.

"It hurts pretty badly," he answered. "Is it broken?"

It wasn't, she explained, but there might be an internal wound. She would check back later, but for now he should be careful.

"Don't take too much interest in caring for me," Jon said slyly. "People might get the wrong idea."

Once she was gone, he quaffed several acetaminophen pills and collapsed into sleep. Sometime after midnight, he woke, his leg cramping in agony as Indonesian pop music blared from a house across the road where his friend Ben Blikololong lived with his father, Ignatius, his common-law wife, and his boy and girl. On many Friday nights, Jon had joined Ben and other young men drinking tuak and swaying to this same music sieving through blown-out speakers. It was a ritual that Ben called "disco." (No girls ever joined, as Lamaleran society would not permit it.) Now, as Jon swatted at malarial mosquitoes and tried to endure the pain branding his calf, he feared he would never join their carefree ranks again. A worry that had attacked him immediately on the jonson — would his fiancée still marry him? — returned to torment him in the smothering darkness.

Jon pulled a purple sarong patterned with pink flowers over his head, cocooning himself from the moonless night, as if he might burst from its chrysalis transformed. His fiancée, Honi, had given it to him. Other men teased him for its floral pattern — Lamaleran men wore checkered sarongs — but Jon had asked Ika to fetch it for him that evening. Over time, its rosy coloring had darkened with dirt, until it appeared ocher, and its threads had fuzzed. Honi's scent had long ago been overlaid by his sweat and the grime of village life, but if he closed his eyes and sniffed, sometimes it seemed he could just smell her.

Jon had met Verokia "Honi" Jaga at the end of the previous year while building the elementary school in Loang, a village near Lewoleba. There he had flirted relentlessly, intoxicated by all the new young women, in part because in Lamalera there are relatively few. Parents often keep their sons home to whale while sending their daughters around the volcano for school, after which the girls frequently choose to pursue office work rather than butchering fish, gathering firewood, and carrying water from the well. Thus, the ratio between the sexes has skewed in the tribe, and young men compete for a small pool of romantic partners, many of whom are disallowed because they are closely related.

In Lamalera, Jon's only romance had left him with an amateur tattoo of his ex-girlfriend's face sneering from his shoulder, after Ben Blikololong had needled battery carbon mixed with coconut oil into Jon's skin one drunken night. When Jon and the girl later broke up, Ben added horns to make the permanent mistake a devil, though the girl's name remained under the portrait. (Jon had also gotten several more tuak-induced tattoos from Ben, including an octopus that was no more than a circle radiating squiggly lines.)

Jon had no luck in Loang, but shortly after he finished building the school and moved to a new project in Lewoleba, a girl from Loang texted to ask if he wanted to be introduced to her friend Honi. Jon and Honi started messaging. They were the same age, twenty-one. She was visiting her village, near Loang, from a monastery on another island, where she was training to become a nun. Their first meeting was at Lewoleba's port, a popular spot for young couples to watch the sunset silhouette a nearby volcano, and they drank from the same lopped-open green coconut with straws.

Honi was afraid Jon would not like her because she was short and had curly hair, whereas Indonesians prefer straight locks. But she appreciated his easy conversation and humor, as well as his praise of her looks. For his part, Jon was smitten by Honi's delicate skin, as a fair complexion is a mark of beauty in Lembata, but he also sensed she had a good work ethic. The most important thing for him about his future partner was that she be hardworking and accept the humble conditions of life in Lamalera.

Through the month of December, their texting and calls intensified. Then one day, Jon received a call from Honi's mother demanding to know if he was her daughter's boyfriend. Honi was no longer planning to return to the monastery, her mother told him.

So, on a Sunday morning near the end of December, without telling his construction-site boss he was leaving, Jon rode on the back of a motorbike to Honi's village, where she waited for him on the roadside. It was only the second time they had met face-to-face.

"Don't be shy," he told her. "Where's your house?"

Honi expressed surprise that he was not afraid to meet her mother. Jon, like all Lembatans, knew that to meet her mother would signal that they were formally dating, which was tantamount to an engagement.

"I've come," Jon answered. "Whatever happens, will happen."

Honi led him off the main road to a small bamboo house roofed with dried grass. Her mother welcomed him, for her father had died a long time before. After Jon was introduced, Honi's mother asked, "You aren't afraid to meet me?"

"If I want to become engaged to Honi, I have to," Jon said.

Jon and the loquacious mother ended up chatting into the evening, too late for him to return to Lewoleba, so he slept on the dirt floor. The following morning, Jon left to spend Christmas in Lamalera, but shortly thereafter he received a call from Honi. When her younger brother had returned from Lewoleba to discover that his sister's boyfriend had slept in their home, he had considered it a breach of his honor, and beaten Honi. She feared he would take more serious revenge later, after drinking, and told Jon, "I'm searching for my plot in the graveyard." Jon gave her directions for how to ride the auto to Lamalera.

The half week they spent in Lamalera together would be their only substantial time together before Jon's injury. Honi instantly befriended Ika, and his grandparents doted on her. She and Jon attended the Christmas sermon together and pressed their foreheads to his elder relatives' knuckles, a sign of respect, as if Honi was already family. They walked beside each other so close "their sarongs kissed," as the Lamaleran expression says.

But two days after Christmas, Jon was called back to his construction job early because his bosses were furious about his earlier disappearance. Honi returned home and soon informed Jon that without the stipend she had received as a nun-in-training, her subsistence farming mother was struggling to make ends meet and pay her younger brother's tuition. She needed to contribute to her family's income until her younger brother finished high school and could work. Recruiters scour eastern Indonesia for poor girls to labor as maids in the cities, so she soon signed a three-year contract to serve in a four-story mansion in western Indonesia.

The next and last time Jon saw Honi was in May, when he escorted her to a nearby island to catch a ferry that would circle the archipelago. They were sorrowful to separate, but long engagements were not uncommon in Lembatan society, especially when one partner took a job off-island. They telephoned as ardently as only new lovers can. The elder whalers began to note that Jon was drinking tuak less frequently and netting for flying fish by himself if the jonson did not go out. Having a woman, they gossiped, was making him more of a man.

When Jon informed Honi of his disaster, she wept and promised she would still marry him. But she could not come home early, she said, because her brother's schooling depended on her and she would be paid only at the end of the year, a strategy that employers use to keep servants from running off. Jon could not help doubting her truthfulness, perhaps because he questioned his own worth if he could not hunt.

SIX DAYS AFTER THE DISASTER, in early July, as a fiery sunset fumed into an ashy evening, Frans climbed the stacked-stone staircase to Jon's house, where he had since been stretchered. Jon and his family, like many other Lamalerans, believed in Frans more than they did the government nurse: when Grandmother Fransiska had broken her hip, it was the shaman they had called. Still, they had been hesitant to summon him this time because they already owed him fish. But when Jon's condition worsened, Ika implored Frans for help.

In the cramped shack on the cliffs, the shaman balanced sideways on a plastic lawn chair in the tight space beside Jon's bed. He had said not a word about the debt, for he would never withhold his treatment from someone in need. The town's diesel generator had not yet chugged on. Mercury evening filled the glassless window like a silver pane. Whining mosquito wings vibrated the dusk. Frans palpated Jon's right leg while asking a doctor's boilerplate questions—"How does this feel? Does this hurt?"—but it was obvious something was very wrong. Jon's ankle had swollen until it was nearly the same size as his calf. His Achilles tendon had contracted, pulling his heel upward, so that it was difficult to tell where the leg ended and the foot started. A storm front of a bruise shadowed his leg from his knee all the way to his toes. Each time Frans squeezed, a groan whistled between Jon's clenched lips.

Frans ordered Ika to fill a bucket with water. When she returned, he dipped his crucifix in it and mumbled a prayer, transubstantiating the well water into a holy liquid. Then he submerged Jon's turmeric-stained bandage in it. While Frans re-bound the leg, Jon locked his jaws.

Frans stood over Jon and raised his once broken arm, showing off its immovable, defunct thumb and what appeared to be an extra elbow.

"See this arm?" he said. "It was hit by a whale's tail." At the time, visiting foreigners had wanted to bring him to the hospital, Frans said, "but the end of the road at the hospital is always amputation." He instructed Jon not to remove the binding or let someone from the opposite sex touch it, and to avoid eating pork or dog meat. Most important, Frans reminded Jon, he had to follow the Ways of the Ancestors or he would not heal: a healthy spirit meant a healthy body. He promised to return in a few days to renew his blessing.

Frans was confident in his ministrations, but many other Lamaler-ans were unsure if the Ancestors would heed his entreaties to heal Jon. Whalers whispered that the reason Jon had been crippled had nothing to do with his inattention, ropes weakened by years of soaking in salt water, or chance. Instead, he was suffering because the tribe had angered the spirits by failing to honor the Wujons. An even more specific rumor also explained why the Ancestors had chosen to punish a Hariona man rather than someone from another clan: the ghosts disapproved of that clan recently renovating its boat shed so that it deviated from the ancestral blueprints.

So SAY THE STORIES OF the Ancestors: The Hariona clan arrived in Lamalera several generations after Korohama, fleeing their village in the wake of a conflict with their neighbors. But by then the beach was packed with boat sheds, and the Harionas had nowhere to park their téna.

However, the Nudeks, one of the original Lamaleran clans, took pity on them. The Nudeks say they leased to the Harionas one of their three boat sheds in exchange for the newcomers swearing to live as their younger siblings. According to the Harionas, they paid the Nudeks a spectacular elephant tusk and promised them a share of each whale they caught in return for ownership of the boat shed — and they never swore subservience. Over the centuries, the terms of the original agreement have grown hazy. But by that May, Krispin Kia Hariona, the chieftain of the Hariona clan, had become convinced his Ancestors had bought the boat shed outright. He called his men together to widen it so that a new jonson could be squeezed alongside *Boli Sapang*.

The boat sheds are open, airy structures without walls, their palm-leaf roofs supported by pillars made of silvered tree trunks, and they are packed so tightly together across the beach that it is possible to use them as a shaded walkway, only breaking cover to cross the footpaths leading to the village. Under Krispin's direction, Jon and the Hariona men shifted over the boat shed pillars five feet — right into the trail that had demarcated the structure's western border. This passage was known as the Path of Blood because when the Ancestors slew an enemy tribesman, they would drag his corpse along its length before displaying it in the village square.

But one man who usually worked alongside the Harionas was absent that day: Laurencius "Jogo" Nudek, the chief of his clan. Jogo was a de facto member of the Harionas because the positions of the two clans had flipped over the centuries. The Nudeks were the hereditary shipwrights of the tribe, and their relative wealth had allowed them to send their children to school in the 1980s before other clans, meaning their future harpooners became paper pushers. Today, the two Nudek téna have been scrapped, and Jogo and the only other Nudek whaler sail with *Boli Sapang*. In contrast, the Hariona clan, which still has few resources to send children abroad, numbers about twenty-five families in Lamalera, which crew their own téna.

Jogo was known as the town's affable wag. At festivals he drank tuak until his bulbous nose glowed red and he told off-color jokes. On hearing about Krispin's plans, however, he was enraged. He interpreted it as an assertion that the Harionas owned the boat shed, rather than rented it from the Nudeks. A few days later, Jon, Krispin, and a few other men were lashing palm-leaf tiles to a roof extension when Jogo showed up. Krispin had the physique of a Buddha and was in his seventies, but he refused to back down to Jogo, who was in his forties and had the muscles of an action hero. The chiefs got into a shouting match. Afterwards, Jogo switched téna and stopped accepting the whale jerky that the Harionas continued to offer him, and word had it that he and his mother, a bad-tempered widow notorious for her curses, were brewing some voodoo in revenge.

Near the end of June, pain began crackling from the right knee to the right shoulder of one of the Hariona elders. Past sixty, he was already nearing the time when most Lamaleran men passed, so the causes could have been natural, but people noted that his right side suffered just as the Harionas had expanded the right side of the boat shed.

Then Jon's right leg was crushed, convincing some Lamalerans it was not only the living who had hexed the Harionas but the dead: especially Yakobus "Boso" Belida Oleona, a lamafa who, nearly a century before, had leapt off a hâmmâlollo to spear a whale and never surfaced. But whenever storms sloshed the sea, Boso would exit the uncomfortable whirlpool and return to his former house, following the footpath that ran along the western edge of the Hariona boat shed — at least until the Harionas altered it and offended him. As Jon's leg continued to swell, everyone agreed that he would fail to heal until the boat shed was fixed. And the Lika Telo increasingly worried that the Ancestors were angered by the dissension among their descendants and began pressing Krispin for a resolution before everyone was punished.

At first, Krispin blamed Jogo's mother for cursing Jon. Eventually, however, he and his men returned the boat shed to its original form. And yet, with Jon's health still fragile nearly two weeks after his injury, the chief ordered his clan to assemble at the Hariona Spirit House.

As a golden afternoon grayed and most Lamalerans carried slop buckets to their pigs, the Hariona clan dressed in their best sarongs and walked to their Spirit House. Along the way, some stopped to check a sheet of paper nailed to the trunk of the banyan tree in the town square on which was handwritten the results of the nation's presidential election.

That morning, 87 percent of the Lamalerans had voted for Joko "Jokowi" Widodo — Indonesia's new president — by puncturing ballots with a nail beside his name. The whalers had supported him because they admired how he had bootstrapped himself up from being a carpenter, and although he was Muslim, a political necessity in the world's most populous Islamic nation, he was regarded as sympathetic to Indonesia's embattled minority Christians, among whom the Lamalerans counted themselves. Moreover, few Lamalerans had given any thought to his campaign promises to revive faltering national economic growth by heavily investing in ports, roads, and other infrastructure in eastern Indonesia as a means of opening the region's untapped forests, minerals, and fisheries, and thereby replenishing the resources that had already been consumed in the country's overpopulated core. Which is to say that none of the Lamalerans knew that by nailing Jokowi's name, they had encouraged a process that would soon transform their lives.

A team of Hariona men carried Jon down the cliffs to the Spirit House, tucked at their base. There was nothing to distinguish this house from neighboring brick houses with rusted tin roofs, but to the Harionas it was the holy abode in which their Ancestors dwelled whenever they visited from the sea.

Jon was installed in a chair in the center of the main room, and though the small space was packed, everyone kept as much distance from him as possible, as if he were contagious. By dark, the entire clan had assembled. Krispin barricaded the front door with a crossbeam. A naked halogen lightbulb glimmered feebly, no brighter than the candles guttering in the corner.

To quiet whispers, the elders hissed, "The ceremony! The ceremony!"

From outside, the swish of the surf drifted through cracks in the glass windows. Everyone sat silently, heads bowed.

Then a fist rattled the door. Jon, who faced the entry, looked up.

Krispin heaved his bulk off a spindly plastic chair, strode to the door, and pressed his ear to the wood. The reedy voice of an old man seeped through it, but everyone knew that it was really Jon's soul speaking. The voice asked in formal Lamaleran to enter the Spirit House. Krispin questioned what the spirit wanted. Jon's soul once more begged to be let in. Again, Krispin queried. The call-and-response was repeated a third time before Krispin lifted the wooden crossbar.

Into the room crept a gaunt old shaman, smelling of brine, his scraggly white beard dripping seawater. He had just swum out into the Savu Sea to reclaim Jon's soul from the waves, where the Ancestors had imprisoned it after the whale had taken it. Then he had apologized to *Boli Sapang,* the clan's téna, for any offense they might have caused it, and washed it with holy water. Now the old man rained salt water on Jon as he leaned over him. In a singsong whisper, he asked forgiveness from the unseen Ancestors and pulled on a forelock of Jon's hair three times. Next, he dipped his thumb in a bowl of coconut juice and drew a cross on Jon's forehead. The symbol gleamed in the dim light. It ran down Jon's face like tears.

The spooky tension eased — Jon's soul had been returned to his body. Then the witch doctor circled the room, thumbing the cross on the forehead of every Hariona.

The ritual was known as the Cleansing of Harmful Language. For the Lamalerans believe the power of words is literal. This belief is so central that while whaling, Lamalerans use a whole different vocabulary, so as not to attract misfortune: for example, if they were to say "knife" while at sea, the sharp properties of the word could cause their rope to be severed, so they say "spoon" in its place. Thus, when Jon had been carried wounded onto the beach and his female relatives had bewailed him as doomed, he had become so, and when the Nudeks had cursed his clan, ill luck had glommed on to him. The rite that had just been performed, however, had erased those hexes and — even more important — restored the unity of the tribe.

Suddenly, Jogo escorted his limping mother into the room. Earlier that day, Krispin had carried a jerrican of palm wine to Jogo's house, and they had drunk it together while the Hariona chief apologized. Now Jogo winked at everyone with the swagger of a man who had spent the afternoon drinking and who had just been vindicated. He was also happy because Jon was a close relative, as Jon's grandmother had been a Nudek before marriage, and so he had felt terrible to see Jon suffer. The Nudeks were followed by Hariona women bearing platters heaped with whale meat boiled until it turned from purple to black; steamed manta stomach, which tasted like tire rubber covered in Vaseline; red rice mashed with crushed corn kernels; and a bowl filled with a soup tinted green by moringa leaves. One of Jon's cousins bore around a jerrican of tuak to the men.

Neighbors crammed the house, and a festival atmosphere replaced the solemnity. Ben Blikololong, Jon's friend who lived across the road, stumbled into the room in his green polyester election monitor's uniform, red-eyed, his curly hair sweat-matted to his forehead. Still drunk from the tuak the town council had given him as a salary to oversee the voting, he yelled, "Jon is the best!" Soon Ben and the other young men were discussing the probable victor of the semifinal World Cup match between the Netherlands and Argentina, which they would watch that night via one of the town's newly erected satellite dishes. One hooligan had even razored the uniform number of the Argentine forward Lionel Messi into his buzz cut, an act that had impressed Jon though it had earned the young man a smack and a lecture from Ignatius.

The one person who did not appear to be having fun was Jon, who sat with his right leg held stiffly in front of him as if trying to trip someone with it. The only time anyone paid attention to him was when they stopped to dip their thumbs, ink-stained from voting that day, into his cup of tuak, and draw a cross on his forehead.

By eight o'clock the Nudeks, the Harionas, and their respective friends had divided themselves between opposite sides of the room. But it was a tiny village, and everyone had to see each other every day for the rest of their lives, so civility still reigned, except for Jogo's mother, who openly gloated that the "sea had given proof," referring to Jon's injury as "his souvenir, his reminder." When Jogo left, he carried home fifty strips of whale jerky and forty slices of whale skin, the rent he had until now refused for the boat shed.

Afterwards, Jon sat with Ika and his grandparents in the front yard, bathed in the platinum glow of the pregnant moon, peering down at the beach to see if sea turtles were coming to lay their eggs, which they would forage. There were times when he acidly resented having to act as a father to his grandparents and sister. But as he overlooked the gold foil sea, he felt only the desire to provide for them. He tried flexing his leg. It seemed to him that it already moved more smoothly. There was hope yet that he could become a lamafa.

Four nights later, around three o'clock in the morning, Jon's cell phone alarm chirped him awake. Tonight he was finally healthy enough to negotiate the cliffs that had kept him trapped in the house. For weeks he had watched everything happening in the village below as if he were peering into a terrarium, but he had remained isolated, for when he would yell down to his friends on the road below, they were usually too busy to scale the heights. He could not yet put much weight on his right leg, so it took him nearly fifteen minutes to traverse a quarter mile, sliding down the stairs on his butt, then, once he reached the bottom, kangarooing along for a few hundred feet before having to rest his left leg.

When Jon hobbled into the courtyard of a teacher who had used his government salary to purchase a satellite dish, everyone yelled, "Jon!" But he had to sit on the courtyard bricks, because none of the thirty-five men thought to vacate their chairs. Everyone was too fixated on the World Cup final. Ghostly soccer players, streamed from a projector, flowed across the box spring draped with a sheet. The spectators were mostly young men, but they had been joined by a few elders who had lived abroad, including Kupa, the member of the Lika Telo who had declined to visit Sipri. Soon Jon was joking and shouting. He did not care who won: what mattered to him was cheering with his peers—and the more than one billion other people watching the game across the globe, shown in shots of crowds hypnotized by colossal screens in Berlin, Buenos Aires, New York, and Hong Kong. In all, 3.2 billion people, or nearly half of humanity, had seen at least one World Cup match. Watching made him feel, if only briefly, that he was part of the modern world.

At halftime, spiffy motorbikes zipped across the sheet, racing along floodlit highways in nighttime metropolises. Lips glossy with ruby lipstick sucked a drumstick of Kentucky Fried Chicken in pornographic slow-motion. Half-Indonesian, half-Caucasian models demonstrated skin-whitening cream that could turn a swarthy complexion fair. Unlike the game, the ads made Jon feel that life in Lamalera was poor, ugly, and backward, and that he was cut off from modernity. Maybe, he thought, he could have all that if he lived in Jakarta.

The second half ended with the score knotted: 0–0. During the first overtime, the Lamalerans jumped and yelled at every pass, shaking fireworks of embers from their cigarettes, but neither team managed a goal. With less than two minutes left in the second overtime, however, a pass arced over the Argentine defense and a German forward volleyed it into the goal.

For a moment: silence. In the jungle bordering the courtyard, an orchestra of insects and amphibians tuned up.

Then the fans of Germany yelled into the faces of the Argentina supporters: "Germany! Germany! Germany!" Shoves were exchanged. An Argentina supporter pulled the plug on the projector, and the machine toppled to the flagstones with a crash. The courtyard blackened.

The house's owner yelled angrily for everyone to leave. Bats boomeranged across a saltpeter predawn sky. Rusting motorbikes grumblingly carried young men home, past their fathers and grandfathers walking to the beach. These were the die-hard whalers who still sat in front of their téna each morning, on the very occasional chance that a full crew of paddlers could be assembled, so one of the ancestral boats could launch instead of a jonson. The elders watched the darkness peel off the ocean to reveal its waves, while the youth returned to their beds.

As July entered its second half, Jon began to pogo on one leg from the beach to the highest cliffs of Upper Lamalera. He even earned the temporary nickname "Pocong," for the legendary Indonesian mummy-wrapped zombie who locomotes by hopping because his legs are bound together. His recovery, while real, was frustratingly slow. He created an amateur physical therapy regimen for himself, spending hours each day stretching and exercising his right leg. As the swelling receded, the tendons of his toes emerged from the loaf of his foot, but pain was still lodged in his calf. He was not a patient person even in the best of circumstances. Now he was going stir-crazy. His agitation to put to sea again was compounded because the dried whale jerky and flying fish that he had stored away for an emergency were running low.

When a baleo sounded on July 15, now nearly three weeks since his injury, Jon leapt to answer the call. He hoped to man an oar — after all, his arms were healthy — but *Boli Sapang* was fully crewed and no other téna invited him. Instead he watched in desolation as the fleet pulled home a large bull. The next morning, soon after the whalers had begun butchering their previous catch, spouts were once more sighted, and this time the fleet's luck was even better. They returned after dark with a trio of teenage male whales, one of which had been taken by *Boli Sapang*. As soon as the sun rose again, the beach was packed with nearly every Lamaleran sharpening their flensing knives on convenient boulders, for even though Jon and many others had not helped spear any of the whales, the Ways of the Ancestors ensured they would partake in the bounty through a ritualized division and sharing of the meat.

First, the elderly shipwright who had built *Boli Sapang* incised lines into the gray skin of the whale the téna had caught, effectively diagramming the animal into portions to guide Jon and the other Hariona men's knife work. Then whalers who were more mobile than Jon threw handfuls of sand onto the slick hide to give their feet purchase and clambered atop the corpse. The two-foot-long blades of their duri were designed to penetrate the whale's foot-thick blubber, and they quickly cut stripes into it at three-foot intervals, from the blowhole to the flukes. A hole was bored at the top of each stripe and a cord threaded through the opening, after which the whole plank of blubber was easily peeled away by Jon and other hunters yanking on the rope. Through repetition of this process, the Harionas flensed the corpse to its core. By the end, only the flippers retained their skin, so that they rested against the flesh like mittened hands trying to cover a naked torso. Until then the whale had been curiously odorless, but now, with the sun heating the shucked meat, the reek of death swamped the beach. Over the course of two hours, the men chipped away at the tons of exposed flesh like ants deconstructing a loaf of bread, piling steaks in neat pyramids in front of their boat shed.

Once the top half of the whale had been filleted, it was time to flip the corpse, and every able-bodied man nearby grabbed ropes lashed to the corpse as if preparing for an epic tug-of-war. *Jo-hé!* called Krispin, the Hariona clan leader, "Heave-ho!" At first it seemed implausible that the hundred or so men could accomplish anything. But then the opposite lip of the whale started to rise. *Jo-hé! Jo-hé!* The Lamalerans fought it upward by inches, with others wedging logs beneath it to prevent it from slipping back. Finally, the corpse teetered at a precarious angle while the tribesmen leaned almost horizontally, held up only by the tension of the rope. Then the whale flipped, and the impact shook the beach like a minor earthquake.

When the second half of the deboned, deflated whale had finally been added to the pyramid of steaks, the Hariona clan sat in a circle around its tower of meat. Then the lamafa began carrying bricks of flesh to each of his clanspeople in turn, so that everyone got an equal portion. This was the foundational Lamaleran ritual: the division of the *umā,* the portions of the shareholders. Every téna (and jonson) is organized as a corporation, with each crew member receiving one share, or umā, and umā are also assigned to non-hunting clan members, such as widows, to ensure that everyone is fed. In certain cases, individuals receive multiple umā. The lamafa, for instance, gets a double share in recognition of his more dangerous work, as well as a third one, the *ķélik,* to give away as a reminder from the Ancestors that his job is foremost to feed the tribe, not himself. (Should a lamafa eat his own kélik, the Ancestors will cause his head to swell until he cannot support it and he has to drag it along the ground.) An individual can also own several umā for performing multiple responsibilities. Frans possesses two umā for *Kéna Puķā,* one as the blacksmith for its harpoons and one as the ship's captain. Because *Boli Sapang* has about forty umā, Jon would have received approximately a fortieth of the dozen or so tons of whale meat if his clan had taken the animal alone. But because another téna had pitched in, the catch was evenly apportioned between the two clans, so that his share was cut in half. Other prey, from swordfish to leatherback turtles, are split according to variations on this system as well. All of this means that an umā is a Lamaleran's most important right and badge of identity.

The Gifts of the Ancestors had been so bountiful that day that most Lamalerans received an umā. However, the handful of clans that had not landed a harpoon still were provided for by the Ways of the Ancestors. As afternoon regressed into evening, Ika and the other Lamalerans who had received shares bore steaks to relatives, neighbors, and friends in the unlucky clans—gifts that went under a variety of names, but that were most often called the *běfānā.* The reasoning behind each individual act of generosity varied—from reciprocating previous běfānā, to honoring family ties, to providing charity—but together they embodied the Ancestors' directive that all Lamalerans should share their personal good fortune with the tribe. By the end of the evening, probably around 90 percent of the village had received whale meat.

The běfãnā is a major reason that anthropologists rate the Lamalerans as one of the most generous societies in the world, significantly more so than Americans or Europeans. In 1999, anthropologists asked the Lamalerans to participate in an experiment called the Ultimatum Game, which measures the altruism of participants by seeing how they share a pot of money between themselves and another person. Across twelve countries and four continents, anthropologists played the game with fifteen different traditional societies, from African hunter-gatherers to Amazonian swidden farmers, as well as modern citizens. By comparing the results, the anthropologists examined how cultural norms of generosity differed between far-flung peoples. In industrialized countries, they found that participants were self-interested, keeping most of the money for themselves. About two-thirds of the Lamaleran players, however, divided the money evenly—and the other third actually gave more away than they kept—turning an experiment designed to draw out selfishness into an illustration of altruism. Of all the peoples, the Lamalerans were the most generous, and anthropologists credited this to the openheartedness they regularly practice in dividing whales.

Such altruism is essential to the tribe's survival, as anthropologists have determined that the běfãnā evolved to smooth out the boom-and-bust nature of whaling. In a standard year, the Lamalerans catch twenty sperm whales. As there are twenty-one clans, that works out to about one per clan annually. Researchers have calculated that an average-sized sperm whale yields about 15,000 pounds of meat, which can satisfy the protein requirements of around a hundred people for a year. This means that the tribe normally catches just as many whales as it needs to feed its fifteen hundred members and still have a small surplus to trade. However, one clan might land two whales one year and none the next, while a fellow clan might take no whales the first year but two the second. If the clans did not share, unlucky clans would starve while lucky clans gorged, until the formerly lucky clans hit a dry spell and starved as well.

The běfãnā, then, serves the practical purpose of redistributing surpluses where they are needed through gifts, which are eventually reciprocated. All hunter-gatherers practice a form of this virtuous cycle to some degree, as cooperation and sharing are essential to their survival, which is a large part of why foraging groups are more egalitarian and generous than industrial societies. Anthropologists have used these facts to argue that modern humanity is actually worse off than their forebears. But for Jon and the other Lamalerans, such common sense is just the Way of the Ancestors.

ALTHOUGH JON WAS A MEMBER of one of the most generous societies on earth, he was not immune to the interpersonal spats that afflict the rest of humanity. Some sixth sense had made Honi suspicious that Jon was cheating on her, and Jon resented her constant texts and calls demanding that he avoid the tribe's women, even the cousins with whom he was close friends. Often their arguments raged until they were interrupted by the cliff-hanger of one of them running out of *pulsa,* phone credits. Then the next day, terrified they had done irreparable damage to the relationship, they would make up in a series of frantic texts or calls.

Honi was right to worry, though her fears were overblown. While Jon was not stepping out on her, he had been experimenting with a rudimentary version of Facebook. Using a BlackBerry so old that many of its keys had been replaced by letterless rubber cutouts, Jon had sent friend requests to every girl listed as living on Lembata. Thirty-four answered. Jon commenced texting with them. To his friends, Jon insisted he was just passing the time. After all, the chance of his meeting any of these girls in person was remote. But one day Honi got wind of his antics from a friend and called Jon, putting on the big-city accent she had learned since leaving Lembata, and pretending to be a girl interested in meeting him. Jon failed her loyalty test. Soon his Black-Berry buzzed with a message from Honi's younger sister: "Don't bother my older sister again." Moments later, a second message arrived: "She has a new boyfriend who is better looking, richer, and more loyal."

Unfortunately, Jon could not answer because he was out of pulsa. He begged his friends for phone credits, but when he had collected enough, Honi did not answer his calls. When they finally spoke, days later, Honi asked if he wanted to be in a relationship. Jon told her that if she desired it, he did as well. But she demanded that he speak his feelings first, and when he would not, she hung up.

Jon told his friends that he had just had his heart broken for the first time. "Some people go crazy," he said, "but not me. Now I won't be able to be hurt again." He would be calm, he declared, because he was an adult. But the truth was that his heart ached worse than his leg.

A few days later, Honi called Jon, crying.

"If you want to go with the other guy, you can," he told her. "I'm not forbidding you to come back to me." That was his last dig at her, and soon they were once more engaged.

Not long after that, Frans paid his weekly visit to Jon's house. As afternoon silted into night, the shaman rubbed down Jon's leg with holy water and declared that his powers had nearly healed it. Soon Jon would hunt again.

Chapter Five

THIS, MY SON, IS HOW YOU KILL A WHALE

July 16, 2014

Ignatius — Ben

The Blikololong boys grew up with a perfect view of their father's back. Most days, Ignatius stood at the tip of the hâmmâlollo, his toes hanging over the edge, his heels on the bamboo, while his sons crouched on the bottom rung, watching intently for his signals.

Ignatius had a beautiful back. He rarely wore a shirt, and his muscles — impressive and naturally proportioned, their animal strength having been earned over a lifetime of physical labor — merged and broke ranks, then melded again. The sun had tanned his skin an almost-purple black. Even when the sea rioted, he rode the rollers with only the slightest bend in his knees, his hands clasped behind him, every bit at ease as a gentleman strolling his grounds. Sometimes he would shift his weight and the arch of a foot would flash, white, naked, vulnerable. For hours on end, he scrutinized the waves far and near, paying attention to everything but his sons — Yosef, Ondu, and Ben — waiting behind him for his sign.

In addition to being one of the most famous harpooners of his generation, Ignatius was the greatest ata mola, shipbuilder, of his time:

by 2014, roughly a third of the téna fleet was his handiwork. He would spend days hand-adzing the boards of a téna so that when they were finally fitted together — one, two, three, like the pieces of a puzzle — the other hunters would tap the hull with their knuckles and murmur approvingly, "It needs no pith," meaning no palm gum and fibers were needed to seal them.

He was renowned for working tirelessly. Even resting, he would whittle fishhooks out of brazilwood or weave a basket from lontar palm leaves, making the weft and warp so snug that his wife could carry water from the well a kilometer away without losing a drop. If someone was building a house or a téna, he would help whenever he had a free moment, asking for no payment but a few glasses of tuak. He took the time to dissect whale carcasses with young hunters, showing them where to puncture a bellows-like lung or perforate a boulder-sized heart, a practice that had earned him the proud nickname "Professor Harpoon."

His gentle humor, wisdom, and knowledge of the Ways of the Ancestors made him a favorite informal judge to settle disputes between men in the village. The women of the tribe, young and old, teasingly flirted with him. The only intimidating part of him was the way his joyful intensity rebuked any malingerer and his effortless perfection implicitly censured any mistake. In the whole village, there were only two people he could not seem to get along with: his eldest son, Yosef, and, on occasion, his youngest son, Ben.

No one could say, however, that Ignatius did not teach his sons well. The same perfectionism that he focused on crafting a téna, he applied to rearing his children. He instructed them in the Ways of the Ancestors as he had been: exactingly, severely. As a boy, if Ignatius made a mistake while adzing boards for a téna, his father would smack him. Such tough love was standard at the time and still is not uncommon in Lamalera. But his terror had never lessened his love for his father. He had revered him in an Old Testament way: with a mixture of awe, dread, and puzzlement. Perhaps it was no surprise, then, that he expected the same militaristic deference from his own sons, no matter how cheerful he was with everyone else. In harpooning, sailing, shipbuilding, rope winding, whale butchering, and all the other skills of a Lamaleran man, he made sure they excelled. (His one regret raising his sons was that he never tried to hide his love of tuak from them, and that they took his occasional drunkenness not as a lesson to avoid imbibing but as permission.) As Ignatius saw it, though, in demanding perfection, he was preparing them for the world's tribulations as best he could.

ONE SUNDAY MORNING AFTER CHURCH, in April 2014, all three of Ignatius's sons gathered in front of their father's home. Juvenile palm trees clawed their way out of rotting coconut shells, which lay where they had fallen months before. Stingray tails had hung so long on bamboo racks, they had leathered into horseshoes that could never be unbent. Sperm whale ribs as thick as logs were scattered across the dirt yard, and pillars of vertebrae had avalanched. Once, Ignatius's wife, Teresea, had kept all of these trophies in orderly stacks and scraped them clean of meat until they shone as white as children's teeth. But now, since her death the year before, threads of blackened flesh, so rotten that even day geckos would not scavenge them, dangled off fresh bones.

Yosef, the eldest son, informed his father that he and his brothers were ready to take over *Demo Sapang,* the clan's téna, which the family led. He said they wanted to let their father rest after a lifetime of labor.

But Ignatius was not interested in doing the small stuff. "I'm not just going to mind the grandchildren and weave sails," he said, insisting he was still made for hard work. His body remained as rigid as a weight lifter's, and he often showed it off, wearing only a sarong wrapped around his waist. But his nearly seventy-year-old face was bunched with creases and he had gone bald except for tussocks of white hair fluffed over his ears.

"You're old," Yosef told him.

Ignatius regarded his sons with red-rimmed eyes and sucked on his cigarette, a Marlboro Light. His cheeks, having only three blackened teeth to prop them up, hollowed extra deep with the drag. His sons—all three of whom smoked—had been after him to quit recently because of his chronic cough, but he had ignored their suggestions. Still, when he could afford something better than palm-leaf cigarettes, he had begun to prefer Marlboro Lights, for their numbing menthol, over his old favorites, Marlboro Reds, which exacerbated his cough. "I'm still strong," he argued. "If none of you answer the baleo, then I'll pick up the harpoon myself." Then he blew smoke toward his descendants.

Ignatius's promise was not an idle one. He continued to captain *Demo Sapang,* though he had mostly turned over his spot on the hâm-mâlollo to Yosef, instead wielding its steering oar. Yet three years earlier, when his sons had failed to get to the beach fast enough, there had been a day when he had launched *Demo Sapang* without them. Finding the téna gone, his sons had asked the wives who were watching the horizon, "Who took it out? Who's the harpooner?"

"Your father," the wives said.

Everyone laughed. No one was certain exactly how old Ignatius was, but it was believed that he'd been born around the end of World War II, meaning he was likely nearly seventy.

When the téna returned, Yosef questioned who had harpooned the sperm whale being dragged into the bay. "Your father," came the wives' answer once more.

Today the rest of the argument between Ignatius and his sons went the usual way. Yosef promised that they were trying to honor Ignatius, but Ignatius answered that he was not ready to quit. Besides, he felt that he could not retire until Ben slew his first whale and became a lamafa. Since time immemorial, Ignatius's ancestors had been harpooners. And by then, people were saying that one of the last true lamafa bloodlines was the Seran Blikololongs, which made Ignatius feel it was even more important to keep the tradition going. Occasionally he would grumble about the tribe's repeal, in the 1990s, of the law that defined lamafa as a hereditary position, and blame the present-day breakdown of the old hierarchies on it, as now men whom the Ancestors had never meant to hold power controlled positions of authority.

If he stopped going to sea, Ignatius demanded, who would teach Ben? Yosef offered to instruct his youngest brother, as he was nearly twenty years older than Ben. But Ignatius seized his adze, signaling the conversation was over, and ordered his sons to help him hew logs for a new sampan.

As the three of them followed their father to the boat sheds, Ignatius said something his sons did not know how to respond to: "Besides, your mother has passed. If I die at sea, I'll join her."

IGNATIUS STARTED LATE ON THE ROAD to becoming one of the great harpooners of his generation. His father, Willibrodus Demon, after whom his middle son was named, had been a harpooner, and Ignatius had stood behind him at the base of the hâmmâlollo when he was a teenager, fitting the correct spearhead with the right bamboo shaft and adding a second harpoon after his father had landed the first. He was naturally left-handed, but as the sinister side was believed to do the work of the Devil, his father would smack him if he forgot to lift his harpoon with his right arm. (In the end, this retraining was only partially successful, for after his father died, although Ignatius would spear large targets like whales with his right hand, for flighty prey like dolphins he would switch to his left.) Willibrodus said little while they hunted, but when they were scooping rice off the communal palm-leaf plate each night, the old man would lecture his son on his mistakes.

Years passed. Ignatius married. He fathered Yosef; Willibrodus Demon II, who died from malaria as an infant; then Willibrodus Boeang "Ondu" Demon III; five daughters; and, finally, Ben. Other clans offered to let him harpoon for their téna, but he was intent on taking his father's perch on *Demo Sapang*. As his father aged, he substituted for him more often. Finally, when Ignatius was about thirty, his father joined the Ancestors. Before he passed, his father made Ignatius swear that he would guard *Demo Sapang* until it could be entrusted to his own sons.

Many years later, when *Demo Sapang* had finally succumbed to the cumulative battering of whales and time, Ignatius disassembled it, saving what boards he could. Then he felled gigantic banyan trees in the untouched jungle to the east and floated them down the coast. He built the new *Demo Sapang* as a copy of the old one, mimicking it down to the smallest internal dowel. He even incorporated a few boards from the old *Demo Sapang* into the rebuilt one, to transfer over the spirit that had inhabited every version of the Blikololongs' téna, from the very first. Onto its prow he chiseled an Asiatic lion's face, the symbol of the clan, for they did not yet have paint in Lamalera.

The first whale Ignatius slew on *Demo Sapang* had two nuggets of ambergris inside it, each about the size of a coconut, which the tribe interpreted as a sign that his career would be blessed. Soon it was being said that he never missed — not even with spinner dolphins, the most difficult and agile of prey to spear. At night, he dreamed about whaling. Even in church, while listening to the sermon, he replayed strikes in his head. In his time, he took twenty-two whales as the first harpooner, scratching their number into the wooden wall of his house — and helped other lamafa take dozens more. Yosef and Ondu grew up standing behind him at the base of the harpooner's platform, as he had stood behind his father. Ben came late, nearly a decade after Ondu, but soon he too was apprenticing at sea. One day, Ignatius promised them, they would take his place.

"THIS, MY SON, IS HOW you kill a whale," Ignatius told Ben, when he was thirteen. He held aloft the *kāfé kotekĕlema,* the great harpoon head, nearly a foot of black iron, overlaid with a red patina of rust. The edge had been honed so many times that it had become an uneven silver razor, and the inverse scales of hammer blows, which had shaped it from rebar, patterned it. The weapon had none of the industrial perfection of a pistol, which kills impersonally from a distance — instead, in each nick was a war story that Ignatius and Ben knew intimately.

Ignatius handed Ben the weapon. It was even heavier than it looked.

"Can you feel it?"

Ben knew his father meant its perfect balance, its strength, its spirit. Ignatius had told him that the soul of the harpoon head was linked to that of both his Ancestors and the Spirit House, and through them to his own soul.

Ignatius showed Ben how to screw the spearhead into a bamboo V-clamp inside the neck of the *lekā kenāda puā gāda,* the great harpoon shaft, which had been polished smooth and oiled not by a thousand hands before Ben's but by the same hands gripping it thousands of times. Sixteen feet long, the weapon almost tipped Ben over. Even once he steadied himself, he could not keep it from swinging every which way, as if it had a life of its own. When he tried to corral the right side, the left would run amok.

Then Ignatius gave him the piece of advice he would always remember: "What is most important is not the strength of the lamafa's arm but the strength of his mind and heart."

This meant something to Ben, as he had always been smaller than the other children. Only recently, though, had he realized that everyone in his family was undersized, including his father. The Seran Blikololongs possessed the wiry bodies of runners rather than the gladiator builds of many of the other lamafa.

"The movements of the harpoon reflect the movements inside of you," Ignatius counseled. "Move with the harpoon, not against it. Your inner and outer balance is more important than brute power."

The majority of Ben's formal instruction in the art of harpooning took place that afternoon. Ignatius guided him through each of the seven harpoon heads, nine ropes, and ten harpoon shafts, and then methodically explained the situations and prey that each combination was used for — ballista bolt–like harpoons for large prey like manta rays and long, light throwing harpoons for dolphins. Occasionally, after that, when they encountered a new, rare type of prey—dugong, Cuvier's beaked whale, false killer whale—Ignatius would explain its anatomy as they butchered it on the beach. And at night, he would lecture on Lamaleran mythology and tell instructive tales of old hunts while his sons scooped up fresh fish and red rice using coconut shells, for Western dinnerware had not yet arrived in Lamalera.

But mostly, Ben stood behind his father and watched how he balanced on the hâmmâlollo with a tiger's grace. He noted the hand signals used to direct the materos during the chase. He marked when his dad leapt and how the experienced hunter javelined the harpoon. Sometimes, while they ate whatever Ignatius had slain that day, his father would add a few words of clarification, explaining why he had aimed in front of the lateral fin instead of behind it, or how he knew that the manta would resurface to the left of the téna rather than the right. But for all the years of Ben's apprenticeship, the most action he was involved in was "doubling," adding a second harpoon after his father had already sunk the first, and only for smaller prey like dolphins or mantas.

By the beginning of the hunting season in 2014, Ben had helped harpoon all types of sharks and small rays, but he could not call himself a lamafa: he had yet to command a jonson or a téna and spear prey from it. He was twenty-seven. His brothers had become lamafa before they turned twenty. Ignatius promised that soon Ben would get his chance. *What is most important is not the strength of the lamafa's arm but the strength of his mind and heart,* he would remind himself. What he loved most about the saying was the implicit acknowledgment that he and his father shared a spirit that transcended their bantamweight bodies. Eventually, however, he began to wonder if the lessons, more than teaching him simply to mimic his father, were supposed to make him his father. Then he would try to stare past his father's shoulder blades to the sea.

* * *

RAISING HIS SONS, IGNATIUS HAD to confront a choice that his father did not: whether to send them to the government schools opening across Lembata. The decision about Yosef was easy because in the mid-1970s Lamalera had only an elementary school. An eldest son was expected to follow in his father's footsteps, and so Yosef left the classroom for the sea before sixth grade.

A decade later, the advantages of an education were becoming clear as the first parents to send their children abroad to get schooling and then work started to receive cash-filled envelopes when the postman led his donkey laden with mail over the volcano. Ignatius had few reservations about dispatching his five daughters to high school abroad, instructing them to become nurses and send money home. But he was more conflicted about his son Ondu's desire to attend high school: he believed his son had the right to choose, but in his heart, he thought Ondu should become a lamafa.

Reluctantly, he shipped Ondu to boarding school on Timor, the province's capital island, but Ondu proved to Ignatius that he "deserved his grandfather's name" when he tried to hitchhike hundreds of miles back to Lembata after taking offense at the school's attempt to serve him a meal made from the pith of a palm tree, which in Lamalera is considered pig feed. This confirmed for Ignatius that the Savu Sea would always call his sons home. And it was an early sign of how effortlessly Ondu would take to the Ways of the Ancestors, becoming a respected lamafa and village leader, and uncomplainingly accommodating his father's every desire, so that although he was Ignatius's most attentive son, he was the one the old man busied himself with the least.

When Ben was sixteen and asked if his father could pay for high school in Lewoleba, with money sent by his sisters and funds that Teresea occasionally earned selling whale jerky in Lewoleba, Ignatius assumed his son would not be gone long. Ben would have to join *Demo*

Sapang during all his school breaks, Ignatius told him, so that he would always know how to be a fisherman. "And don't come back fat," Ignatius said, "or embarrass me by forgetting how to tie your knots, you understand?"

One morning soon after, Ben fit his belongings into a battered backpack, pressed his forehead to the knuckles of his father and his mother, and rode the auto over the volcano. When he returned three months later on break, he was the living manifestation of all of Ignatius's fears. His hair had been cut into a mullet, and he wore punk clothes and an earring. A tattoo of a devil's face — done professionally, unlike Jon's — flamed on his shoulder. Ignatius bit his tongue and kept faith that the Ancestors would guide his son home. When Ben next returned, he brought three-foot-tall speakers, from which he played Indo rock until he blew them out, after which he would still make them perform into the wee hours like a scratchy-voiced singer.

Then one afternoon, a little less than three years after Ben had left for school, he rode the auto home with Anastasia "Ita" Amuntoda, a girl from the Kedang tribe, which occupied the far side of the island. Ita was heavily pregnant. At first, too afraid to face his parents, Ben hid at Ondu's house, in Upper Lamalera, for the night. The sanctuary did not last long, as the next day Ondu informed their father of what had happened. When Ben brought Ita to his father, the old man looked away. Ignatius could not speak. He was mad about this disaster, but he did not know whom to blame.

That was the end of Ben's schooling. Ignatius would no longer pay, and the principal shouted Ben out of his office when Ben asked to return, using money he earned himself. He drove trucks in Lewoleba for a few years to make a living and avoided Ita and Ignatius in Lamalera. He bitterly mourned his fate, and the loss of his hopes of attending the police academy after graduating high school.

Ben's despair, however, was nothing compared to Ita's. To that point, she'd had a middle-class Indonesian upbringing, watching translated Disney cartoons on TV, filching candy from her parents' dry-goods store, and planning to go to university off-island. But now the pregnant sixteen-year-old was forced to dwell at Ignatius's house because her own family would not let her return until she was married, and they were demanding an exorbitant bride price as a means of punishing Ben. With the father of her child on the other side of the mountains, she knew no one in the tribe. Instead of being a carefree high school student, she had to cook and clean for Ignatius and Teresea and, soon, her baby. Teresea and the other women were kind to her, and they tried to teach her the Lamalerans' ways, but since she was used to simply turning on a spigot or lighting a propane stove, the tasks of carrying water from the well and chopping firewood exhausted her. She shied away from the bloody work of butchering whales, as she'd previously only ever cleaned a chicken. Meanwhile, the nasal local language seemed impossible to master. She dreamed of somehow returning to her old life in Lewoleba, maybe one day even still attending university, and leaving the whale hunters behind her like a bad dream.

When Ben would return home for holidays, Ignatius kept pressuring him to resume his apprenticeship on *Demo Sapang*. Ben resisted, but eventually he hit a dry spell of work in Lewoleba and had no choice except to move back to Lamalera. However, even with Ben installed in his childhood room again for the long term, he seemed curiously reluctant to resume his harpoon training.

Ignatius wondered: Why did his son not want to become a lamafa? When Ignatius was young, that was every whaler's dream. Why should that change just because bulldozers had carved a road through the jungle and airplanes the shape of tiny harpoon heads pulled contrails like white ropes through the oceanic sky? He knew the Ancestors were proud of him and his sons, but he could not tell if Ben felt the Ancestors' satisfaction too.

On July 16, 2014, at noon, Ben watched a jonson race back into Lamalera Bay, skidding along so fast that each time the boat hit the front of a wave its prow lifted off the water and scattered spray when it slammed down. An early return meant either that a hunter had been hurt or that sperm whales had been sighted. When the man at the prow hoisted a harpoon shaft and a burst of wind unfurled a white shirt tied to its tip, the Lamalerans had their answer.

Baleo! Ben roared, along with several dozen other men.

They shouted until the cry repeated from the houses up the hill. The men on the beach stowed the nets they had been fixing, doused the fires that had heated half-forged harpoon heads to a molten glow, and shoved half-built sampans to the corners of boat sheds, then ran to their téna.

In the village, kids hollered as they ran through the streets and old women cast down their canes to cup their hands around their yelling mouths. The baleo was not a unified cry, all fifteen hundred voices in the village raised at once. Rather it was a rolling chorus that started on the beach then spread outward, as each person who heard it took it up for a few seconds and then cocked an ear to confirm the message had been picked up farther on. The baleo echoed its way up the cliffs, expanded into a choir once it reached Upper Lamalera, then broke into a chain of lonely voices in the orchards, until concluding in a faint refrain in the hamlet of Lamamanu a mile above. At about the same time, shouting from the east confirmed that the news had been received in the outlying villages, and children were being dispatched as messengers to men felling trees in the jungle or spearfishing in far-flung coves.

As whalers sprinted across the beach, raising puffs of sand with each step and leaping over rib bones, Ben stood unmoving. Even Jon was hobbling from téna to téna, trying to convince the incredulous captains to give him an oar. Ben faced a choice. Normally, it was his duty to drive *Kanibal,* the family jonson. But Ignatius was over the mountains today, on a mission to Ita's parents that Ben had been trying not to think about. Without his father, a nerve-wracking possibility had materialized: Could the hâmmâlollo fall to him? Ondu was away at a wedding. Yosef had bought a jerrican of tuak earlier in the morning and retreated to one of his hiding spots. If Ben wanted to become a lamafa, he should sieze command of *Demo Sapang*. He might not get another chance this good for a long time.

Finally, instead of running to *Demo Sapang*, Ben sprinted to the shed behind his father's house, where the fuel drums were stored. While the beach resounded noisily, he waited peacefully as gasoline siphoned through a rubber hose into two jerricans. He loved driving *Kanibal* rather than rowing on *Demo Sapang*, thrilling to the power of the jonson's engine in his hand — even the boat's name, taken from an Indonesian horror movie rather than the tales of his Ancestors, was a victory over his father.

When both twenty-liter jerricans were full, Ben hoisted them onto his shoulders. By the time he reached the sand, Ben's second uncle, Stefanus Sengaji Keraf, identifiable even from a hundred yards away

Ben driving Kanibal

by his bushy beard and crooked right arm, which had been shattered by a whale and healed without a cast, stood on the hâmmâlollo of *Demo Sapang* as it floated in the bay.

His clansmen had *Kanibal* up on log runners at the waterline, waiting. A team of men pushed the boat through the surf while he primed the Yamaha Enduro engine. He motored *Kanibal* alongside *Demo Sapang,* and the two ships were roped together. Then the jonson dragged the téna out to sea, its outboard motor laboring but tireless.

Finally, Ben spotted Yosef, two téna back, squatting on the hâmmâlollo of *Boli Sapang.* Without Jon, the Hariona clan was still down a man, with barely enough to row a téna. They must have invited his late-arriving brother to guest-star as their lamafa, Ben deduced. He felt a pang of guilt: for the first time in years there was no Seran Blikololong leading *Demo Sapang.* But he felt it was better that he did not become the lamafa that day: it would only make his impending betrayal of his father worse.

As RECENTLY AS A DECADE AGO, whenever Ignatius traveled from Lamalera to Lewoleba, he would rise before dawn to trek over the mountains. As he walked through the cassava fields above the village in the dark, he would take care not to step on any seedlings if it was the wet season, but if it was the dry season, he would stamp a straight line of footprints through the ash of the annual swidden burn-offs. Sunrise would find him swatting away bees in the cashew orchards of the mountain tribes. By noon, he would be pressing through the tangled jungle along the ridgelines of the volcano. Then all afternoon he would scramble down a root staircase, not fighting gravity but letting it draw him downward in a near run. The footpath would be busy with families returning from market bearing rattan backpacks bulging with goods, local women carrying firewood wrapped in vines on their heads, and farmers leading horses bearing old rice sacks filled with freshly picked coffee berries. At the end of the day, shortly after dark, after a slog of about thirty miles, he would arrive foot weary in Lewoleba.

But on the same morning his sons would answer the baleo, he rode an auto over the volcano. The converted dump truck was stuffed with nylon sacks of whale jerky or cashew fruit, and passengers squeezed around them. Together, the salty reek of dried whale, the cloyingness of the drupes, and the yeasty scent of human sweat blended into an overwhelming funk. Dust like a sandstorm billowed through windows without panes. Dangdut music screeched through blown-out speakers that the driver played at maximum volume nonetheless.

Occasionally, Ignatius glimpsed the Savu Sea below, as smooth as if it had been planed. Once he would never have missed such a perfect hunting day. But recently he had been coughing constantly, enough that he had trouble sleeping, though that was not the only reason his rest was disturbed. He had been daydreaming, nightdreaming, about his wife: almost a year earlier he had found her body lying in the bedroom like a piece of clothing she had taken off.

What a wife Teresea had been! The mountain tribes had feared her as a fierce bargainer. She had never complained about working as hard as he did for their family. She had been a kind, firm mother to their eight children. For over half a century, she had been his partner. He missed her gossip about village news and her jokes, the way she would filch his cigarettes and then deny them to him until he almost begged. Recently, he had been imagining that she was still alive. Some afternoons, when he climbed the stairs from the beach to his house, he met her again — not *her,* of course, but there she was, coming down the stone steps, the stairs on which they had passed each other every afternoon of their courtship, their encounter the product of careful timing played off as chance, singing in her raspy yet sweet voice as if soloing for God, and it was like he was still wondering how to ask her parents for her hand in marriage.

Except it was not his chosen one but Ika, Jon Hariona's sister, greeting him with a "Good afternoon, Grandfather," and spiriting on her way, her head so still that the bucket filled with laundry balanced atop it did not wobble despite her dancing hips. Teresea and Ika's resemblance was uncanny: both had short curvy figures and long kinky black hair, though Ignatius preferred Teresea's pale skin and plumpness to Ika's dark complexion and skinniness. The favorite pastime for each was singing in the church choir. Teresea had even grown up in the house next to the one Ika would later inhabit, so that when Ika descended the stairs it seemed to Ignatius that she was Teresea, stepping out of the past.

Ignatius and Teresea's romance had started with eye contact and escalated to chats on the stairs, but soon he began delivering extra fish to her parents, and Teresea would stop by his house to help his elderly mother butcher his catch. They sought permission from their parents to attend the *Oa* dances, held every Saturday night under the banyan tree in the village square.

Every week, the ancient tree was transformed into a chandelier by whale oil lanterns — and later, pressurized gas lanterns — hung from its gnarled branches. Under the dangling flames, the girls of Lamalera joined hands to form a huge circle and then spun clockwise. From the shadows, the boys watched as the girls' sarongs bloomed. Then the girls released one another's hands and turned to grab the forearms of the waiting men. Ignatius always inserted himself next to Teresea, so that their fingers braceleted each other's wrists.

They themselves provided the music, eerie ululating chants that created the beat for the dance and sounded like lullabies meant not to ease a baby asleep but to spook her awake. Like the square dances of the American South, Oa has a simple repetitious structure — a 1-2-3 step advance and retreat, followed by a slide sideways — with each movement called out by its participants. For hours Ignatius and Teresea sang stories of ages long lost, which still described the present, and danced so hard they wore grooves in the earth, revolving like a gear in the clock of time. The whale oil lanterns flattered everyone with candlelight and a faint honey-like smell. Only their hands touched, but Ignatius found it erotic enough that it set his heart spinning. He would scratch Teresea's palm with a fingernail, a Lamaleran sign of favor, but one so subtle no person could censure them for it.

Today, however, as Ignatius rode the auto over Labalekang, all he had left of Teresea was a black-and-white photograph, already fading, in which she posed like a person who had never seen a camera before, stiff and guilty looking, so that it had captured her physical features but not her teasing, giddy soul. The banyan tree, meanwhile, was no longer illuminated every Saturday night, and the Oa was resurrected only for festivals.

No doubt all this reminiscing was prompted by the approach of Ben's wedding, just two weeks away. The goal of Ignatius's journey was to finalize the bride price for Ita. The negotiations with her parents had been ongoing for six years, ever since Ben fled their high school in Lewoleba with Ita in tow, and had continued even while the young couple birthed first a daughter and then a son. Ignatius had already made four trips, and Ondu had served as an emissary eight times.

Ignatius hoped the visit would be a success, but he feared it would unfold exactly as it had before: The Amuntodas would welcome him warmly and shut the metal garage door of their dry-goods shop to armor their conference against intrusions. Then they would offer him Marlboro cigarettes and Tugu Buaya packaged coffee, but he would smoke confetti tobacco hand-rolled in lontar palm leaves and ask for coffee pounded from native beans to prove he was not ashamed of being from the villages. Next they might show him around the shop, and he would have to compliment them on how everything was displayed in glass cases and wrapped in plastic, though he felt this was just a way to drive home the point that vegetables at the Lamaleran barter market were stacked on the ground. Meanwhile, Ignatius would try not to self-consciously compare his patched sarong and flip-flops stitched with fishing line to Ita's father's tailored slacks and patent-leather shoes.

Once they had exhausted all pleasantries, Ita's father would ask if

Ignatius had brought a *gading,* an elephant tusk, though the only things he was carrying were a hollowed-out bamboo tobacco container and a knife tucked into his sarong. The problem was, Ignatius, like almost every other Lamaleran, could not afford a gading. When the Amuntodas asked after the size of the elephant tusk he had paid for his own wife, he acknowledged that it was the length of a full *gudi,* a specialized dpa measurement used for gading, equal to the distance from the center of a man's chest to the fingertips of his extended arm. But that had been more than four decades earlier, when every family had a few gading stored away, imported over the centuries along the ancient trade routes from western Indonesia, where elephants roamed the jungles. Eventually, Indonesian laws had ended the ivory trade, and Chinese traders had bought up all the heirloom tusks, driving up the price of gading to about three thousand dollars, more than many villagers would earn in a decade.

Although Ignatius would haggle with Ita's parents in the language of gading and gudi, everyone knew the vocabulary was metaphorical in the present day. After a few sallies, he would offer the standard price: about a hundred dollars cash, with a few pigs and goats thrown in. But Ita's parents, while unfailingly polite, would imply that their daughter was worth an actual gading.

Ignatius always struggled to control his frustration. Of course Ben's actions had not been honorable and the Amuntodas deserved some recompense for that, but he was sure that they were punishing their daughter and his son out of spite. Worse, they were endangering the souls of Ben and Ita by forcing them to live in sin.

But even if a date was set, there was no guarantee it would endure. Shortly after Ita moved into Ignatius's house, the Amuntoda and Seran Blikololong families had agreed on a bride price far cheaper than a gading. Ignatius had even paid ahead of time for an auto to bring forty-five members of his family over the mountain for the wedding. But then the Amuntodas canceled without warning just a few days before the ceremony, claiming that a relative had suddenly died, though Igna-

tius believed they just wanted more money. Ben and Ita were humili-
ated when a priest stopped the parish's mandatory marriage-preparation
class and announced to all the engaged couples attending it that Ita's
family had asked for them to be removed.

As the auto crested Labalekang, Ignatius rolled yellowed palm leaf
around a line of tobacco flakes and hoped this time would be different.
Ita had been dropping hints lately that an overture would be accepted.
Her name and Ben's were in the church log for July 31. Before he died,
he wanted to see Ben become a lamafa, but watching his youngest son
walk up the aisle would bring him almost as much joy.

BEN HAD MAXED OUT THE engine of *Kanibal* for two hours straight,
dragging *Demo Sapang* all the way into the heart of the Savu Sea,
standing as he steered so that he could better glimpse the distant
spouts. As they approached the pod, Ben counted the number of times
the whales spouted: twelve, thirteen, fourteen…When he was close
enough to see the individual droplets in the geysers, the flukes of six
whales pointed skyward and then sank with barely a splash.

The whales had exhaled fifteen times, which, according to the
Ancestors' wisdom, meant that they would remain underwater for fifteen minutes. The ocean was all fractal waves, featureless in their simi-
larity, but since sperm whales fountain at a forty-five-degree angle in
the direction they are traveling, Ben knew to follow the aim of the last
spout — southwest — like a compass needle. Reckoning their speed in
relation to the amount of breath they had stored, he slowed *Kanibal* so
that its pace was just a little faster than that of the hidden whale. His
calculations led him to a patch of water indistinguishable, to the outside observer, from the rest, and there he idled the engine while the
remainder of the fleet spread like a noose across the Savu Sea.

They waited. Waves rhythmically high-fived the hull. Stratospheric
winds plucked cirrus clouds apart and wafted their shredded tufts
west. Each second, like a wave, repeated the shape and rhythm of the
last. Time stretched to its breaking point.

Waiting for the whales to breach during a hunt requires a special Zen. It is impossible to be a hundred percent attentive every second, or the pursuer will exhaust himself before the quarry even arrives. The Lamaleran trick is to slip into a reverie of total awareness, an almost-slumber where the body rests while the unconscious crunches every seabird skimming the ocean, each waltzing partnership of wavelets, every shadow oiling the current just beneath the surface.

But Ben was too worried to fix his full attention on the hunt. It was early afternoon, and by now his father and the Amuntodas had already decided his fate. But it was not just his marriage prospects that unsettled him. The shame of living in sin had bothered him at first (even as he enjoyed the notoriety among the other young men), but that had long ago faded. And though he still brooded on the spitefulness and racism of his future in-laws, who he was certain hated him as much for not being from the Kedang tribe as for getting their daughter pregnant so young and out of wedlock, that was not what agitated him now. What Ben could not stop thinking about lately was an offer he had received from an old friend with whom he had driven a *bemo,* a minibus, in high school: come to the tourist mecca of Bali and work a new bemo route with him.

The freest time in Ben's life had been driving the doorless vans through the streets of Lewoleba, swerving through traffic to pull up in front of anyone waving from the roadside, always on the lookout for cops because he did not have a driver's license. He had taken the job to help pay for his high school enrollment fee, but soon he found himself skipping classes to take extra shifts, for the vehicle had become the coolest part of his life.

All the bemos driven by their teenage male drivers announced themselves with flair like "Son of God" spray-painted in swirling silver letters or a decal of the Virgin Mary plastered beside one of a stripper. Ben pasted magazine cutouts of Britney Spears and Jennifer Lopez onto his dashboard, for though he was not sure exactly who the women were, that was not the important thing about those pictures. He cranked up the giant speakers under the back seats until they thumped so powerfully that dust would spill from the roofs of houses as the van passed. He liked to imagine that his bemo was no different from a rolling club, and he was the passengers' very own DJ, spinning Western hits and dangdut, Indonesian pop music spiced with Bollywood trills and synthesizers. Whenever a pretty girl got on, he selected a love song, and it was like he was speaking right to her. He got "DJ" tattooed in six-inch Gothic letters across his back. He never told Ignatius about his work.

During that time, Ben heard tales of Bali. So many tourists thronged Kuta Beach, he was told, that walking its sandy length was like traveling the world. Clubs, beer, and drugs abounded. DJs too. Some Indonesian men even got foreign girlfriends. They would share their weed with you. You did not have to marry them to have sex. When he occasionally met foreigners in Lewoleba, he asked them to tell him about the women in their countries.

The first week in the city, he had been intimidated by the unfamiliar faces—there were none back in his village—and the bustle, but before long he decided he never wanted to return home. Plumbing meant he did not have to walk a kilometer to the well to fetch jerricans of water. And twenty-four-hour electricity allowed him to watch European soccer games late into the night. In Lewoleba, no one boiled rice over a wood fire. An acquisitiveness that he had not experienced in Lamalera, where most possessions were shared, kindled in him: he yearned for his own TV, sound system, and motorbike. He learned how to be cool, turning his baseball cap around and pledging allegiance to Manchester United over Chelsea Football Club.

At first, he enjoyed school, excelling in social studies and German, but soon his attention wandered. He lived with relatives beside a police barracks, and began hanging out with the officers, attracted by their masculine swagger, their action-hero stories. They taught him to box and to drink. He covered for them when their wives inquired about their mistresses. Soon he was planning to become a policeman after graduating high school, though he never told Ignatius about that either. Policemen were rich enough to buy Honda motorbikes. Movies about their exploits were featured on TV. There were no policemen in Lamalera.

But the best part of Lewoleba was the girls. They did not have to dress with Lamaleran modesty. And there were so many! In the village, boys outnumbered girls, as any parent who could afford to do so sent their daughters over the mountains to school. He was tortured by unquenchable fantasies.

Ita sat at the same table as he did in Lamalera High School One. He was a natural artist—in Lamalera he had tattooed whales, harpoons, and wet-dream angels on his friends with a needle and battery carbon, with generally more success than his drunken mistake on Jon. He had passed Ita torn-out notebook pages covered with panoramas of Lamalera Bay, sketches of his sisters and mother, and a portrait of her, omitting her cross-eyed gaze and focusing instead on her cutely upturned nose, her sable tresses.

Ever since Ben had been forced to return to his tribe, he had taken every possible odd job that would bring him back to Lewoleba for a few weeks, from working on construction crews to driving bemos. But as he waited for the whales to resurface, he dreaded telling Ignatius he wanted to leave Lamalera. He knew exactly what his father's reaction would be: grief and anger. But the worst part would be his bafflement: his father could not conceive of why a man would not want to become a lamafa, or why his youngest son would not happily spend his youth taking care of his father. (In Lamalera, it is the obligation of the youngest child, not the eldest, to care for his parents.) His betrayal would seem all the crueler because his father would not recognize the need driving it. But if only his father understood him, then he would agree that Ben had to move to Bali.

Whatever the outcome of the negotiations today, Ben had a plan. If his father had succeeded in arranging the marriage, Ben would say he was going to Bali to support his wife and children. And if his father had been denied, he would say he was leaving to earn money for the gading.

The yawps erupting from his peers yanked Ben back to the hunt. Cataracts were pouring off a breaching sperm whale. Ben jammed the engine through its gears, and the rope between *Kanibal* and the téna strained. He powered the jonson toward the whale, paralleled it, and then as he passed it, swung *Kanibal* hard to the left. When the nose of the téna had reached the whale's tail, he swung *Kanibal* hard to the left. The sudden shift of momentum catapulted *Demo Sapang* forward just as the rope was undone. The oars of the materos chopped the water, nudging the ship ahead of the other téna, and his uncle Stefanus raised his harpoon.

Now Ben was no longer part of the chase.

WHEN YOSEF HAD HEARD THE BALEO, he had tipped back his jerrican of tuak and gulped down the rest of its ripe, yeasty contents. But out on the sea, as the sperm whales breached, he showed no ill effects of the alcohol, balancing ably on the hâmmâlollo of *Boli Sapang* while scream-ing orders at his crew. He was dissatisfied when *Demo Sapang* raced ahead of his téna, because he knew he would not get a shot at the forty-foot female whale both were chasing, though he was also proud that the Blikololong men were proving stronger than the Harionas. But then Stefanus, the lamafa standing in for him, missed a potshot, with his harpoon bouncing harmlessly off, and the animal dove. Yosef began storing up insults to hurl at him once they were ashore, for he had likely deprived both clans of a chance at a whale. By the time the two ships made it back to the fleet, the remaining whales had also escaped, except for one, which had managed to flip the first téna that had harpooned it but not disable the next three. To avoid further dividing the prize, the captains of the successful ships were waving away others.

The sun branded Yosef as he brooded that he could have spent the last three hours in the shade of a palm tree emptying another jerrican of tuak. Despite his renown as a lamafa—most Lamalerans agreed that he was a better harpooner than his father and some even said he was the best of his generation — he was just as famous for his prowess as a drinker. Any time he got his hands on some palm wine, he would not call a group of friends but steal away to savor it alone. He had a reputation for starting fights when sloshed, so many people did not invite him to parties. He had what might have been the first signs of liver problems: constipation and searing stomach pains after a drinking bout. Still, he could bring back dolphins with spear holes tunneling all the way through them.

Without fail, he butchered such trophies in front of Ignatius's house to make sure his father saw them. Since Yosef was a boy, he had been listening to people talk about how perfect his father was. Some people even said that his father was a better drunk than Yosef was: instead of getting belligerent, an inebriated Ignatius was as likely as not to wander to the beach to adze boards for a sampan. This competitiveness, and a lifetime of deeper resentments, occasionally boiled over into fights between the two of them that would wake the entire village at midnight with curses echoing off the cliffs.

Yosef had been conceived out of wedlock, and when Teresea's parents had found out, they sequestered her in their house during the pregnancy and dismissed Ignatius's emissaries by naming an outrageous bride price. They hoped she would marry a wealthier suitor with connections to their family. Even when Yosef was born, in November 1968, they would not let Ignatius see his son.

Ignatius was so disappointed that, without slipping word to Teresea, he exiled himself to the distant island of Flores, where he worked at a coconut oil factory, scraping the white flesh from fibrous shells and then using a press to squeeze out the juices. Eventually, Teresea discovered where he had gone and wrote him: *I will love you until I die. There is no other man for me in the world.* Ignatius began smuggling letters to her, along with a portion of his salary, by addressing envelopes to her sympathetic friends. In return, Teresea sent fata biti, smashed popcorn, the treat Lamalerans always long for when away from home, and more professions of love. Every month, Ignatius put aside as much of his wages as he could to pay for the gading her parents had requested.

Finally, after five years, Ignatius wrote to Teresea's parents, informing them he had compiled the bride price. He received no reply. But a letter from a Blikololong relative soon informed him that his uncle's skull had been crushed by a whale and that *Demo Sapang* needed to be rebuilt. Ignatius decided that no matter what happened with Teresea, it was time to return home. When he did, with the money and the backing of the town priest, Ignatius finally won over Teresea's parents. On December 21, 1973, the two were married.

But Yosef barely knew Ignatius, much less as his father. During his formative years, Yosef had bonded with his grandparents instead. Even after Teresea joined Ignatius's household, Yosef would often sleep at his grandparents' home. But eventually Yosef had to join *Demo Sapang,* and there, as fathers are apt to do, Ignatius drove his firstborn harder than the rest of his crew. Yosef felt his father unfairly criticized him while being bafflingly easy on everyone else. When the new *Demo Sapang* was built, Yosef would storm off when his father highlighted how his work deviated from the Ancestors' perfect model. Even when, at seventeen, Yosef became the youngest lamafa of his generation, he did not believe his father was proud. No matter how many whales he killed or how many sampans he built to Ignatius's directions, his father never seemed satisfied.

Most of the time, Yosef was polite if reserved with his father, but when he got drunk, he werewolfed. As a young man, he broke the harpoon shafts on *Demo Sapang* and threw rocks at Ignatius while yelling, "You're not my real dad!" But even as an adult, he would regularly get drunk and berate Ignatius. Ignatius believed Yosef's tantrums were the influence of Teresea's parents, who had whispered to him that he was the offspring of the suitor they had favored. Ignatius wept openly after the fights, and his wife and other sons comforted him, promising that they knew Yosef was his. Once he even disowned Yosef, though he finally relented. After each conflict, they spent weeks avoiding each other, a difficult task as they lived only two houses apart, but they eventually eased into hunting together again, until inevitably the same fight and unspoken reconciliation repeated. And so they passed the decades, trapped in a vicious cycle of recrimination and love.

Yosef's conflicts with his father were not his only worry. His bad temper kept him from finding a wife until late in life. Once he did, two of the children she bore died of disease before they turned six. Their ghosts hounded him. Even more, he could see that his father would soon pass, leaving him the head of the family, but he also feared that no matter how great a lamafa he was, he still lacked the ability to provide for them in a changing world, where his skill with a harpoon was of diminishing importance.

A snort like a giant nose being cleared of a cold brought Yosef out of his reverie, and he sprang to the tip of the harpooner's platform. A lost sperm whale calf had just breached a hundred yards away. A gift from the Ancestors. Téna cut each other off in the scramble to strike first.

"Row like you want to feed your families!" Yosef yelled at his materos, paddling the air with his arms to rouse them.

Another téna, *Kelulus,* a rebuilt version of the ship destroyed in the 1994 hunt of the devil whale, was on course to cut off the fleeing child. Crouched on its hâmmâlollo was Yosef "Beda" Ola Bataona, a star young harpooner. The materos for the two téna pulled as furiously as teams in a head-to-head crew meet. The whale strained to stay just ahead of *Boli Sapang,* too harried to gather enough air in its lungs to dive. Yosef lifted the kāfé kotekĕlema above his head and waited to see if the materos would close the last few feet or if the whale would escape. His mind was clean, empty of worry and anger, clearer than tuak could ever wipe it. His anxieties resolved into a single directive — plant the harpoon two feet below the dorsal fin. That knowledge came from his father, who had learned it from his father, who had learned it from his father — truth as it was supposed to be: unchanging. It was on the hâmmâlollo, where the lamafa must stand alone, that Yosef felt closest to Ignatius.

The whale began to rise toward Yosef's harpoon—then juked left into the path of *Kelulus*. Beda leapt and planted his harpoon shaft in the whale like a flagpole. Normally, Yosef would have been furious at losing his prey, but when a calf is caught, its mother will often try to save it. In hopes of this, *Boli Sapang* and the rest of the fleet paced *Kelulus* as it was dragged west. Sure enough, a shadow swelled in the depths, like a meteor falling up, erupting from the water. The calf stopped, turned to rub its nose against its mother's. The mother crunched the harpoon rope in her mouth, but though her teeth were six inches long, they were blunt, made for crushing, not cutting. As the fleet encircled mother and child, the two whales faced inward, their foreheads touching, their tails aimed outward, attempting to create the marguerite formation, named for its resemblance to the daisy-like flower. But though a full pod of six or more whales can form a 360-degree wall of tails, the mother and child were only two petals, and plucked as easily.

Yosef waved *Boli Sapang* in at a perpendicular angle to avoid the whales' flukes, which hinge vertically and have a limited horizontal range. He did not even have to jump but just rammed the kāfé kotekĕlema straight down into the mother. An inevitability entered the hunt once he had landed the first harpoon, especially when the mother did not manage to dislodge the spearhead or break the rope during her first dive. The lamafa of the téna *Praso Sapang* added a second harpoon, and the already slim chances of the mother escaping were halved. With two harpoons secured, the Lamalerans let the mother exhaust herself dragging the téna a mile across the ocean. When the mother tried to smash the téna with her tail, the crews turtled up beneath their boats' thwarts until she tired.

An hour later, when the floodlight rays of the afternoon sun started to acquire a candlelight glow, the mother whale was still dragging *Boli Sapang* and *Praso Sapang* in circles. Yosef called for Stefanus, his uncle, who had been waiting nearby on *Demo Sapang,* to add another harpoon. When Stefanus struck, the whale rolled so violently that she

The Lamaleran fleet battles the mother whale.

wound the ropes around herself like a giant spool, yanking *Praso Sapang* into the rear of *Demo Sapang* and shattering the boat's aft. With these two téna now crippled, Yosef lashed a duri to the end of a harpoon shaft and began stabbing the whale three feet headward of its lateral fin. Because not even the strongest Lamaleran can deal a death blow through foot-thick blubber and the even denser flesh beneath, hunters kill their prey with a thousand pricks delivered to the same spot, trying to bore a hole to the vital organs. He attacked relentlessly, as if powered by an inexhaustible rage.

Yosef had yet to capture a whale on *Demo Sapang* in 2014, and if he failed to do so, it would be the first year since he had become a lamafa, nearly thirty years before, that he did not take a whale on his father's téna. His tribesmen whispered that he was losing a step. He was nearing fifty. The average Indonesian male died at about sixty-seven, more than a decade before U.S. men, which meant physical decline often started far in advance of that.

A Lamaleran riddle asks when a harpoon truly injures a whale. The whale might thrash at the first blow, but many elders say that this reaction is more from surprise than agony, as a person might jerk back on jamming a splinter into her finger. Is it the seventh, the sixteenth, or the fifty-first jab that really starts to hurt it? It is no single blow, the elders will point out, that brings a whale down, but the accumulation of small wounds.

Yosef had defeated all the beasts of the ocean, but he could not win the fight against time. His six-pack had started to bunch into a pot-belly. Every night, the cataract spiders spun a few more strands of cobweb over his retinas. Lately, his harpoon had a disquieting tendency to glance off its target. He knew he should not drink so much tuak, but the liquid blurred his fights with his wife, the loss of two of his children, the disobedience of his remaining offspring, the need to borrow money from off-island relatives to pay for their school fees, his father's declining health, and the impending obsolescence of the lamafa. If Ignatius's training him to become a lamafa had been an act of love, it had also doomed him. He planned to force his son to finish elementary school and continue to high school, but how could he convince him that the path of a lamafa might soon dead-end when Lamaleran society told him otherwise?

Yosef stabbed until at last he pierced the bunker of flesh and his lance perforated the mother's intestines. When the whale exhaled, blood rained on him and flecks of flesh tangled in his hair. Who would not want to be numb to the thousand cuts? Maybe bleeding out was not so bad after the initial pain. It might be like slowly sinking under a rising tide of tuak. A blissful, gauzy fade-out, where time loses all proportion and a death of hours or years can feel like only minutes.

Eventually, the whale shuddered and vomited twenty-foot-long streamers of flesh: giant squid tentacles. Afterwards, its tail stopped twitching and its blowhole leaked an algae-like liquid, and the only sound was the slap of waves against the téna and the sizzle of an ember as Yosef smoked a cigarette. Then he grabbed a rope, inhaled a lungful of air, and dove into blood so dense he had to feel his way around the colossal corpse. He kicked deeper, and suddenly, he was underneath the red. The water was colder, aquamarine, and clear. Crimson curlicues wafted off his skin. Below him was fathomless darkness. Fragments of whale drifted into it, and scavenger fish vultured after them. The whale's massive blood-streaked eye was open, staring into the depths. Yosef looped the rope twice around the spindly jaw and shoved it closed so that water did not infiltrate the stomach and sink the body. Then he swam upward, guiding the rope toward the evening glow.

As he broke through the waves, the first stars opened their eyes. He knew that the clan chiefs would give away jerricans of tuak to the men who guarded the beached whales until dawn, and that was what excited him as he swam out of the cloud of blood and into untainted water, where he bobbed, letting the Savu Sea cleanse him.

FOUR HOURS EARLIER, AN AUTO bearing Ignatius home had fought its way rock by rock up the north face of Labalekang in full sunlight. The vehicle was crammed with passengers and cardboard boxes filled with goods bought in town. The hooves of a goat tethered to the roof rang like a tap dancer's shoes. Dust swirled through the cabin, settling softly like a shower of sifted flour. It was oppressively hot.

Ignatius, propped against a pillowy bag of unhusked rice, had been nodding off. Ita's parents had tried to extort him—demanding not only the original payment for themselves but another thousand dollars for one of their relatives who had helped raise Ita. He had refused, but not with the anger he had expected. Instead, he had been almost apologetic. Facing those two paired against him, he was heartsick for his wife. Still, he planned to write to the bishop in Larantuka, who, he was sure, would see through the Amuntodas' greedy schemes and order the marriage.

The auto crested the shoulder of Labalekang. The sun had already pendulumed far to the northwest, and the cabin cooled as it entered the shadowed, southeast quadrant of the mountain. As the vehicle luged down the fine sand of the road, a cape of dust spraying behind it, Ignatius kept thinking about his children.

Ben always assumed that Ignatius was mad at him for having children before marriage, but after the first hot surge of feeling, Ignatius had been unable to remain angry at his son for a fault he had committed himself. And Ignatius was still bothered by how Ita's parents let her live in sin. He was sure they must not think about her feelings, because how else could they exploit her as a bargaining chip for six years while trying to squeeze a few more rupiahs out of him? How could any parents treat their child like that? Everything he had ever done had been for his family, past, present, and future, his Ancestors, children, and grandchildren. His sons had not turned out exactly how he had planned, but he never had a sampan or a téna match his perfectionist expectations either. Yet he had always—*always*—loved each and every one of his creations. And none of them had proven better than his sons. Both Ondu and Yosef were lamafa and ata mola. And Ben was on his way to joining them. His sons! His sons! If his wife was in heaven, well, at least he would see his sons soon.

At that moment, he had no idea that *Demo Sapang*'s keel had been crushed by *Praso Sapang,* that his téna was taking on water, that a whole team of men were bailing it furiously while it struggled to shore. He did not know that he and his sons would not be able to launch when the baleo sounded the next day because they would be amid repairs, that they would miss a glorious hunt, with every clan but theirs and one other taking a whale. Most of all, he did not realize his youngest son planned to leave Lamalera.

BEN, LIKE EVERY OTHER LAMALERAN, knew all about sperm whales and family loyalty. When the calf had been harpooned, he correctly predicted that the mother would not abandon it. But what really stuck with him was watching the child's tail slap ineffectually at Yosef as his eldest brother dispatched the mother, before the juvenile too was killed.

Though the Lamalerans have accepted that they must kill whales to survive, they do not take their lives callously. They recognize them as cognizant, feeling, soulful animals. And in viewing them as reincarnations of their Ancestors, they have anticipated what science is just figuring out: that the intellect of sperm whales approaches that of humans. Sperm whales have the biggest brain of any creature in history. Their gray matter even features extremely rare neurons called spindle cells—also found in humans—which govern communication, compassion, and the ability to feel suffering. They live in widely spaced groups that display distinct methods for hunting squid and child-rearing, such that researchers consider them to have discrete "cultures," just like humans. Moreover, each whale has a personalized set of clicks used to identify itself—and thus its own "name" and perhaps even "whalehood." All of which makes certain philosophical provocateurs challenge the uniqueness of personhood, for if a sperm whale has culture, language, and self-awareness, what is the true dividing line between humankind and this other mammal? Is the sorrow of a whale calf for its dying cow any less real than a human son for the loss of his mother?

Later that night, as the téna towed their catch home through the darkness, Ben could not forget the calf's suicidal bravery. Had it wished, as a lance rammed its soft organs repeatedly, that it had tried to save itself? Ben wondered if a mother whale ever regretted trying to save a child, especially if the effort doomed its other children. After all, he had seen many times a cow whale try to save one calf, leaving its other children to mill about, a decision that almost invariably resulted in the whole family being slaughtered together.

Perhaps sometimes it was better for a mother to abandon her children or a child his parents. Sometimes the only reward for loyalty was the same harpoon piercing both of your hearts. Blood of my blood, flesh of my flesh. It is not the strength of the lamafa's body that is most important, Ignatius had said, but that of his mind. However inspirational his words, they also hid a subtle condemnation: *If you can't do it, it is not the fault of your body but your mind, your very soul.*

Ben knew that he would miss the constellations above the Savu Sea on nights like this: so many stars gleamed that the light they cast was brighter than moonshine, and the Milky Way twisted in a three-dimensional helix from horizon to horizon. There was the Pointer, as the Lamalerans called the Southern Cross, its northernmost star burning a sulfurous orange while the line of three stars below pulsed a frigid blue, directing the fleet toward the village. The breeze had warmed. Plankton fluoresced a soft green where rollers slapped *Kanibal*'s hull.

More than the stars, he would yearn for his daughter and newborn son. Once he had established a new life in Bali, he would send for them. On the beach, whale oil lamps and torches were massing, terrestrial constellations guiding the téna in. But for Ben, Lamalera would not be home much longer.

Chapter Six

THE LAUGHTER

July 2014–September 26, 2014

Ika

One night in late July, as Ika was sitting in the dark on the stairs of her house and singing along to Indonesian Christian pop music playing off her cell phone, her rare respite was interrupted by a pig squealing. At the bottom of the house's terraces, one of her family's hogs had gained its liberty by tearing free of the rope threaded through holes punched in its ears — the customary way Lamalerans leash their swine — leaving the cartilage in shreds. Pigs are like the investment accounts of Lamalera, as each family raises several for years until they can be sold or slaughtered at a marriage or funeral, when a porcine offering is required. Losing this escapee would be catastrophic.

Ika sprinted down the stairs, cut the animal off before it could reach the jungle, and beat it back into its wallow with a stick, all while shouting for help. Jon had been going to bed when he heard the squealing and was slow to descend the stairs because of his still-nagging injury. The rest of the neighborhood men were away or drunk, but half a dozen women rushed to join the blockade.

Ika waded into the reeking slop, wielding a rope weaponized with a slipknot. Pigs in Lamalera are not the domesticated hams of U.S. farms. With their muscular, streamlined bodies and canine-looking snouts adorned by tusks, Lembatan hogs are likely descended from captured wild boars. This particular beast had been fattening for years in anticipation of being eaten on Jon's wedding day, and it weighed well over two hundred pounds—more than double Ika's weight. In the weak beam of a cheap flashlight directed by another woman, Ika tried to snag the escapee's hoof in the lariat, but whenever it grunted she shied away.

Finally, Jon limped up to the women and yelled, "Wait till it picks up its hoof and then just put the rope on!"

After several more tries, Ika noosed the animal's hoof, but when she yanked, the slipknot jammed, and the pig kicked off the rope, dousing her in mud and shit. Everyone froze, expecting her to start cursing or crying. Instead, she tipped her face to the sky and unleashed her raspy laugh, which rolled on and on, until Jon snorted. Ika turned, splashed to the edge of the wallow, and held out the rope to him. He slapped her, not with all his strength, but with enough force that the smack rang.

Ika did not cry or say anything. Instead, she dropped the rope and withdrew into the shadows behind the tamarind tree.

Jon stared down the other women until they backed away, then picked up the rope and retied the slipknot. He stalked the hog, hobbling on rocks like stepping-stones to stay above the mud. When the pig shifted its weight, he casually lassoed its rising hoof, jerking the noose closed before it finished its step. Then he tied the rope to a boulder. Without a word, he returned to the house.

The other women asked if Ika wanted to wash at their homes, but she waved them away—she would always have to go home in the end anyway. She waited until Jon had been inside long enough to fall asleep. Then she emerged from the darkness, spattered with crusted filth, and climbed the stairs.

A FEW WEEKS LATER, in mid-August, on the Saturday that a war would unexpectedly break out between southern Lembata's tribes, Ika woke while stars still sequined the sky. It was market day, the highlight of the week. Excitement tickled her heart. Would this be the day her life transformed? she wondered. Would the right young man notice her?

Quietly, so as not to wake her family, she rose and pulled on a Hello Kitty T-shirt, her favorite. Then she piled sheaves of whale jerky and dried flying fish into a rattan basket, coiled a dish towel on her head, and settled her load atop it. Like every other Lamaleran woman, Ika rarely carried anything—whether a plate of rice, a butcher knife, or a bundle of firewood—in her hands. Instead, she portaged whatever it was atop her crown. Unable to drop her chin to check her footing, she toed her way in the dark down the stairs, joining a parade of giddily whispering young women who were also balancing baskets.

While the older women, mummified in sarongs, packed them-selves into an auto, Ika and the young women trooped out of town and toward the village of Wulandoni, following the aurora of a flashlight. The budding sun found them humping their loads past deserted beaches and through the overgrown ruins of villages, the former homes of tribes who had been wiped out by conflicts or had abandoned their homelands for cities. As flocks of birds greeted the dawn with orchestral chatter, the young women gossiped about the bargains they would win, the men they would flirt with, and all the other adventures of the Wulandoni Market.

Ika relished her time with other young women, whom she had not been able to see much since she had left elementary school after her grandmother fell and broke her femur. When her grandparents had informed her that she would have to disenroll from sixth grade, Ika protested. "But if not you, who will cook?" they asked her. "Who will barter our fish?" Once, Ika had dared to imagine crossing the moun-tains for high school. But she told herself this was the will of God. Every morning, as she boiled rice on the clifftops, she tried to ignore the uniformed children gamboling on their way to class. Sometimes, in the afternoons, she would sneak down to the beach and frolic with them, but when she came home her grandparents yelled at her. Eventually, she was not so much excluded by her peers as forgotten. She tried to prevent this by joining a traditional dance team, the church choir, and the Catholic youth group. After attending, she would practice a hip twist or a song endlessly as she worked in the kitchen shack. The trouble was that she often had to skip the meetings to cook or clean.

One of the best times in Ika's life had been a camping trip she took the previous year to a nearby beach, with the island's young Catholics association. At home she would have been fetching water from the well. Instead, she played volleyball with other girls and roasted fish the boys had caught over coconut-husk coals. At night, she and the other participants choired around the campfire. Singing was her favorite pastime, the one activity that allowed her to concentrate on praising God and not on her own worries. After the group songs, Father Romo asked her to perform a solo. Climbing atop a packing crate, she shivered with nervousness, but when she opened her mouth, she was enchanted by her own smoky alto. It unnerved her how much she liked being the center of attention. The rest of the night, she had to fend off compliments. Recently, she had started dropping hints about attending the upcoming annual retreat again, but her grandparents would always remind her of her chores and question if it was appropriate for her to sleep unchaperoned near young men.

Work enslaved every day. She woke predawn to cook breakfast, then axed firewood in the hills, before walking nearly a mile to the well — in advance of the sun pushing above the volcano, if she could. When there was no longer any hiding from its blaze, she retreated to the shade of the tamarind tree to shell rice and winnow the chaff until her grandparents demanded lunch. And when Jon returned from hunting, she helped butcher, salt, and hang his catch, which usually took until evening, when she had to feed the pigs, fetch the night's water, and cook dinner. It was only when she lay on a bamboo pallet next to her snoring, musty-smelling grandmother that she had time enough to pray.

She found solace in Jesus and the Ancestors. Confession released any exasperation she built up against her situation. She strove to sacrifice herself as Jesus had. What ambitions she had once possessed, she channeled into Mari, scrimping on the household budget to send her younger sister, who was sixteen years old, to high school in Lewoleba and promising to support her through university. (Jon backed these efforts too, though he also often grumbled about the cost.) The only problem was that Mari did not seem to appreciate the gift she was being given. Mari was more interested in boys and fashion than her academics. Whenever Ika saw her sister's disappointing report cards, she wanted to remonstrate with her and remind her what an opportunity this education was, but she lacked the courage to berate and instead relied on plaintive, tentative comments, which were brushed aside.

How Ika missed school! While she was going herself, she had felt, smugly, that her brain worked differently from those of older women, who thought only of bartering, weaving, and child-rearing, and never of science or the outside world. But recently, she noticed, her interest had begun to wane when her friends talked about algebra or the Second World War, and she realized with horror that she was becoming like her elders. Sometimes she still daydreamed about returning to school. Not long ago, a small technical fisheries high school had opened in Lamalera, the first such institution in southern Lembata, instructing fewer than a hundred students. Although Lamaleran elders mocked the school for failing to teach either math or seacraft well, for Ika it represented an opportunity to hope—though even she had to admit that having a nineteen-year-old join the sixth grade would be ridiculous, never mind having someone in her twenties enrolled in ninth grade.

Ika yearned for an education because she knew what she was missing in the outside world. In the last few years, several of her cousins had graduated high school in Lewoleba and gotten jobs as petty government officials. Visiting them, she had been amazed at how electricity, refrigerators, and rice cookers saved them from having to spend all day gathering wood, smoking meat, and stoking the cookfire. She had been jealous of the weight they had gained—always a goal for Ika, who was perpetually skinny and sometimes appeared nearly starved during lean times. There, it seemed a modern life might be put on as easily as the lipstick they wore. Indonesia had even recently had a woman president. If only Ika could find a way to cross the mountains permanently.

Whenever the frustration became too much, she tried to laugh. She was a naturally buoyant person—a *tukang tertawa,* a "craftswoman of laughter," in her own words. She laughed so often that it contributed to her perpetually hoarse throat. It was a laugh as unique as her singing voice: tittery and scratchy, high and yet resonant with deep notes. It usually started as a shiver, as if she was being tickled, then hijacked her whole body, until it bent her double and squeezed out her breath, until she threw her hands up in the air as if signaling surrender. That cascade of hilarity seemed to say, *Aren't we all ridiculous?*

Ika holding the family Bible

Ika laughed when Jon spent money that would be better saved for Mari's school fees on cigarettes or tuak. She laughed each time her grandparents slid down another rung of infirmity and indignity. She laughed at her own persistent desire to join the camping trip. But lately that laugh had become more difficult to summon. When she could manage it, it was less gaily amused than angry and mocking. It was not like her laugh after the pig had spattered her in filth, a laugh that brushed off misfortune to revel in the absurdity of life. Rather it was like her laugh in the days after Jon slapped her, notes that rang false while trying to cover her humiliation and scorn. But the market — one of the very few enjoyable things in her routine — had the power to change that.

AFTER NEARLY SEVEN MILES of walking, the Lamaleran girls approached the village of Wulandoni. The trail merged with a dirt road, and they joined crowds of mountain women toting repurposed cement bags stuffed with cassava. Autos honked foot traffic out of their way. Men rattled past on motorbikes. (In rural Lembata, the elders considered it inappropriate for women to ride the machines because they had to spread their legs to straddle them.) Amid the bustle, Ika giggled loudly and gesticulated with her arms, all the while gyroscoping her body to stabilize the basket atop her head, a performance meant for the boys sneaking glances at her.

Ika was so caught up that she did not notice the dozen or so tense-looking men just outside the market spatulating raw concrete onto a three-foot rebar pillar, the kind used to mark boundaries between Indonesian towns. Nor did she mark the angry crowd massing around them. If she had, she might have discerned that the nervous construction workers were not native to that village but hailed from a neighboring tribe, the Luki, the only Muslims and Paji native to that southwestern corner of the coast. The massed men fingering their machetes, however, were from the Nualela tribe, natives of Wulandoni who lived by the beach and farmed the hills above and who, like the

Lamalerans, are Christian and Demon. And she might have recalled the two tribes were traditionally enemies.

BUT EVEN IF IKA HAD NOTICED the gathering confrontation, the Wulandoni Market was such a stable and long-standing arrangement that it seemed impossible that fighting should mar it. For almost two centuries, since around 1830, after a Lamaleran hunting trip gone awry, the women of southern Lembata had been regularly meeting in the same palm grove to barter.

So say the stories of the Ancestors: One day Dato Lama Nudek harpooned a gigantic bull whale from his téna. Over a day and a night, the whale dragged the Nudek clan before breaking the harpoon rope. But Dato would not give up. His clan patrolled the islands east of Lembata, until they spied men in bark clothing butchering a beached sperm whale. When the Lamalerans attempted to claim it, the scavengers argued that any whale could have washed up there, and challenged the Lamalerans to send forth a champion for a duel. In the end, the Lamaleran fighter was killed when an artery in his thigh was severed by a machete blow. But Dato managed to reclaim the whale anyway by yanking out his iron harpoon head from an open wound and brandishing it as proof. The men in bark clothing dispersed and the Lamalerans then spent a week butchering the whale, storing its oil in bamboo tubes, and camping on the beach until the flesh was jerkied and they could sail for home. By the time they rounded the Ata Dei Peninsula, just down the coast from home, Dato and his men had run out of water, so they landed in Labala Bay, near present-day Wulandoni, to reprovision. They dispatched runners to tell the mountain tribes to bring them rice, corn, and cassava in exchange for their whale jerky and oil.

While the Lamalerans have easy access to fish, whales, and other marine life, it is difficult to grow vegetables on their arid, rocky shore. The mountain tribes, on the other hand, receive enough rain to grow a rich harvest of vegetables and fruits, but lack reliable sources of meat, as they raise few animals, and there is little prey worth hunting in the jungle. Over the centuries, then, the coastal and mountain tribes of Lembata have developed a symbiotic trade essential to the survival of each, exchanging their surpluses for the others' needs. This networking has led to alliances that bind groups on opposite sides of the Demon and Paji—and Christian and Muslim—divide, unifying what are otherwise contentious tribes.

The trading between the Nudeks and the mountain tribes went so well that all agreed to a biweekly market under the same palm trees. In time this market became the economic pillar of the region, as well as a place for youth to court and elders to resolve intertribal politics. Even during the headhunting epoch, before colonial authorities ended the practice, it was generally considered neutral ground because neither the coastal tribes nor the mountain tribes could afford for it to shut down. When the Gregorian calendar was imposed by the Dutch government in the early twentieth century, the Wulandoni Market was formalized as occurring every Saturday morning. For almost two hundred years, the market continued uninterrupted—until August 16, 2014, that is.

That day, after Ika passed the Luki construction workers wielding their crowbars and the Wulandoni farmers gripping their machetes, she joined a gossiping group of Lamaleran women squatting in the shade of a few palm trees. With several autos carrying mountain tribe women still en route, the bartering had not yet commenced.

A friend passed Ika a handful of bright green *sirih* peppers, leathery *pinang* nuts (a.k.a. betel, or areca, nuts), and a wooden bowl packed with slaked lime made from burned coral. Ika stuck her finger into the ash, coated it, and sucked it clean. Then she bit into the sirih and pinang, and chewed the mixture like a tobacco plug. Soon she was pausing in her conversation to spit out what looked like bloody vomit, for the ingredients had reacted and turned crimson. Whenever she laughed, she revealed teeth that looked as if they had been chewing raw meat. The mild stimulant is as ubiquitous among the region's women as cigarettes are among the men, and already Ika had red striations on her teeth from this practice, while the older women's teeth had been stained a permanent crimson or black.

As Ika chatted with her friends, gangs of men, some young, some old, cruised past the unmarried women, pointedly staring at them. Ika's gaze darted across their unknown faces. In Lamalera she knew every man's name and history, and had found them wanting, but at the market there was at least the possibility of a worthy romance. Lately, Ika had begun to see her future in the old women squatting in the dirt beside her, withered as the jerky in their baskets, and though she told herself to focus on caring for her family, she had started to wonder if there might not be a way to escape that fate. If an older man stopped to talk, Ika and her peers would tease him, "You're too old!" or "We'll tell your wife!" But if a confident young man asked for help in selecting the best mangoes for his grandmother, well, a girl might be persuaded to stroll with him.

Many Lamaleran bachelors had noticed Ika's muscular arms and legs, her angelic singing, and her untamable laugh. For years she had warned her friends that boyfriends only gave girls headaches. She even avoided the parties where youth courted. And the previous hunting season, after several young men had asked Yosef Boko for her hand, she had explained to her grandfather that she was not ready yet for marriage: a husband would distract her from caring for him. (Privately, however, she had also found flaws with each bachelor — one had a reputation for uncontrollable anger, and another, though rich, was lazy.) But recently she had begun to see marriage as a way to reroute her fortunes. If the man she happened to fall in love with lived outside the tribe, was rich enough to own a motorbike and smart enough to hold a modern job in Lewoleba, there would be nothing wrong with that, would there? She had even started giving her cell phone number to young men from other villages at the market and texting with them, though she was careful to never let this go too far and keep it secret from her grandfather, who would only rage that she was following in her mother's footsteps.

But that morning, no young man succeeded in enticing Ika to walk with him. When the late autos finally rumbled up in a cloud of dust and the government overseers in their ill-fitting polyester suits shrilled their whistles, Ika joined the hundred or so other coastal women marching into the market with their baskets of dried fish. On the dirt field, a similar number of mountain women awaited them, the older kefela dressed in handwoven sarongs with motifs identifying their tribes, while their juniors wore pajamas decorated with Disney cartoon characters, favored for their breathability. Ika strolled past piles of vegetables, occasionally squeezing cassava hairy with roots, weighing a corncob in her palm like a gold bar, or sniffing a stack of methanol-smelling sirih peppers. Except for a handful of kiosks that sold a small selection of dry goods, there were no proper stores on Lembata's south coast, so the market was the only opportunity for families to stock up on fresh food.

Eventually, Ika's eye was caught by a pyramid of twelve small green tomatoes, with which she planned to flavor a dolphin stew, on the tarp of a woman with a powdered face, a dowry's worth of gold jewelry in her nose and ears, and an Islamic headscarf—a woman from the Luki tribe. Elsewhere, the Catholic-Demon girl and Muslim-Paji woman might have viewed each other as enemies, but their tribes had found common ground at the market for almost two centuries, and so Ika thought nothing of holding out her basket, from which the woman selected a single knot of dried whale, after which Ika scooped up the tomatoes. Then Ika moved into a group of mountain women, quickly exchanging her meat for more produce, as there was no bargaining, for the conversion rate had been stable for centuries: a six-inch strip of jerky for a dozen bananas or other fruit or vegetable. The key to getting a good deal was exchanging smaller pieces of dried meat for larger ears of corn.

What had changed, however, was the duty required by the Indonesian government. When Ika had entered the palm grove, an overseer had demanded from her 1,000 rupiah, or about ten cents. It was not a huge sum, but for people who had few ways to get cash, it was nevertheless a burden, especially when compounded with end-of-year taxes. All of this was an effort by the government to draw the barter regions of southern Lembata, and similar economies across Indonesia, into the national economy and a single citizenry. The challenge for the government, which purports to honor the cultural diversity of its people, is that subsistence whalers and other traditional peoples pay few taxes and often do not think of themselves as Indonesians first. The government's solution to that has been to issue taxes that can be paid only in cash, forcing indigenous people into construction, plantation, and housekeeping jobs to earn money, strengthening their national ties while weakening their tribal ones. It has required children to go to school, where they learn Bahasa and Indonesian history instead of traditional knowledge. Animists have had to label themselves as belonging to one of five world religions, such as Catholicism or Islam. Tribes that have resisted, unlike the Lamalerans, have been denied state benefits. Of course, the Indonesian government is not the first to do this. This strategy of incentivized assimilation has been pursued around the world for millennia, from the Romans to the Americans, to forge disparate far-flung groups into a nation.

The inroads that the modern economy was making into Lembata's barter economy were evident in the southern corner of the market, where a number of itinerant traders had parked pickups they had driven over the mountains from Lewoleba that morning. Ika ignored them because the outsiders would accept only rupiah for goods they sold out of their truck beds: soap bars, matches, coffee packets, fishing hooks, factory-stitched sarongs, skin-whitening cream, and big-ticket modern goods like pots and pans. These items were not just kept in a different physical corner of the market — Ika also separated them in her head, using foreign words and Western base-ten math to count steel knives, while with indigenous goods she employed the native word *munga,* a unit of six that is the foundation of Lamaleran math and the barter economy.

The Wulandoni Market. Muslim women in headscarves sit in the front two rows. Behind them squat rows of Christian women with their hair uncovered.

Around nine a.m., more than an hour after Ika arrived, a baleo echoed through the market, set off by a telephone call. The few Lamaleran men in attendance packed themselves three to a motorbike and raced home. Back in Lamalera, although Jon had continued to heal, he was not quite healthy enough to take up a paddle on a téna, and so he was assigned to drive the jonson that towed *Boli Sapang*. But at least he had finally rejoined the hunt.

By midmorning, Ika had filled her basket with cassava, stumpy milk bananas, longer flute-like Bugis bananas, and the tomatoes as small as baubles. She had even sold a bit of dolphin jerky to a Lewoleba trader for about a dollar a strip, money she planned to save toward Mari's school fees. As she left the market, she again overlooked the young Luki men racing to finish their half-built pillar while the crowd of angry Wulandoni natives continued to swell around them. But she did stop to contemplate a construction project that dwarfed any previously attempted in southern Lembata: a half-built seawall and a line of concrete pillars rising out of the bay, with bulldozers and backhoes parked onshore. The government was building a port. It was a year away from completion, but when it was finished, it would open the isolated coast to development. Merchants would be able to avoid the expense of trucking goods over the mountains, and the port would also offer regular ferry service to the provincial capital. Ika fantasized that she might get on one of those massive rusty ships and ride it over the horizon, whether for good or just a holiday, she would decide at the time.

But there was no point in wasting too much time daydreaming: she had to get home to cook lunch. The autos were parked farther down the road, beneath trees bleeding sap that old men harvested as a type of glue, and she turned over a bit of the money she had earned for selling the dolphin jerky to one of the drivers. She had decided to indulge herself and ride the seven miles home, as she wanted to return rested. In Lamalera, there was endless work to do.

After Ika left, several of the Luki men continued to spade concrete onto the rebar pillar, while their fellows formed a defensive perimeter. The more progress made on the pillar, the more enraged the crowd of Wulandoni men grew, for it was the kind used by Indonesian towns to demarcate their boundaries. Although the Luki lived in Pantai Harapan, a village not far to the east, by erecting this pillar they were claiming ownership of the future port and of Wulandoni itself, an escalation of a long-running land dispute between the two towns.

Enmity was not new between the Nualela and Luki tribes: once, they had headhunted each other, as Demon and Paji groups generally did. But even during times of ancient warfare, their barter had been considered protected, since the Luki are mostly fishermen, while the Nualela are primarily farmers, so both needed the other to survive. The safe zone of the Wulandoni Market had even eased tensions when in the late 1970s, the government relocated both tribes from their widely spaced historical homes to the same stretch of bay, after a tsunami had destroyed the original Luki village and the Nualela were resettled from their former mountaintop fortress to the more accessible beach as part of a welfare program, now that Indonesian soldiers guaranteed the peace.

For decades, the two tribes coexisted mostly happily. Tensions started to grow, however, once the Luki began selling some of their fish in Lewoleba and using the money to buy whatever they needed from fellow Muslims there instead of relying on their Christian neighbors back in Wulandoni. This decoupling was driven partly by global politics, as Luki youth educated off-island were exposed to news about Muslim–Christian conflicts in the Middle East and elsewhere in Indonesia, and shared what they learned with their tribesmen. (The Christian tribes, of course, were no less influenced by the international news cycle, and Lamalerans regularly joked about the "Islamic State of Luki.") As the years passed, both sides thought of themselves less as Lamaholot, the overarching ethnicity of the region, which included both Demon and Paji, than as opposing sides in a worldwide war. Whereas once the tribes were careful to respect their trading partners, both sides began to squabble over access to springs and farmland.

Then, in mid-2014, after the new president, Jokowi, kept his campaign promise to help develop eastern Indonesia, construction on the port began, and suddenly Wulandoni Beach, a previously unremarkable patch of sand, became the economic future of the south coast of Lembata. The Luki revived an old claim that the government had granted them all the land surrounding Wulandoni, though they could not produce the paperwork. The Nualela countered with a paper trail going all the way back to colonial maps showing their ownership of the beach, for though they had historically lived in the hills above it, they had controlled the territory down to the waterline. The arguments escalated from shouting matches to lawyered-up court dates, until finally the Luki men began building this pillar.

As the market that day was winding to a close, a senior Wulandoni administrator, from the Nualela tribe, ordered the Luki men to stop. They answered by bludgeoning him with their fists and tools, then retreated to their village. The mayor of Wulandoni rushed the wounded man around the volcano to the hospital in Lewoleba. The police there brushed off the mayor's complaints, saying Wulandoni was too remote for them to do anything, and besides, the following day was Indonesian Independence Day — it would all just blow over.

But the next morning, as several hundred attendees at a flag-raising ceremony stood outside Wulandoni's church, a shirtless young Luki man ran onto the field from the direction of Pantai Harapan. The crowd found the crazy boy amusing until they realized he was waving a machete. Then a cavalry of motorbikes rumbled down the road behind him, each of their Luki riders similarly armed. The crowd fled screaming. About fifty Lamaleran high school students, who were visiting for the celebration, barricaded themselves in the church. As the Luki mob smashed the rectory's windows with rocks, those within weepingly informed their families in Lamalera via cell phone that they were about to be murdered.

But in their initial assault the Luki did not actually use the machetes on anyone, only chased the Nualela from town. Then they ransacked the mayor's office, apparently looking for the Nualela's land deeds. When they could not find the documents there, they burned down the house of the vice mayor, where the papers were sometimes kept, though they had been relocated to Lewoleba weeks earlier. Later, there were rumors that Luki assassins wielding bows and arrows had chased the mayor through the town as he raced away on his motorbike.

Most of the Lamaleran men were butchering the sperm whales they had caught the day before when they heard the clanging of the gong that had once called the Ancestors to defend their cactus walls. They assembled at the Bataona Spirit House, where Father Romo told them, "Don't do anything violent. But show the people of Luki that Wulandoni isn't alone, and that all the Christian villages are behind them!" A troop of about fifty men marched out of town, though many others, including Jon, Frans, Ignatius, and Ben, stayed behind to finish butchering the whales before their meat spoiled, as at this point calls had informed them that the Luki attackers had retreated. All across the region, hundreds of Christian men were arming themselves with spears, machetes, and bows and arrows, and hurrying to Wulandoni.

When the Lamalerans arrived in Wulandoni, still spattered with whale gore, clutching their duri, they found police officers patrolling the town. Someone had dialed the authorities in Lewoleba, who had rushed a pickup load of cops over the mountains. But those few policemen were not enough to control the scores of Lamalerans, Nualela, and men from other Christian tribes, who were massing beside the dry creek that divided Wulandoni from Pantai Harapan. Soon, on the other side, the men of Luki gathered as well. Who attacked first is contested along partisan lines, but by late afternoon the two sides were swinging machetes and firing arrows. According to many witnesses, the police fled. In the end, the body of a Christian man was abandoned near the bridge, his lips sliced off to reveal his shattered teeth and his gored belly leaking his innards. Several others on both sides were seriously wounded.

The situation did not calm until soldiers wearing the red-and-black armband of the Indonesian Special Forces rumbled into Wulandoni the following morning, now two days after the inciting incident at the market. The Indonesian government is highly sensitive to conflicts with religious overtones, aware that they have the potential to become flash points in a diverse nation, where the Muslim majority often clashes with the significant minority of Catholics, Protestants, Hindus, and Buddhists. The tactical unit stayed for several days before they turned the security back over to an expanded police force. Though open conflict did not flare up again, stories circulated of Christian and Muslim boys bow-hunting each other through the hills. Several Luki men were jailed for the murder of the Christian, while a few Nualela were arrested for burning Luki fishing boats several days after the main conflict. At night, Lamalerans stood guard with bows and arrows on the road to Wulandoni. The market itself remained shut.

Once several weeks had passed, a peace embassy from Luki apologized to the mayor of Wulandoni, blaming the attack on a few tuakcrazed youth. But the Nualela felt that the assault had been carefully orchestrated, citing the men who had hunted the mayor as well as the attempt to burn the deeds. And the family of the deceased was not prepared to forgive his death. The overture was rebuffed. Later, when the Luki specifically asked for the Wulandoni Market to be reconvened, the Nualela again refused. The decision was about more than protecting themselves now. The Christian tribes were punishing the Luki, effectively imposing an economic blockade, for the Muslims had no one else on the coast to trade with. Luki families began leaving Pantai Harapan to stay with relatives in Lewoleba and search for work there. Instead of restarting the Wulandoni Market, the Christian villagers agreed to meet among themselves every Friday on Lamalera's soccer field.

AND SO, EARLY ON THE MORNING of September 26, six weeks after the incident, Ika carried a basket of jerkied flying fish past a bamboo goal and across a dirt expanse toward a few dozen Lamaleran women squatting in tree shade. Meanwhile, the only Muslim trader who would arrive that day, a merchant from Lewoleba, laid out flip-flops on a blue tarp. The kefela had not yet arrived. As the Lamalerans spewed sirih pinang and gossiped, one older woman complained that Dato's centuries-old promise had been broken, and all the other crones agreed that the Wulandoni conflict was the result of the outside world meddling with the Ways of the Ancestors. True, tribal tensions had existed before money, taxes, and land disputes, but the barter economy had enforced a kind of equality: there was no taking advantage of someone else, only exchanging excess for excess, so that everyone was better-off. Now life seemed like a zero-sum competition. Better that the Wulandoni Market had endured. Its end, they proclaimed, surely prophesied worse things to come.

But Ika was secretly pleased: the new market saved miles on her commute. And as much as she venerated the Ways of the Ancestors, it was increasingly clear that those rules favored men and the elderly at her expense. She would not mind having outside influences open for her a few of the city-girl freedoms she had seen on the Indonesian soap operas. From the heights, she looked across the glassy bay, so windless that the sampans dotting it had not even bothered to raise their sails, to Wulandoni and the unfinished seawall, smudged with blue haze. Today, she was feeling pessimistic about escaping Lamalera. Her grandparents had forbidden her to attend the annual young Catholics retreat. But another possibility had occurred to her: even if she never left the tribe, the modern world might one day make it to her. Change was coming, but she feared that it would arrive too late for her to take advantage of it. The best she could do while waiting was laugh.

Chapter Seven

THE WAY OF THE LAMAFA

September 2014–November 2014

Jon

One dusk at the beginning of October, Jon piloted the jonson *VJO* toward a cataclysmic sun. With his left hand, he gripped the tiller of the 15-horsepower engine, while with his right, he shaded his eyes as he scrutinized the horizon. He had sat out the hunting season recovering from his injury, and now that he was finally healthy, he yearned to erase the memories of his weakness and prove to the tribe once and for all that he was no kefela. The best way to do that would be to spear something. He scanned the scarlet waters as if he could will a manta ray to leap. He dreamed of taking the next step toward becoming a lamafa soon: He believed his return to full health proved that his injury had been punishment for his clan's transgressions and not his own. The Ancestors owed him one for making him endure as a sacrificial lamb.

Meanwhile, three other men sat chattering on a mound of green nets overflowing the hold: Andreus "Anso" Soge Bediona, Jon's close friend, a cheerful, mop-haired fisherman in his early thirties; Marsel, Anso's taciturn silver-haired older brother; and Bernardus "Boli" Tapoonā, the charcoal-skinned, heroically muscled son of a legendary harpooner. They never bothered to glance at the water, for they knew that even if prey was sighted, there would be little time to run it down before darkness fell.

Besides, now it was Léfa Bogel, the Lazy Season. The sperm whales had finished migrating past Lembata, and the heat had clarified to its annual peak, a near cremating intensity that bent the air with mirages and gave every hour a siesta weight. The once lush jungle had withered in the autumn of the tropics, so that leaves spiraled to the ground and crawled over one another in the evening winds, rustling like a migration of insects. The well ran dry, and women had to clamber down the sea cliffs with their buckets to suckle from a briny spring that bubbled forth at low tide. Dust constantly thickened the air, invading nostrils and mouths, making it impossible to stay clean. Even the friendliest villagers started quarreling. This was, historically, when men spent the days sprawled in the shade of the boat sheds, slurping lukewarm, fizzy tuak, shirtlessly savoring the rare breezes wafting off the surf, rather than putting to sea under the furnace sun.

But the introduction of outboard engines had changed that. Since 2009, at the urging of Fransiskus Gonsalés "Salés" Usé Bataona, a Lamaleran expat intent on modernizing the village economy, men had increasingly been using the motorboats for a new type of hunting that allowed them to avoid the punishing daylight altogether: driftnetting, an industrial fishing technique that was transforming the Lamaleran way of life and undermining the Ways of the Ancestors.

It was for this work that Jon skimmed the jonson west, while the lilac sky blackened and Labalekang shrank as if the weight of the clouds stacked atop it were pushing it beneath the sea. For a few minutes after the water gulped down the sun, the peaks of the six volcanoes picketed across the horizon shone with golden alpenglow. Then the air became gritty with darkness. Stars ignited. Jon's stomach staggered at each jolting swell — that afternoon he had shared a jerrican of tuak with the other men while mending nets — and three times he vomited over the gunwale, as his friends chuckled, "Kefela!" But no one tried to take over driving for him. *VJO* was the jonson that Jon had guarded since Salés entrusted it to him during his teenage years while the businessman pursued opportunities outside the tribe.

Once Jon found an eastward current deep in the sea, he cocked the motor out of the water. Bejeweling the darkness, tiny with distance, shone the headlamps of five other driftnetting jonson. Jon enflamed the light strapped over his baseball cap. Then, from an old soda bottle, he sprinkled water blessed by Frans onto the nets and the three men kneeling on them. The drift net was coiled in a colossal rope in *VJO*'s hold. For forty-five minutes the four whalers unspooled the webbing in a shuffling dance, until a trail of white foam floats stretched nearly a mile back to a winking scarlet beacon.

At last, their work completed, Jon and the others chewed whale jerky and tried to light cigarettes, though the bruising wind kept snuffing their lighters. They made the usual jokes—lying about who was having an affair with which pretty girl—but soon the babble died. Despite rolling like logs over the deck as two-foot swells rocked the jonson, they slept soundly. Shooting stars sizzled across the heavens. The darkness of the ocean and sky merged, as did the bioluminescent plankton and the stars, so that *VJO* seemed to be drifting in an interstellar current. As it grew colder, Jon drew Honi's sarong tighter, as if wrapping himself in her arms.

Since Jon and Honi had gotten back together after breaking up over Jon's Facebook flirtations with other girls, the two had been enjoying a honeymoon period. At first, Jon had been secretly jealous that Honi got to leave Lembata for a city, but once she explained the on-the-ground realities of her life, he only felt bad for her. Instead of being recruited to a glamorous metropolis like Jakarta, she had been sent to a bland, polluted million-person industrial sprawl on an outlying island. She had to spend her every waking hour sweeping the four-story mansion of her employer or cooking for his family. When her biweekly day off came around, she was usually too tired and intimidated by the crowds outside to explore. Instead she called Jon, and they passed hours fantasizing about what their shared life would look like once she returned, nearly two years hence. Even when they ran out of things to say, Jon would tuck his phone into his left breast pocket and keep the line open, just listening to the susurrations of her broom across the tile. With the phone in his shirt pocket, it was as if sounds of her were emanating directly from his heart.

In the witching hours, Jon woke to spluttering. "Dolphins," someone murmured, come to raid their net for small fish. But rather than worrying about the thieving, they were actually excited, for they hoped one would become entangled in the twine, though the "clever fish," as they were sometimes called, were usually canny enough to avoid it, and soon the men fell back asleep.

The drift net that lurked in the current below marked a recent and major shift in the livelihood of the Lamalerans that was threatening the primacy of the lamafa, and one Jon had unknowingly helped to jump-start. Net fishing itself was not new. The method had been introduced to Lamalera in 1973, when the United Nations' Food and Agriculture Organization paid for a Norwegian fisherman to live in the village for two years, with the goal of modernizing the Lamalerans' fishing techniques, which would improve their haul, and thereby the nutrition of the mountain tribes who relied on them as well. The tribe happily adopted the small-gauge gill nets they were offered, and today still use similar tools in the coral gardens close to shore. (The Lamalerans rejected some proposed modernizations, though, as breaking too much from the Ways of the Ancestors, such as employing a motorboat armed with a cannon that fired explosive harpoons.)

The Lamalerans, however, began to practice a whole new type of net fishing shortly after 2003, when the expat Salés returned home. Salés, Jon's patron, was descended from one of the Lika Telo, the Big Three clans. But his father, who had traveled the archipelago assisting the town's Catholic priest, encouraged him to give up his aristocratic inheritance, first to attend seminary and then to study law at a university in Jakarta. After several years, however, Salés missed the sea. He quit his job as a manager in a water-bottling company and apprenticed himself on a fifty-ton Javanese trawler, where he learned to use long-lines and drift nets — the arsenal of an industrial fisherman. Then he returned home in his early thirties, convinced that he could bring his people into the modern age, helping them and creating a legacy that he never could in the city, where he had been part of the anonymous masses, while profiting at the same time. In Lamalera, he built *VJO* and filled the jonson with massive drift nets whose five-inch weave was sized to catch tuna and swordfish weighing hundreds of pounds rather than the tiny flying fish the tribe had previously sought with their two-inch-gauge gill nets.

Salés, who was not married back then, and whose younger male relatives had followed in his footsteps to attend school over the mountains, soon recruited as his deckhand a boy who had no father demanding his time and affection: Jon. Eleven at the time, Jon still sometimes apprenticed on his uncle's jonson, which practiced traditional harpoon hunting, and its crew of old salts mocked the drift nets. But as Jon saw the effectiveness of the new tools, he increasingly joined Salés rather than his uncle. Instead of spending hours searching for difficult-to-spot prey, burning gas chasing it, and then hoping the lamafa struck true, he and Salés would spread their nets, go to sleep, and then wake to manta rays, swordfish, tuna, and dolphins snagged in their web. Soon Salés trusted Jon to deploy the nets and work the outboard motor without supervision, for Salés had become involved in other ventures that kept him from going to sea: first arranging credit for his tribesmen to buy outboard motors as the tribe's jonson fleet expanded, then opening the village's first gasoline depot to supply them, and finally loaning out more money so other whalers, convinced of the drift nets' effectiveness by his and Jon's success, could purchase them. Within a few years, Salés had become involved in ventures all over the island, including buying a fleet of autos that he hired out to drivers. Often he disappeared over the mountains on unexplained business for weeks at a time. The tribe was so impressed with him that he even was elected mayor for a short stint, though everyone quickly found that public office did not suit him, and he returned to wheeling and dealing.

Salés became so busy that eventually he asked Jon's grandfather, Yosef Boko, for his blessing to have Jon captain and care for *VJO* in his absence. Later he would joke that he had chosen Jon because he was "small but potent, like a fire pepper," but really Salés had been impressed by Jon's desire to prove himself in a society where people normally deferred to the hierarchy. Jon was stunned by the invitation: in his teens he would run his very own jonson—though only in the drift-net season—while harpoon hunting with other motorboats the rest of the year. Of course, Salés's patronage came with heavy responsibilities. Jon devoted himself to maintaining *VJO,* "shampooing" the engine, disassembling it and soaping down each bolt, every few weeks. If he anchored the boat in the bay overnight, he slept on the hâm-mâlollo to make sure it did not get shipjacked by another tribe. Salés also effectively transformed Jon into his representative in the village, requiring constant updates on tribal news. Lastly, Jon had to give three-fourths of any catch to Salés's spinster sisters, who lived in Lamalera. In exchange, Jon got to keep the other fourth of the catch. Moreover, when his family really needed something, like malaria medicine for his grandparents or help with school fees for Mari, Salés often provided it. But perhaps the greatest blessing of holding the keys to *VJO* was that over the years Jon grew into one of the best jonson drivers and driftnetters in Lamalera, skills that became progressively more important as the tribe transitioned from their traditional livelihood to a more modern one.

By 2010, just seven years after Salés had introduced them, almost every whaler in the village owned at least a 50-yard section stitched into one of the kilometer-long drift nets, woven out of dozens of such pieces. The new technique in turn drove the rise of the jonson, as clans bought engines to power the boats far enough from the coast to make the nets effective. In 2014, the practice had become so widespread that the Tobo Nama Fata—the Council on the Beach that preceded

the opening of whaling season — took the step of banning it during
Léfa to ensure that the Lamalerans were not nocturnal when they
should be harpooning the Gifts of the Ancestors by day. Only once the
whales finished their migration in September would it be allowed.
That year, Salés registered *VJO* and its crew, including Jon, as a small
corporation with the Indonesian government, so that he could win a
small-business grant to buy new nets and another engine, a move that
other teams were soon clamoring to copy. Just as the téna had been
outmoded by the more efficient jonson, so harpoon hunting was
quickly being superseded by drift nets.

A LITTLE AFTER FIVE A.M., as the emerging sun outshone the eastern
stars but the western half of the sky still lay in night, Jon and his com-
panions awoke and reeled in the drift nets. The first sections yielded
only several two-foot Pacific mackerel tuna, but the foam floats of the
next portion had been pulled underwater. When the men hauled the
net to the surface, they discovered a seven-foot swordfish. The sail of its
silky black dorsal fin was torn, the lenses of its huge yellow eyes were
misted with blood, and a tattered flag of ripped net had twisted around
its lance of a nose — the majestic creature was dead. It took all four
men to wrestle the several hundred pounds of fish over the side. Then
they had to double the tail back to fit it in the hold. It was so entangled
in the nets that onshore they would have to cut it free, but no one would
mind the afternoons of restitching that would follow: it was a windfall.
Over the next hour, reeling in the rest of the net, they discovered a
four-foot swordfish, a dozen or so more mackerel tuna, and a hundred-
pound yellowfin tuna. The good haul highlighted the efficiency of
driftnetting: in about ten hours of light work, Jon and the others had
taken in more than a thousand pounds of meat.

They had just finished coiling the nets when the harrumphing of a
large motor echoed across the glassy water. A schooner twice as long as
VJO chugged out of the west, its ax-blade prow slicing directly at them.
It flew no flag, though from its construction Jon could tell it was from

Sulawesi, an island some seven hundred miles to the north. With no way to outrun the schooner, Jon swung *VJO* around to face it. The other men located their duri. Piracy was not unknown in the Savu Sea, and the water otherwise lay empty for miles around. As the mystery vessel approached, Jon discerned a quartet of men on the foredeck, all of them sunburned and salted, with the grimy appearance of having been at sea for days. Before their feet lay two huge sharks, and blood slathered the white decks.

Jon hailed the ship in Lamaholot, the regional language, but the men answered in Indonesian, the national language, which all citizens speak. They were Bajo Laut, "Sea Nomads," members of an ethnic group that once ranged in flotillas across eastern Indonesia and the Philippines, rarely ever setting foot on land. (Scientists have found that the bodies of the Bajo Laut have adapted to such an extent to their marine lifestyle that they have better eyesight under the water than terrestrially based humans, as well as an improved ability to hold their breath while spearfishing, which they do for hours a day.) But like the Lamalerans, the Bajo Laut have had their traditional lifestyle overhauled by modernity, and most of them have now settled in stilted houses on barrier islands, to which they return after the commercial-fishing expeditions that have replaced their marine hunter-gatherer lifestyle.

The four Bajo Laut men yelled across the gap between the ships, asking if Jon had caught any tuna — they had been chasing the schools hundreds of miles south from their homes, planning to ice them for export as sushi to Japan or America. Jon and the others held up their catch. The Bajo Laut did not want the mackerel tuna but asked for the yellowfin. In return, they offered the mako shark and tiger shark displayed across their foredeck. The predators' teeth had been pried out, leaving them with gummy old-man smiles, and their fins and tails had been hacked off, as the Bajo Laut would sell those pieces on the lucrative Chinese black market, but the rest of the meat was intact, as it was essentially worthless to them, since no one would buy it. Tuna, however, is a $400 billion business, the most lucrative fishing industry in the world. For the Bajo Laut, exchanging five hundred pounds of shark for a fifth of that weight in tuna made sense, as it also did for the Lamalerans, who cared only about how much meat there was to eat and were not even aware that they could sell the yellowfin. With the deal agreed to, the sea nomads tipped the dead sharks from their higher deck onto the lower jonson, where the corpses struck the deck like anvils, heavily rocking the boat. Then the Lamalerans passed the yellowfin hand to hand across the gap as gingerly as if it were a baby. Then the Bajo Laut set off to chase the dwindling tuna schools toward Papua.

They were not alone in raiding the Savu Sea, which is part of the richest marine ecosystem in the world, the Coral Triangle, sometimes called the "Amazon of the Oceans." Unfortunately, the northern and western legs of the Triangle run through what are industrialized regions of Indonesia and the Philippines, and have now mostly been reduced to barren seascapes, so only the eastern area, in which Lembata lies, remains relatively untouched. But as ocean resources closer to home have become depleted, fishermen from across Asia have begun plundering one of the globe's few remaining robust fisheries — including the earth's most valuable remaining tuna fishery — which just happens to include the Lamalerans' traditional hunting grounds.

The pillaging had begun five years earlier, when small ships from an island three hundred miles away from Lembata began using old World War II artillery shells and homemade fertilizer explosives to bomb the Lamalerans' reefs, collecting fish carcasses by the hundreds and leaving the coral gardens in ruins, this after having already destroyed the atolls between their home and Lembata en route. When the Lamalerans tried to intervene, bombs were thrown at them, and the remote island had no effective coast guard to call. Then came other homegrown opportunists, like the Bajo Laut, and after them rusty trawlers from Taiwan and Southeast Asian countries flying false Indonesian flags and illegally unleashing up to thirty miles of line baited with as many as 12,000 hooks in an effort to extract tons of marine life from the Savu Sea every night. And that was all before Jokowi's government began to push Indonesia's own national fishing fleet there, building out infrastructure and offering monetary incentives to fulfill his campaign promise of jump-starting the national economy by exploiting the natural resources of eastern Indonesia.

Because fishing yields have always fluctuated for the Lamalerans, at first they were hesitant to blame their dwindling catch on the interlopers. Besides, the very idea of a fishery declining is foreign to the Lamalerans, for if whales and manta rays are gifts from the Ancestors, the only way to exhaust them is by using up the spirits' goodwill. But the evidence was hard to controvert. Once, sharks had flocked to wounded whales, allowing the hunters to harvest a second bounty, but that never happened anymore. And the giant manta rays, which always had been the second most important prey for the tribe, providing up to two tons of meat apiece, had become rare. Likewise the population of smaller rays, such as bōu and mōku, had plunged — by as much as 87 percent, according to some estimates.

By 2014, even if the Lamalerans had not yet decided exactly what was causing their catches to fall off, they needed to replace the lost meat, driving them to hunt traditionally less important species, like dolphins, and employ more modern fishing techniques, like driftnetting, in turn putting yet more stress on the Savu Sea's fisheries. But even if the Lamalerans had better grasped what was happening to their ecosystem, there was little they could have done. Besides cutting the reels of foreign long-liners at night, which the Lamalerans did not do to protect the environment but to steal the hooks and buoys attached to the miles of fishing line, they had no real way to deter pirates.

This backdrop meant that as Jon lugged his windfall of swordfish, shark, and mackerel onto Lamalera Beach, he felt doubly vindicated: not only that the Ancestors had favored him, even while his tribesmen struggled, but also that driftnetting was paying off. On the sand, he and the rest of the crew divided the fish into six stacks of meat. Five of them were arranged according to the Ways of the Ancestors: one for each of the four crew and Salés. But there was also a pile of about five pounds of swordfish and mackerel that the Ancestors had never licensed. These fish Jon sold to a waiting kefela man for about a dollar, enough to pay for gas for the next driftnetting expedition with a small profit left over. The fishmonger would then resell the fish in his mountain village at a small markup. For Jon the transaction was a good deal. He had few other ways to get cash, and the flesh would have been eaten otherwise. If the entire swordfish had been up for auction in Japan or America, however, it would have likely sold for several thousand dollars, and the yellowfin tuna exchanged with the Bajo Laut earlier in the day would fetch an even higher price, for high-grade sushi meat could sell for thousands of dollars a pound.

Most Lamalerans were not aware of this. But Salés was. At about that time, he was busy traveling to Jakarta and Kupang, meeting with seafood-export businesses and government officials to secure low-interest loans and grants for a proposal to construct an internationally certified fish factory on Lembata. He was even requesting funds to build a tanker to ship the bulk of the catch out to Jakarta, where it could be routed around the world. The next year, when the port at Wulandoni was finished, he planned to make a killing connecting Lamalera and the outside world.

EACH MORNING, AS JON PILOTED *VJO* home from driftnetting, he visored his eyes with one hand to scan the blue savannah for spouts, splashes, and dorsal fins. But he told himself not to want too badly the opportunity to use the assembled harpoon waiting on the rack. There is a saying in Lamalera: *Preme ki,* Hope, but not too much, reflecting the belief that the whales would never come if the people demanded them. And yet it was impossible not to hope, for even trying not to hope was its own way of hoping.

When fate failed to yield him his big break, he started recruiting a lamafa to *VJO* so that he could hunt during the day as a *bereung alep,* a second harpooner — an apprentice, in his case — before driftnetting at night. The man he wanted was Yosef "Ote" Klake Bataona, one of the most promising young lamafa, whom children already pretended to be when playacting. At over six feet tall, Ote towered above the other Lamalerans. He had an action-hero body and shins barnacled with scars. A spring-loaded power propelled his movements, and he made a game of easily swatting flies out of the air. On the hâmmâlollo, he wielded with a single fist the great harpoon for sperm whales for which other lamafa need two hands. Resting, his acne-pitted face usually glowered.

As fearsome as Ote appeared, however, he was teased constantly by other men for being in his early thirties and still lacking a wife. "Champion harpooner at sea, but he can't stab anything on land," a man drunk on tuak might yell as he walked past. "I bet his harpoon's too small to spear anything!" another might add. (Lamaleran has as many specialized words to describe harpoons, stabbing, and hunting as Eskimos do snow, and thus may be the richest language in the world for penis jokes.) If teased enough, Ote would retort that he was married to his harpoons. He didn't want a wife, he insisted. He prayed

Ote astride the hâmmâlollo of VJO

184

only that God would grant him success in the hunt. Besides, Ote's fatherly energy was centered on caring for his aging mother, his spinster sister, and his nephews and nieces, whose parents had left the island years before. His favorite nephew, who was four, had even forgotten his biological father and told everyone it was Ote.

But Jon knew that despite his friendship with Ote, it would not be easy to convince him to work for *VJO*. From the beginning of the year, many other boats had already been courting his services. Ever since the hâmmâlollo was no longer passed from father to son, attracting a lamafa to a boat had become like a free-agency market in a professional sports league. The Ways of the Ancestors, of course, prescribed the share each crew member received, and thus no one could entice a harpooner with the promise of more fish. Accordingly, captains sought to recruit lamafa by offering them well-run ships to lead, which would catch more prey over time, and advantageous personal and clan alliances.

Ote's branch of the Bataona clan had shrunk until it could no longer launch even a jonson, much less a téna. Over two decades on other people's boats he had worked his way up from deckhand to freelance lamafa, filling in across the fleet whenever some clan's permanent lamafa was unavailable. At the end of the previous year, Frans had called Ote to lead *Kéna Pukā* after its elderly lamafa fell sick, and Ote had proven himself by taking a sperm whale. A few months later, that same lamafa formally announced his retirement by visiting Ote's house one evening to ask on behalf of the Bediona clan if the young man wanted to take his spot on the hâmmâlollo. Throughout the conversation, Ote made sure a picture of his late father sat beside them, as he wanted his father's presence at the proudest moment of his life. An agreement was all but formalized, but the next day another clan sent an emissary to ask if Ote wanted to become their lamafa instead, pointing out that they had a younger crew. A flurry of meetings followed. Frans promised that Ote would have time to grow under his command and that the Bediona crew would not castigate him if he made mistakes while learning to lead a téna. In the end, Ote chose

Frans and *Kéna Pukā,* not only because the materos of the second clan had a reputation for complaining endlessly if a lamafa missed but also because he respected Frans, who was known to run a tight ship.

Ote had a successful first Léfa in charge, taking another sperm whale, several whale sharks, and many different rays over the course of the season. But by October, with *Kéna Pukā* no longer regularly putting to sea, Jon convinced Salés to offer Ote *VJO*'s *leka,* the ownership of its harpoons and the formal status as the lamafa of the craft, which not even a clan chief or captain can compel the lamafa to give up. Technically, Ote did not yet own the leka for *Kéna Pukā,* for the emeritus lamafa would retain it for several probationary years until it could be determined that Ote was worthy of a lifelong appointment. That made Salés's offer impossible for Ote to turn down, for the height of a hunter's career is to become one of the thirty or so *leka lamafa,* one each for the fleet's active téna and jonson, answerable for both the hunting success and the spiritual health of their craft and crew.

Until that point Ote had borrowed harpoons from whichever lamafa he was replacing, but to make his own set for *VJO,* he climbed Labalekang to the precipitous ridges where bamboo forests swayed in the mist, and cut sixteen different shafts, each sized for its type of prey and purpose. Then he carried the poles to the shore, pressed out their bends with rocks, let them sun-dry, fire-hardened their joints, and finally wove rattan collars around their ends to reinforce them. A few days later, Jon and Salés ceremonially baptized Ote and the bamboo with holy water. Then Ote placed his harpoon on *VJO*'s rack, bonding his spirit to that of the boat. Jon was ecstatic: not only had he managed to get one of the tribe's most promising harpooners to lead his craft, but he had also figured out a way to learn from the best.

ONE MONDAY IN MID-OCTOBER, the first day *VJO* would launch with its new lamafa, Ote chased his favorite nephew, Luto, across the beach as the mulleted and rat-tailed four-year-old pursued his screaming sister, waving booger-covered hands at her. When the boy paused to mine more ammunition from his nostril, Ote scooped him up with a single arm and then thumbed a cross on Luto's forehead, trying not to laugh as he warned his young charge to stop antagonizing his sister. Meanwhile Jon and the rest of the crew shouted at him to hurry up as they pushed *VJO* into the shallows. But by the time Ote loped over to *VJO,* Luto had already rearmed himself and was chasing his sister once more, cackling.

VJO slid out of the bay as if across a mirror, the water so glassy that Jon could see his reflected face. As the boat motored into the heart of the tribe's hunting grounds, each crewman surveyed a separate quadrant of the horizon, while Ote stood atop the hâmmâlollo, his fingers boxed around his eyes, rotating all the way around like a periscope. Rather than standing behind the lamafa, as the second harpooner traditionally does, Jon sat at the back, steering the outboard engine, for he best knew the machine and the quirks of the beat-up, slightly lopsided old boat, the naked boards of which were starting to warp and were stained with rust bled from nails.

As *VJO* advanced, flying fish fired themselves out of the ocean ahead of it, their wings glimmering like tiles of mica, their glide contoured to the waves so that they always remained several inches above the sea's undulating peaks and valleys, until they needled back into their element. But for nearly an hour, as the crew traveled farther from shore, the Savu Sea stretched around them, empty of any animal of consequence. Sometimes whole days can pass for the Lamalerans without sighting worthy prey. Oceanic life clusters around plankton blooms, schools of feed fish, and nutrient-rich upwellings that are often invisible from the surface, which means that sometimes even the world's richest marine ecosystem seems as barren as a desert. For the Lamalerans, then, most time hunting is spent waiting until they glimpse a distant splash or a spangle of sunlight glinting on a fin, with their uncanny ability to pick out such details in the ever-similar but ever-changing sea.

Suddenly, Ote yelled, "Bōu!"—a yellow devil ray—and snatched a harpoon off the rack. Jon swung the boat right, following Ote's outstretched finger. The froth as the lamafa hit the water obscured whether he had struck true, but then the line started hissing over the hâmmâlollo. Ote did a pull-up to regain the platform as brothers Anso and Marsel applied gentle pressure on the rope, resisting the bōu enough to inflict pain but not enough to risk jerking the flange out. Soon the shadow in the depths had turned back and resolved into a shape that outsized even Ote. As it spun figure eights, Anso pilfered a length of rope each time the animal approached, gradually shortening its circuit. Meanwhile, Jon screwed together a harpoon. It was his job, as the bereung alep, to "double," to land the second weapon. Ote also assembled another harpoon, but he let Jon step onto the hâmmâlollo.

The water was so clear that, from above, it seemed to Jon as if the ray were flapping through air. Blood smoked from around the iron embedded in its back. The situation was the equivalent of an underhand pitch: the manta on a short rope, the ocean calm, with unlimited time to strike. He was confident—he had hit harder targets before, including the manta with Narek—but if he delayed too long his friends might mock him. He leapt. When he surfaced, a harpoon line was churning out—but not the one attached to his weapon. Somehow he had missed. On board, Anso and Marsel were trying to rodeo the beast but had almost been dragged overboard by its great strength. The miss was especially humiliating for Jon because he had now created the possibility that the harpoon would yank loose from the ray as it fled. *Lolong,* Ote yelled, a specialized word in Lamaleran indicating that Jon had stabbed too far in front of the ray.

In Lamaleran, there are specific words for describing everything from a lamafa missing because of slipping on the wet boards of the hâmmâlollo (*segalit*) to being thrown off-balance by an unexpected wave while attacking (*sleder*). *Pleba* means to hit a target so hard the harpoon head exits the other side of the animal, while *lobut* means that the harpoon—head and shaft—passes all the way through the prey. Then there is *todeh,* perhaps the most derisive word in the Lamaleran language, as it denotes a harpoon's failure to enter, and can describe not only a lamafa's inability to pierce a whale's hide but also a married man's failure to conceive children (which made it a favorite taunt for other Lamalerans to hurl at Ote). These ultra-specific words allowed Jon and Ote to compress paragraphs of information about the hunt into a few syllables. More than that, though, they were also linguistic microcosms of a whole way of life, and will be among the first words to vanish if the Lamalerans' culture weakens.

It took Anso and Marsel a full ten minutes of coaxing the ray before it was within striking range again. Standing on the hâmmâlollo, Ote eased his harpoon into the ocean but kept it still as the ray neared the boat. The animal's eyes on their stalks swiveled to look at its tormentors above, ignoring the weapon. Ote waited until the ray passed just inches beneath the spearhead, then casually skewered it. Lessons from lamafa were often demonstrations rather than lectures, and Ote was pointing out how to avoid being misled by the refraction of the water by placing the ray and the lance in the same plane of light, as well as reminding Jon it was not always necessary to jump. A lamafa was like an arrow in a bow of the jonson; if he missed, it took time to reload.

The ray somersaulted and was trying once more to flee when Jon leapt from *VJO* and impaled it mid-flight. This strike was every bit as impressive as his miss had been embarrassing. The ray disappeared in a cloud of blood roiled by its frantic wingbeats. With three harpoon lines now secured, the crew no longer feared the ray escaping. They hauled it against *VJO*. Then Jon set his duri between its horns, leaned on the blade, and sawed. At first, the wings tattooed *VJO* like a drum, and soaked Jon in red froth. But when the high-pitched squeaking of the knife across the skull ended with a soft crack, like the opening of a coconut, the flailing stilled. The men caught their breath. Wavelets plashed against the hull.

Jon finishes off the yellow devil ray with his duri.

Because the ray was too large to drag on board, they had to pierce its wings with hooks and tie the hooks to the boat to support it while they treaded water and sliced around the bottom of its gills to dislodge the head as a single piece, after which they axed the wings off the torso. In the end, they stacked four portions of the ray at the bottom of the boat like a disassembled puzzle. For a time the corpse still shimmered, as if with an underwater enchantment, but before long the sun dried its silky skin to road tar and its bulbous eyes fogged, like burned-out lightbulbs.

A kilometer away, another jonson, aimed east, was chasing prey they could not yet see, though they could make out the harpooner and his spear silhouetted against the lilac backdrop of the Ata Dei mountains. Ote blessed everyone with Frans's holy water, the crew said an Our Father to thank the ray for its sacrifice, Jon rip-corded the engine, and they raced to rejoin the hunt.

*   *   *

IN THE MONTHS THAT FOLLOWED, Jon practiced the techniques he saw Ote using while seconding on dolphins and devil rays. He copied how Ote shuffled his hands up and down the shaft to extend or retract the harpoon, depending on his distance from the target, and how the lamafa placed one palm under the butt of the harpoon to add maximum distance to the throw. He learned how to hyperventilate himself into a frenzy before striking large targets like manta rays to ensure that his blow pierced their thick hide—but also how to slide into a Zen state when attacking flighty dolphins, where accuracy was more important than power. But it was not just the physical skills that Jon had to master before he could become a lamafa. The Way of the Lamafa paid less attention to hunting techniques than to the cultivation of a spiritual balance between the harpooner and the world, for if a lamafa honored the Ancestors and defended the unity of the tribe, the fish would surrender themselves willingly to him.

Still, Jon sometimes found following the Way of the Lamafa confusing. Because there was no official rulebook, only an oral tradition of guidelines, it seemed to him that the Ancestors had missed offering even the faintest suggestions about many modern-day situations. Should he not use a cell phone, as certain elders suggested, even though he saw some successful lamafa chatting on them? Did he really have to keep anyone from touching his feet, lest they disrupt his spiritual balance? Privately, he decided the prohibition against a lamafa having sex during Léfa was probably just superstition (though with Honi several hundred miles away, he did not have anyone to test it with anyway). It also seemed to him that the Way of the Lamafa required him to be superhuman sometimes: How was anyone supposed to keep from having angry thoughts against his clansmen occasionally? Unlike Ben, he did not have a father to guide him. And as excellent as Ote was in action, he was not a great talker or philosophizer. Eventually, Jon decided that he would have to assemble his own Way of the Lamafa from the many existing traditions.

Through November, Jon's harpooning improved, but as the first moist winds of December ruffled the Savu Sea, he realized he would not become a lamafa that year. Thousands of miles to the north, on the roof of Asia, the Gobi Desert was cooling, exhaling western winds that would blow south, pick up moisture over the Pacific, and usher the monsoons to Lamalera by Christmas. Clans began to rig up the rope systems that would lift the téna and jonson off the ground and into the eaves of the boat sheds, to dodge the storm surges that would reach the retaining wall at the back of the beach. Jon looked at the desiccated branches of a gum lac tree and told himself to be patient. In four months that wood would be festooned with felty red buds releasing vivid green leaflets, the seas would calm, and the tribe would hunt again. Then, he promised himself, he would become a lamafa.

PART TWO

2015

Chapter Eight

A NEW YEAR

April 2015–May 2, 2015

Frans — Sipri

For the Lamalerans, time is a spiral, more cyclical than linear. Seasons wheel. Sperm whales migrate. A living person departs but returns as an Ancestor. Each time the gum lac trees birth new leaves from their buds, the truth of the Old Ways is reestablished. Léfa always returns.

During the rainy season, the village had seemed sepulchral, with muddy dogs splashing through otherwise empty alleys and storm-driven waves gnashing the deserted beach. Wives and children huddled in damp houses, triple-wrapped in sarongs. With many men having joined construction crews on the other side of the mountains, only a scattering of sampans fished near shore, ready to sprint home if a typhoon blew up. A téna crew could always be scrambled, though, if sperm whales passed the island and the seas were peaceful enough. The wettest months, January through March, were called the Hunger Season. That year, excessive rains had rotted the cassava of some mountain tribes before it could be harvested, and during the succession of damp days the Lamalerans struggled to sun-dry their meat before it sprouted maggots. To feed themselves, the tribe dipped into the *mata gapo,* huge rattan baskets stuffed with corn and rice, which had hung all year above the hearth, the smoke killing any infiltrating weevils. But people still grew skinny, and the flu proliferated.

April arrived at last, and the Southern Hemisphere winter chilled the Australian deserts, forcing dry winds north across Indonesia. The sea calmed, and the whalers streamed home. Now the beach bustled with men forging harpoons and crews recaulking their ships with dried tree pith in preparation for the whaling season.

As usual, Frans had *Kéna Pukā* ready and hunting ahead of the rest of the fleet, but one day, when Ote harpooned a dolphin, the ship's leo, its Spirit Rope, broke. A new leo would have to be woven from jungle materials—a big deal because of its ceremonial importance and the significant time it would take. By the early 2000s, nylon ropes had been substituted for all the naturally made ropes except for the leo, for they were easier to replace (though not necessarily stronger). Frans ordered his men to flay bark from gebang palms and hibiscus trees, while the women of his clan spun endless thread from jungle cotton. These materials were then woven into a single mighty leo by the tribal elders, who joyfully belted work songs they rarely got to sing anymore, while the young men echoed the snatches they could pick up: "Give us strength! Give us tuak!" Over two days, the leo grew inch by inch to its final three-hundred-foot length. Then it was shellacked with the sap of a hummingbird tree, which hardened and blackened when cured with seawater, forming a protective shell around it.

Normally, Frans would have kept a close eye on such fraught work—the rope had to be twisted an exact number of times to win the Ancestors' approval—but he had journeyed four islands away to attend his elder daughter's ordination as a nun. The Perpetual Profession of Solemn Vows, as it is known, was an accomplishment important enough that he would later throw a festival for the whole tribe to celebrate it. Watching her put on the wimple, he was immeasurably proud, but he also felt the same sadness a father does on handing his daughter over to her groom. It made him yearn for Bena, his younger daughter, who was supposed to move home the next year, for all of his children now lived outside the tribe, with his elder daughter at the convent, Bena attending university, and his only son, who had never shown much aptitude for the sea, teaching P.E. at an elementary school on a distant island.

When Frans returned to Lamalera, one day before Tobo Nama Fata, the Council on the Beach, the gathering at which all the hunters set the rules for the upcoming hunting season, he was met by a crowd of relatives. They helped him carry several duct-taped cardboard boxes loaded with rare goods, like spices and cooking oil, to his house, and then they sat together on his porch to drink coffee from and admire a chipped, secondhand enamel thermos he had brought back. Clearly agitated, Frans speechified about the thickets of cell phone towers and cavalry of motorbikes he had seen on the neighboring islands, worrying aloud about when they might reach Lamalera. Other elders complained about the jonson, and soon the assembly began discussing if they should be banned, as Sipri had demanded. One man asked Frans if Sipri would join the Tobo Nama Fata that year, a sly reference to the Curse of the Black Goat, which no one was brave enough to ask about directly. In answer, Frans said nothing but offered a mysterious smile, from which the whalers drew the assurance that all was well, even though they were not permitted to know what had happened. The affairs of the shamans were kept purposefully enigmatic, even for the Lamaleran elders.

ONLY FRANS AND A FEW other clan leaders knew that the Wujons — the Lords of the Land — had rescinded their threat to hex the tribe after another emissary had apologized for the transgression of the Lika Telo the previous year. The Wujons had been especially mollified by the fact that the head of the Bataona clan, Kupa, whose absence had disrupted the ceremony the year before, had quietly been convinced to return to his former home on another island so that a more respectful relative could ascend to his position.

Even more important, Sipri, who had issued the warning, was being pushed out as the Lord of the Land by his fifty-two-year-old son, Marsianus Dua Wujon. Marsianus had felt that his father's threat of the Curse of the Black Goat had been an overreaction, and used it as evidence to argue to his relatives that his father, now entering his mid-seventies, was becoming senile. Marsianus also played on the other Wujons' resentments stemming from the installation of a cell phone tower on their clifftops three years earlier. Because the Wujons owned the land, the cell phone company had paid Sipri the huge sum of $5,000 for building rights. Marsianus and his clansmen had hoped the money would be split. But Sipri kept it all. He needed to buy his stroke-felled wife medicine, he argued, as well as pay for projects, such as rehabbing the Spirit House, that would benefit everyone. Many of his people never forgave him. It was not just the appropriation of the money; it was also his hypocrisy in enjoying the modern conveniences of Lewoleba even as he forced his tribesmen to live archaically. Leveraging all this, Marsianus won his people's support to lead Ige Gerek and Tobo Nama Fata, effectively becoming the chieftain of the Wujons.

Frans and the Lika Telo found it easier to deal with Marsianus. Whereas his father had clung to the old rules without compromise, Marsianus, though still conservative and in favor of a return to sailing and paddling, was less inclined to dispute the tribe's choices. "I have to live in Lamalera and rely on the whales to eat," he once said. "My father does not."

But even as Frans savored having defused the Curse of the Black Goat, across the island a fear nagged at Sipri, as if the Ancestors themselves were whispering warnings in his ear. He had turned over the duties of the Lord of the Land to Marsianus, but was his son really ready to lead the Council on the Beach and perform the Calling of the Whales? At first, Sipri resisted his worries, but as the night thickened, he decided that only his heart was in tune enough with the Ancestors to lead the ceremonies properly. The Lamalerans and Marsianus would not be expecting him, but he had to confront them. The next morning he summoned a nephew to convey him on a motorbike over the volcano.

LATE THAT AFTERNOON, UNAWARE OF his father's impending arrival, in preparation to lead Tobo Nama Fata, Marsianus enthroned himself on the top step of the newly rebuilt chapel in the center of the beach, where the totem of sperm whale skulls had once towered and beside which an eighteen-foot shard of a skull now stood, driven into the sand like a bone monolith. With eyes reddened from a lifetime of staring at the sun glittering on the sea, he watched his people arrive and sit before him. The three chiefs of the Lika Telo knelt at the bottom of the stairs. Meanwhile, a hundred or so whalers kicked off their sandals and squatted in rows on the beach. A boy with one leg, still too young to be self-conscious about his deformity, hopped by blissfully in a game of tag, before an elder yelled at him and his playmates to stop disturbing the preparations for the ceremony.

Ote was among the crowd as well. His gaze tracked two teenage girls sashaying by. Another hunter noticed and teased him: "Your nephew needs a mother." In response Ote plucked a severed crab pincher from the sand and threw it at him, but with a wince—his hands, which had been flayed grabbing a harpoon rope towed by an orca, were bandaged in rags. Ignatius shushed Ben and several other chattering young hunters, as Marsianus rose and smoothed the collar of his blue knockoff Polo shirt. Jon, who had the flu, was resting at home.

To open the Council, Marsianus declared, "I am the Lord of the Land," and welcomed the assembly with a speech stressing that he would hear their problems as a representative of their forebears.

One of the Lika Telo answered: "We are the fishermen. We ask that Ige Gerek happen tomorrow. Please bring our wishes and our hopes to the Ancestors, for we need the whales to come."

Marsianus and the Lika Telo ritually exchanged woven rattan

baskets filled with dried corncobs, palm-leaf cigarettes, and sirih pinang. Then, one by one, the whalers began to inform the Council of their problems. At first, most of the complaints were about specific hunts, as various captains recounted in play-by-play detail how this devil ray or that whale shark had been stolen by a rival crew, and Marsianus and the elders resolved the shouting matches that ensued. Once this rigmarole had been dispatched, the assembly reaffirmed the long-settled rule that only téna could challenge kotekělema, the sperm whale. Then the more contentious issues were addressed. Some men wanted permission to driftnet during Léfa, but the Council maintained the ban through September. The most intense quarrel turned out to be whether they should delay Ige Gerek for a day because it conflicted with a scheduled Catholic Church ceremony. Some elders argued vehemently against it, saying the date had been set by the Ancestors. But eventually it was decided that Ige Gerek would be switched to the day after Misa Arwah, the mass in which the miniature candle-bearing fleet was released.

Eventually, the assembly returned to the much-debated question of whether the tribe should discontinue use of the jonson. At the heart of the discussion was what it meant to be Lamaleran and how the tribe would survive. Jeffery "Jepo" Bataona, who had replaced the truant chief as the newest member of the Lika Telo, suggested the tribe seek a governmental or philanthropic sponsor to pay them a living wage to sail instead of using the engines, so that their traditional knowledge would not be lost. Some elders enthusiastically agreed, but others demurred, saying the youth should not have to be paid to do the right thing. A group of young hunters disputed the idea for a different reason. Even if the tribe could get someone to pay for the whalers to sail and row the téna exclusively, the offer should still be rejected, they argued. With their motors, the jonson were simply more efficient for catching small prey, and besides, the whole world was modernizing.

There would be no official vote on any of these issues, however. A consensus was measured simply by the number and vehemence of those who spoke for or against an idea. Because of this truly democratic governance, which is practiced in some form by almost all hunter-gatherers, the Lamalerans are more egalitarian and democratic than industrial societies — but this equality also makes them very hard to control since they have no formal authority over one another. Even the Lika Telo, though they have the most prestige of any of the clans, have no legislative tools with which to impose their judgments. Social pressure is the only way to enforce the tribe's decisions. Even then, it is impossible to eradicate minor offenses, like someone deciding to drift-net during Léfa. (Though for major offenses, like a murder, the whole tribe can render a consensus judgment, usually involving a shamanistic punishment.) Ultimately, the tribe had no true way to stonewall modernity. Even if Sipri or other hard-liners succeeded in prohibiting the jonson, as long as a sizeable group kept using the engines, nothing could be done.

Of course, the question of what the Lamalerans wanted was complicated because there was no single unified desire. What it meant to be a Lamaleran differed greatly for Sipri, for Frans, and for Jon, and none could agree on which changes were good and which were bad. Jon and Ote considered not having to row for hours under the searing sun a benefit, but Sipri considered it an existential threat. As the discussion wound on, some whalers wandered away, bored, knowing that the lack of a decision was a decision in itself — as it had been every year before that. In the end, the debate was deadlocked. It would have to be taken up again at the next Tobo Nama Fata.

The tortured mating call of a tomcat echoed as Marsianus recited a prayer in archaic Lamaleran, which even Frans and the other elders only vaguely understood, remembering their fathers speaking it at long-lost ceremonies. Heat lightning sizzled on the misted heights of the volcano, but no thunder followed, as if even nature held its breath. Marsianus asked the ghostly Ancestors, who had gathered to watch the ceremony, to return in two days' time for the Calling of the Whales, then dismissed them. As the Southern Cross twinkled to life in a slit of sky left exposed by the dry storm, the whalers recited the Lord's Prayer. Then Marsianus climbed the cliffs to the Wujon Spirit House. There he found Sipri waiting.

CLOUDS SMOTHERED THE STARS, intensifying the night, but no rain fell. By seven o'clock, people had already retreated to their homes and many were readying for bed. Jepo sat shirtless on a bamboo bench in his family's brick courtyard, where Jon and so many others had watched the World Cup the year before. He was playing peekaboo with one of his young daughters, while locusts and frogs harmonized in the jungle behind them. The orchestra crescendoed, then abruptly cut off, sensing an impending disturbance, and in the silence, slapping footsteps echoed in the alley.

Frans strode into the courtyard, head down, shoulders hunched, as if ready to head-butt anyone in his way. Rather than his everyday uniform of tattered T-shirt and soccer shorts—often sourced from suppliers who cheaply purchased factory-damaged or otherwise unsellable clothes from America, so that he had one shirt declaring a Super Bowl champion that had in fact lost—he wore a T-shirt bleached an iridescent white and a neat green checkered sarong. "Stand!" he commanded.

Jepo asked what was wrong and lowered his daughter to the ground.

"We have an important mission. Sipri has just arrived!"

Jepo rushed his daughter into the house, then emerged dressed in camouflage pants and T-shirt, his scraggly goatee wrangled into a rubber band. He hopped on his crocodile-green motorbike and then revved it. Its headlight stabbed the darkness. Frans hiked his sarong around his knees and straddled the back. Then Jepo launched the vehicle up the rocky dirt road that switchbacked up the cliffs. Both were terrified that the elderly shaman had come to execute the Curse of the Black Goat.

Jepo and Frans found Sipri and Marsianus waiting for them in the Wujon Spirit House. With its bamboo walls and grass roof, the building was an anachronism among the village's otherwise brick tin-roofed houses, for the Lords of the Land knew that their Ancestors would not stay in modern accommodations. A single whale oil lantern cast campfire shadows on the walls and illuminated the shamans from above, leaving their eye sockets in darkness. In the year since Frans had seen Sipri, the old man had wasted away even more. The edges of his cheeks stood out so starkly it was as if his crepe-paper skin had been vacuum-sealed over his skull.

Sipri said nothing as Jepo and Frans both gushed about what an unexpected pleasure it was to see him. Jepo said that he appreciated Sipri making the trip and promised to buy a chicken for him to sacrifice at Ige Gerek. Frans handed out imported, factory-made cigarettes, considered higher class than the usual cigarettes rolled from dried palm leaves. Meanwhile, Marsianus sat silently in the corner. Sipri was still afflicted by the medical condition that made his eyes "spicy." Tears fell from them constantly, and he scrubbed them with his purple sarong until they reddened.

Finally, Sipri sighed. "It's lucky I came," he said. "Otherwise the ceremony wouldn't have happened at the right time. When my child told me it was going to happen on the second of May, I was surprised. Changes in the schedule like that are very important!" On learning that Ige Gerek had been delayed, Sipri had raged at Marsianus and declared that it was providential that the Ancestors had warned him to return, or there could have been a disaster. Then Sipri had sent a nephew to summon Frans and Jepo.

Now he ordered Frans, Jepo, and Marsianus to recount what messages the hunters had entrusted to the Lords of the Land during the Council. Sipri had decided that in a few hours he — and not his son — would bring the messages up the volcano to the Ancestors. He warned that the Ancestors were losing patience with the Lamalerans for not giving up the jonson and for failing to honor the Wujons sufficiently.

Throughout the hour-long harangue, Frans worried that Sipri was leading up to the Curse of the Black Goat, and he and Jepo tried to soothe him by agreeing, whenever possible. When at last Sipri fell silent, having exhausted both his listeners and himself, the old man had made no mention of the curse, to Frans's great relief. Jepo concluded the conference by formally asking Sipri to perform Ige Gerek the next day. As they left the Spirit House, Frans wondered why Sipri had failed to follow through with his threat. He decided that the old man must have judged that the tribe was doing a good enough job honoring the Ancestors to warrant only correction, not punishment.

Then Sipri, Marsianus, and the young men of the clan rushed to assemble their offerings, wrapping brown-shelled eggs and sirih pinang in banana leaves, and unpacking the heirlooms of the Ancestors from their rattan boxes in the Spirit House. Though the Lords of the Land would normally have started their climb that night, sleeping partway up the mountain at the hamlet of another tribe, it was now too late to start hiking. The shamans managed a few fitful hours of sleep while the Southern Cross ticked across the night sky like the hand of a clock. Before daybreak, Sipri roused Marsianus and his grandsons to face the Ancestors.

DAWN EXPOSED SIPRI IN THE ORCHARDS. The jungle was still far off, for the Wujons had started climbing Labalekang later than usual. Sipri found the cashew trees around him unnerving: in the dark, he had been able to imagine that their tight rows were still the virgin jungle of his childhood, but with the light, it was impossible to ignore that farms now reached miles up the volcano. Every few hundred feet he had to rest, despite using the Spear of the Dragon, the magical weapon wielded by his spirit forebears, as a walking stick. (In Lewoleba he had recently taken to employing a broken umbrella, stripped of its canopy and ribs, as a cane.) Marsianus powered on, not bothering to wait for his father, the vein between his eyebrows pulsing cartoonishly whenever he glanced over his shoulder. Soon it became clear that they would

A lamafa lands a harpoon while Frans exhorts him on Kéna Pukā.

A lamafa leaps to harpoon his prey.

A lamafa hurls himself off his ship to strike a fleeing sperm whale.

Sperm whales are the largest carnivores in history, with adult males weighing in excess of sixty tons. Here, the modern-day incarnation of Kebako Pukã, *the original téna, endures the battering of a mature bull whale in 2016.*

The Lamalerans hunt other marine animals besides sperm whales, including manta rays, orcas, sharks, and dolphins. Jon Hariona spears a dolphin (above). A lamafa spears another dolphin (below).

The Lamaleran fleet sails home one evening in 2014 after a successful hunt.

The téna Demo Sapang sails into Lamalera in 2011.

The Lamalerans prepare a whale for butchering.

After filleting the top side of the whale, the Lamalerans flip the corpse to get at the meat on the bottom.

After a whale is divided, each Lamaleran slices his or her portion into six-inch strips and sun-dries it. Here, a whaler hangs his portion.

Once whale meat has withered into jerky, it is either eaten by the Lamalerans or carried to the island's barter market by the tribe's women.

At the barter market, one strip of whale jerky can be exchanged for a dozen bananas or cobs of corn.

With corn from the market, Grandmother Fransiska prepares fata biti, smashed popcorn, for Jon.

Lamaleran women make their traditional sarongs with materials sourced from the forest. Special motifs woven into the sarongs tell stories: above, a pattern of manta rays and sirih pinang boxes tell of a successful hunt.

The Lamalerans are officially Catholic. Here, Bena Bediona, Frans's daughter, stands in the village church after practicing with the choir. On the wall behind her, a mural depicts Christ converting the tribe on Lamalera Beach.

The Lamalerans also practice an ancient religion in which they worship the Ancestors and Lera Wulan, the Sun-Moon God. Here, Marsianus Dua Wujon (foreground) *and his father, Sipri Raja Wujon* (background), *the Lords of the Land, summon the whales during Ige Gerek.*

Today, the Lamalerans have synthesized the two religions. They still believe their *téna have souls and perform shamanistic rites by whale oil lantern to honor them (above). In ceremonies like Misa Arwah (below), a Catholic mass overlays a formerly animist ceremony, and the tribe prays to both Jesus and their Ancestors.*

Jon Hariona

Ignatius Blikololong commanding his téna, Demo Sapang

Lower Lamalera, as seen from the cliffs above the town, in the dry season.

The whalebone shrine on the eastern end of Lamalera Beach, kept to honor the whales that sustain the tribe.

The next generation of lamafa practice harpooning.

not be able to reach the promontory where the first ceremony was usually held until too late in the day. Sipri called a halt at one of the lower sacred stones. He strove to make sure that the Ways of the Ancestors were followed, but sometimes he faced imperfect choices: start the ceremony later than the time proscribed by his forebears or hold it in the wrong spot.

He hoped that the Ancestors would understand: he was trying his best, but his body was failing him and so was the world. How could he save the Lamalerans if they would not follow his directions? In the heat of the moment, when he had threatened the Curse of the Black Goat, he had meant it, but after cooling down, he had known he could never follow through. His goal was to rescue his people, not destroy them. But now that his bluff had been called, he had no way to force the tribe to do what was best for them. No matter how hard he tried, change bulldozed onward. He understood that this would almost certainly be the last time he led Ige Gerek. His people! His people! He dreaded what would happen to them after he was gone.

Still, he would go down holding the tribe as closely as possible to the Ways of the Ancestors. He planned to survive the coming year and be there at the next Council on the Beach. And at that moment, there was one thing he could do to fix things, even if just temporarily. He pounded the rusting Gong of the Ancestors with a drumstick whose end was wrapped in red cloth. A tinny echo wavered out, summoning the past. He hoped that when he became an Ancestor, he would finally have the power to force the tribe to do what was right.

THAT EVENING, AS LOW CLOUDS cotton-balled the sky, laying an azure filter over the sunset, nearly fifteen hundred Lamalerans gathered on the beach for the annual ritual of Misa Arwah, the Mass for Lost Souls. The ceremony was the same that year as it had always been: Father Romo reading off in identical order the names of the souls perished at sea; the choir repeating the standard hymns until their throats were scratchy; the priest, his acolytes, and the tribe putting miniature téna filled with candles on the currents, so that their hopes could be borne into the night.

Jon, who was coughing with the flu, did not attend the ceremony. He sat on the clifftops instead, wrapped in a sarong, watching the thousands of flames coruscate below. During the rainy season, he had started to tire of apprenticing to Ote and was counting the days for Honi to come home. Why did he always have to be waiting? He was dreaming again of moving to Jakarta, where he expected, like all the young transplants he saw on Indonesian soap operas, to make it big.

Meanwhile, Ignatius prayed that Ben would at last marry Ita and that he would become a lamafa as well. It felt as if the last year had worn him down as much as previous whole decades had, and he hoped that he would see his son finally achieve these goals before he joined his beloved Teresea.

This year, Ben's hopes were more aligned with his father's. His friend's plan to start a bemo route in Bali had fallen through, and though he had been disappointed at first, over the last few months he had increasingly savored life in Lamalera. Sure, there were times, like when his two young children misbehaved or his father's commands exasperated him, that he still thought about running away to Lewoleba, but he had begun to want to become a lamafa. Perhaps he had crossed some invisible line of maturity.

Freed from fearing the Curse of the Black Goat, Frans prayed for a successful hunting season and the health of his family and clan — and that after his daughter Bena finally graduated from university in a few months, she would not take a job on a distant island and keep her promise to move home, though even if she did, she would probably not arrive until the next year, needing to tie up loose ends abroad.

Ika's hopes were the gauzy dreams of a young woman in love: marriage, children, a home of her own. She had started secretly dating a young man from the village. And though a part of her still hoped to complete her education and live a more modern life, suddenly the prospect of leaving the tribe had lost most of its appeal.

Once the prayers were completed and the candle-bearing boats had vanished into the darkness, the Lamalerans began to walk off the beach without fanfare. Soon only the pious and the wretched remained, kneeling as the wind tumbled sparks around them. Then the tide invaded, drowning the fire field and driving the stragglers back into the sickly halogen light of the village. Smoke fugged the beach. The heavenly chandelier of candles above glimmered as it always has and always will.

THE LAMALERANS WERE BACK ON the beach at dawn, stepping over snuffed matchsticks, candles frozen grotesquely mid-melt by seawater, and a few wracked vessels that the Ancestors had returned to them. They were assembling for Misa Léfa, the Opening of the Sea, which celebrated the future in much the way that Misa Arwah honored the past.

After a sermon, Father Romo, using an aspergillum made from a shaving brush, sprinkled holy water on all the téna, each of which had been decorated with jungle vines. Next, he blessed the ocean with his hands out, as if he were a sorcerer casting a spell. Finally, the Lelaona clan launched the téna *Praso Sapang,* its ceremonial second stern artfully festooned with palm leaves. The rest of the fleet would launch the next day, but *Praso Sapang* always hunted alone on the first of Léfa, for the Ancestors had decreed it so, and its catch would foretell the results for the rest of the year. The crew rowed with the deep strokes of men showing off for their families, chanting to keep time, though not truly singing as in the Age of Song. From shore, the Lamalerans watched the red, white, and blue boat reduce to a twig. Once past the currents ringing the island, *Praso Sapang* raised its bipod mast and hauled the furled sail to its peak, after which the captain unscrolled the palm-leaf sheet with the yank of a rope. The tilted diamond stood out against the horizon like semaphore, signaling that the Lamalerans hunted again.

Everyone waited to see what the Ancestors would send them from beyond the horizon of the Savu Sea. When, forbiddingly, *Praso Sapang* caught nothing, the tribe began to whisper that perhaps the Ancestors were displeased—a judgment with which Sipri concurred, when he heard of it in Lewoleba.

Chapter Nine

NEKAT

May 2015–June 2015

Jon

During the Hunger Season, when the rains gushed from the skies and Jon could rarely harpoon hunt, he watched a lot of TV at a neighbor's house. The standard Indonesian soap opera plot was an enticing one: a young Indonesian moved from his or her rural village to Jakarta and found instantaneous, improbable success. This fantasy glamorized what were in reality the brutal experiences of countless youth who relocated to Indonesia's burgeoning cities, such as laboring for twelve-hour shifts in sweatshops, sleeping on the floor, and then rising to do it again. But Jon had no idea what migrants really went through, and could not help but find his poverty wanting when compared to the televised rock-star urban lifestyle.

Although he still hoped to become a lamafa, he found himself more and more often annoyed with his elders and the Ways of the Ancestors. It was hard for him not to view the Council on the Beach as a relic when the salt-beards did not even follow their own rules; one particularly annoying hypocrisy was that every year they decreed anew that whoever saw prey first had exclusive rights to it, but inevitably conflict would arise when a ship would steal another's fleeing manta ray. In Wulandoni, a finished wharf jutted into the sea, leaving only the customhouse to be built to complete the construction. Jon and other young men hoped that cash-paying jobs would follow once the port was finished at the end of the dry season. But that was too far ahead: Jon wanted the future now.

For the first time, he had an actual escape route to Jakarta, if he wanted it. Salés's older brother, another Lamaleran expat, was an executive at the Indonesian subsidiary of Unilever, in the capital, and when the old man had visited the tribe to participate in Misa Léfa, he had taken a liking to Jon and offered to hire him as a guard at his mansion in the big city. At the time, unsure if the proposition was even serious, Jon had not pursued it. But on days when he was particularly frustrated with life in the tribe, he would summon the old man's number in his phone and consider what might happen if he called it.

Still, Léfa awakened in every hunter's heart a longing for the chase. On the first day that the whole fleet was allowed to launch, Jon drove *VJO* while Ote wielded the harpoon. Though *Praso Sapang*'s solo expedition a day earlier had forebodingly yielded nothing, the whalers managed to forge their own luck, surrounding and slaughtering a school of devil rays, with most boats taking several. Jon won the approval of his elders by doubling behind Ote on three small rays and one manta ray.

That afternoon, whispers fluttered through the tribe that Jon *nekat:* an Indonesian verb that means to hazard greatly to achieve a goal, but which the elders use to describe a young man running to the hâm-mâlollo to double, pushing aside others who have grabbed spears — perhaps leaping in front of even the lamafa himself. "We elders can tell who will become a lamafa," Ignatius declared. "Jon is not fully there yet, but he has that active spirit — nekat — and is getting much closer."

LATE ON THE AFTERNOON OF the season's first hunt, as the sun's final rays flared and then darkened, like a candle that has spent its tallow and is engulfing the wick, Ika descended to the beach to help Jon lug the ray steaks back up the cliffs. Only this time, one of the hunters who had been accompanying Jon, Aloysius Enga "Alo" Kĕrofa, carried the tub of meat for her. The whole way home, Ika could not stop giggling.

In the second half of the previous year, Yosef Boko had been beset with letters asking for his granddaughter's hand in marriage. But Ika had no interest in any of her suitors, including Ote. Realizing she would get no peace, however, until she found a boyfriend, she decided to create a fake one. Most Lamalerans did not find Alo attractive, as the tribe's standards of beauty favored skin that was lighter than his almost charcoal coloring. Even more, Alo was a member of the Kĕrofa clan, which had been poor since the tribe's first chieftain, Tana Kĕrofa, had been usurped by Korohama and banned from owning a téna.

Ika did not mind Alo's low caste, however: first, because she had no plans to actually marry him, and second, because she romanticized it as an injustice that Alo bore nobly. While she knew the Ancestors had decreed the Kĕrofas' unending punishment, she quietly questioned it in the same way she did the fairness of having many opportunities denied her just because she was a woman. While she could never change how the whole tribe treated the Kĕrofas, she felt like her subtle rebellion with Alo righted a wrong in some small way.

Besides, there was just *something* about Alo. Ika liked his muscles, his stylish punk clothing, and the way his white teeth contrasted with his nearly black cheeks when he smiled. But the thing that made her heart flop into submission whenever they met was his silliness. Ever since they were kids, whenever Alo saw Ika on the street, he never failed to let loose a witty jibe, which she would counter. Soon both of them would be guffawing, such that they were labeled "craftspeople of laughter" by the tribe.

One afternoon near the start of the Lazy Season, not long after she had declined a marriage proposal, she encountered Alo on a deserted path to the well, and explained the scheme she had in mind, asking him if he would participate.

"Not your real boyfriend?" he said, laughing.

"My fake one," she insisted.

Alo agreed.

Because he had always dated other girls even while flirting with her, Ika had assumed that Alo liked her only as a friend. She was surprised, after several months of staged romance, when he confessed real feelings for her. (Later, she could not help but wonder if she had subconsciously planned it all along — or if Alo had somehow tricked her.) On Christmas Eve, after the evening service at the chapel, Ika coaxed Alo to their house, where he pressed his forehead to Yosef Boko's knuckles, while blushing and sneaking guilty glances at a scowling Jon, his longtime friend. As Ika made coffee, the three men formalized the courtship — though Jon made it clear that his sister's wedding would not happen until after he married Honi, so that Ika could continue caring for his grandparents until then.

Soon Alo was spending most of his free hours with Jon and Ika, helping the Hariona family build a new house. Alo and Ika always worked near each other. Jon noticed her meticulously sweeping wood shavings one day and joshed her: "Why did you sweep that corner again? Because Alo is there? Be careful you don't sweep him away!"

For years Jon and Ika had not so jokingly worried about their house falling on them, but fixing its insect-chewed pillars and rust-gnawed roof had been impossibly expensive. Then, miraculously, near the end of the rainy season, the neighborhood headman had received a home-repair grant from the national welfare agency, and he had given nearly a thousand dollars to Jon, as the Harionas had the most dilapidated domicile in the area. First, Jon had replaced the rusting metal roof with fresh sheets of galvanized tin. Then he decided to dream bigger, tearing down the entire southern wall of the house. In its place, he erected a scaffolding of green saplings, sketching out an addition that would nearly double the building's size. By the beginning of Léfa, he had constructed waist-high walls from bricks he had made himself, and fixed doorframes in them, like blueprints drawn in the air.

Jon loved wandering among the unfinished rooms, picturing his future. In this suite with wide windows overlooking the bay he would dwell with Honi. In a room with walls all the way to the ceiling, in contrast to the cubicle-like spaces they now occupied, Ika would sleep until she married Alo and moved to his house. Jon's grandparents would rest on the wraparound porch. His children would be proud of their home in a way he had never been.

Normally, Jon tried to live day to day, embodying the Lamaleran saying "Hope, but not too much." Now, however, as his reputation as Ote's bereung alep grew, until it seemed he might indeed become a lamafa, and the house took shape, he began to picture what a permanent life in Lamalera would look like. He stopped using Facebook on his cell phone, turning his password over to Honi, who had been afraid that he was flirting again with other women on it, though he had really mostly been looking at pictures of Jakartan life. No longer did he daydream about accepting the job offer from Salés's older brother. Meanwhile, he and Ika pooled their savings with a neighbor to open a kiosk out of his bedroom, selling penny candy, soy sauce packets, shampoo sachets, and loose cigarettes. People climbing the cliff stairs would shout their needs, and he or Ika would rush to serve them. Some of their modest profits they put aside to pay Mari's school fees, but much of it went right back into buying cement and nails for the house. It might be worth it, he had started feeling, to invest in a life in the tribe, especially if he became a lamafa. Not only would he get more meat for his harpoon work, but after a lifetime at the bottom of the Lamaleran hierarchy as an illegitimate orphan, he was finding that his people's newfound esteem was worth more than all the riches in the capital.

BUT THEN, IN MID-MAY, Ote informed Jon that once *Kéna Pukā* launched he would return to that téna, whose hunting had been delayed by the weaving of the new leo for the Bediona clan. Jon tried to convince Ote to stick with *VJO,* pointing out that though Ote owned

the leka of *VJO,* his position as the lamafa of *Kéna Pukā* was still probationary. But several days later, at dawn, Jon, Alo, and the rest of
VJO's crew watched as Ote and the Bediona clan motored away on
Kéna Pukā, using an outboard engine hung on scaffolding over the aft,
which allowed the téna to perform like a giant jonson.

The motor was a concession Frans had made several years earlier
after a particularly disheartening day when every clan using a mechanical aid had caught a whale, but the hunters staying true to the Ways of
the Ancestors had caught none, and several crew members had refused
to put to sea again if the ship did not modernize. Because several clans,
like the Bedionas, lacked a jonson, the tribe had allowed them to attach
motors to their téna to hunt all animals except sperm whales, though
once the Gifts of the Ancestors appeared, the engines had to be off-
loaded to another boat. Now any téna that put to sea when not hunting
kotekĕlema used this method, though people who had jonson
employed them instead, as they performed more hydrodynamically
with an engine.

Jon looked stricken by Ote's betrayal. He had thought their friendship would win him over. But to the other Lamalerans, Ote's decision
had never been in doubt: the prestige of leading a téna was greater than
that of leading a jonson. Then, in the wake of the star harpooner's departure, a pair of midshipmen also defected. The sensitivity that had lurked
in Jon since his abandonment by his parents flared, and he swore to Alo
that their catch the next day on *VJO* would exceed *Kéna Pukā*'s. He
briefly considered snatching up Ote's harpoons himself, but knew that
would be overstepping. No man could declare himself a lamafa. He had
to be invited by others to lead the ship. Instead, that evening, he set out
knocking on doors, trying to recruit a new harpooner for *VJO.* But all of
the best-known ones gently declined, citing other commitments.

In truth, Jon was not too disappointed, for when the remaining
crew — Alo and another young man who had stayed loyal — showed
up tomorrow, one of them might request that he wield the harpoons.
That night, he slept on the beach so that he would be in a prime posi-

tion to recruit a new crew at dawn. He would need three additional crewmen for a total of six—either a lamafa and two materos or, if he became the lamafa, three materos. Surely among the tribe's more than three hundred fishermen there was a trio who believed in him.

First light revealed buffed, favorable seas. Most of the men who descended to the beach were already committed to boats, but about a third of them were freelancers. Jon, Alo, and the third young man stood in front of *VJO*'s boat shed, billboarding their insufficient numbers. Jon clasped his hands behind his back, pretending to stare out to sea, though really, from behind his mirrored sunglasses, he was monitoring all the unattached hunters on the beach. The sun inched over the cliffs, yin-yanging the beach into lit and shadowed halves. The rays blasted Jon, and soon his shirtless back sparkled with sweat, but he did not retreat. Meanwhile Alo and the other steadfast crew member ducked into the shadow of the boat shed, more to avoid the stares they were getting than the heat. But the older freelancers did not approach. They wanted to work on boats with a track record of success, and with a proven lamafa. Many whalers perceived that Jon wanted to take the hâmmâlollo, but none spoke on his behalf, for while his reputation as a backup harpooner had grown, only he truly believed himself ready to lead a ship.

Ote strolled past Jon without acknowledging him, and then *Kéna Pukā* launched with Ote on the hâmmâlollo, Frans at the tiller, and a crew of mostly white-haired men, who a generation before would have been retired by their age, but who kept working because there was no one to fill their places.

To the west, as *Kanibal,* the Blikololong family jonson, motored seaward, Ben stood at the tip of its harpooner's platform, his hands clasped behind his back, his shoulders scrunched, his knees flexed— in the exact posture his father had once maintained as he rode the hâmmâlollo. Ignatius had given his youngest son his first chance to lead the jonson that day. Jon was happy for his friend, but could not help wishing he was in Ben's position.

As the sun rose higher, more jonson arrowed toward the horizon and the crowd of freelancers dwindled, until the only remaining able-bodied crew were Yosef, Ben's oldest brother, who was hampered by a half-healed foot injury that had worsened his already grumpy disposition so no one was willing to put up with him, and a pair of young bullies who always started fights on boats. Finally, Jon broke his statuesque pose and strode stiffly past the three freelancers sitting in front of the chapel, so close that it seemed impolite when they did not acknowledge him. His reflective sunglasses hid his eyes, but his mouth was a bunched smirk. Sweat slithered down his face and naked torso. Since he was not as strong as Ote or as connected as Ben, he believed his only hope for success was to strive harder than his rivals. What he did not realize was that the other hunters interpreted his bravery as arrogance.

Eventually, after ignoring Jon pass in front of them again, even Yosef and the two bullies were picked for the final téna of the day, which they helped push into the Savu Sea. Like a marooned sailor, Jon watched the fleet course toward the lavender storm clouds mushrooming over the mountainous Ata Dei Peninsula. Instead of circling back to *VJO,* where his two friends waited, he walked off the opposite end of the beach, aiming home, fury and sadness clotting his heart.

Jon felt vindicated when *Kéna Pukā* and Ote returned that evening empty-handed.

But it was not just Ote who was struggling. The whole fleet seemed stymied. Not a single whale had been sighted since Misa Léfa. Some people recalled *Praso Sapang*'s disappointing inaugural hunt, but most blamed a South Korean documentary team that had arrived at the end of April in dump trucks carrying thirty packing crates filled with IMAX-style cameras, a diving compressor and scuba gear, portable stoves, sleeping bags, and coolers of Korean food. This was not a first. The Lamalerans had hosted several film crews before, and are usually happy to welcome outsiders to their village. But the South Koreans roamed the village at all hours, barging into private ceremonies and people's kitchens without asking permission.

The Lamalerans began calling the Koreans *biawak,* a type of carrion-scavenging lizard, and not just because they wore FiveFingers shoes, with sheaths for each toe, which made them look reptilian. Jon was especially disturbed by their use of a drone at all hours, which caused him to suspect they were trying to catch him in embarrassing moments. He actually liked having foreigners take his picture, but only if he first got to coif his hair and put on his favorite Real Madrid jersey. Ignatius became so upset that he stoned a cameraman filming the launch of *Demo Sapang,* though he later sniffed it off as nothing, saying, "I didn't even draw blood." Soon Frans was grimly predicting that the whales would not come until the film crew left.

Tourists and journalists have regularly visited Lamalera, in small numbers, since the 1990s, drawn first by a documentary produced by an anthropologist who lived with the tribe and then by several subsequent films. By 2015, around two hundred foreign backpackers a year overnighted in Lamalera, primarily during Léfa, though many of them, on realizing there were no modern amenities and they might have to wait weeks to see a whale hunt, left after only a day. Meanwhile, a much larger number of Indonesian visitors, probably around two thousand, were being brought to the tribe by government-sponsored cultural tours, as part of a push to expand domestic tourism to the region, but they sieved through the barter market and the village in a few hours, never staying the night.

Some elders feared that the young would be corrupted by foreign customs, such as the visiting women who wore bikinis, but the shortness of the stays, combined with the language barrier, meant that village life continued essentially unaltered. The outsiders did not even really distort the tribe's economy, as backpackers spent only about twenty dollars a day, most of which was captured by the three homestay owners, and the government tour operators collected most of the money from the Jakartans, leaving the village administrators to take about a dollar per head. Having seen many tourists come and go, the Lamalerans tend to treat them courteously, if a bit disinterestedly, and continue on with their lives without much thought.

Except, as the Koreans' month in Lamalera wound to a close, the tribe's normal forbearance was badly frayed. Jon and other jonson captains were even refusing exorbitant offers to take the film crew out to search for the still-absent whales. The Lamalerans enjoyed more than a little schadenfreude that the Ancestors were withholding their gifts. Still, the tribe was being deprived of its most important prey, so when the film crew left, disappointed, near the beginning of June, the hunters were relieved to imagine that their luck might finally turn.

Ote's lack of success on *Kéna Pukā* continued, however, past the departure of the Koreans, so he finally returned to *VJO,* having decided that his problem lay in *Kéna Pukā*'s crew and with their eyes too aged to spot prey. During the interim, Jon had spent the lion's share of his time working on his house and gillnetting for flying fish, and he was ecstatic to be hunting big game again. The reunion did not last long. Frans soon convinced Ote to return by explaining that the harpooner's bad luck had been caused by a mistake in the weaving of the clan's new leo, and that Frans himself had rewrapped its strings, such that the rope now finished not on an even number of twists but an odd number, which symbolized possibility rather than closure. Jon was miffed at the shaman, but the older man had healed his leg, and so he reserved his real ire for Ote. Though in the future they would hunt together again as business associates, the close friendship they had enjoyed while Jon served as Ote's bereung alep was lost.

WHEN OTE ABANDONED *VJO* FOR the second time, Jon decided that, once and for all, he would nekat. He did his due diligence first, again making the rounds asking other lamafa to wield Ote's harpoons, though he already knew they would demur. Once that formality was out of the way he started dropping veiled suggestions to the members of *VJO*'s crew. "I've searched for a lamafa until my head hurt," he said. "Who's left to ask?" But when neither Alo nor the others got the hint, Jon announced that he was done pleading for a lamafa and that he would take Ote's place. He twisted arms until he got five commitments from friends and relatives to be his materos. Even though Jon was disregarding custom, the only enforcer of Lamaleran rules was social opinion, so if a person could get enough people to bend the rules, he could get away with it. But on the evening before they were set to launch, one of Jon's recruits, having second thoughts, needled him about being a kefela and reneged. It was still possible to run a jonson with a crew of five, however, even if it was not optimal, so Jon spent a restless night hoping everyone else would keep his promise. Losing even one more materos would make it impossible to launch.

On May 25, Jon woke before the roosters, pulled on his favorite Real Madrid jersey and newest jeans, and boiled coffee for himself over the wood fire. When Ika rose, she forced him to eat a few handfuls of crushed popcorn, though he was too nervous to take a full breakfast. Then he carried a jerrican of gasoline down the steps in the gray predawn light, almost skipping. *VJO* smelled like a dishwasher in its boat shed, for Jon had disassembled and soaped its every piece the previous afternoon, and double-checked the harpoon lines, spearheads, and bamboo shafts. Now he sat on the harpooner's platform and watched as the pale blue ocean settled out of the dark purple sky, like a heavier liquid separating from a lighter suspension, and waited to see if his crew would show.

A thin elder with a concave chest, a man who was considered retired but had agreed to fill out the ranks, joined Jon first. Next arrived one of Jon's neighbors, renowned more for his drinking than his seamanship. Then came Alo, along with Ika, but they did not whisper flirtatiously, only watched as the sky blushed and was feathered by clouds blowing in over the mountains of the Ata Dei Peninsula. Jon kept glancing toward the road, checking for the fourth and last materos, Bernardus "Boli" Tapoonā, a muscular man with a surprisingly shrill voice. Boli often joined *VJO* for driftnetting, and had been with Jon the day they traded their tuna to the Bajo Laut for their two large sharks.

By now other jonson and téna were already plowing the becalmed sea. As usual, Ote did not even deign to glance at Jon as he launched *Kéna Pukā*.

Finally, Boli's helium voice squeaked from the back of the boat shed. "Who's the lamafa?" he asked.

Because Boli lived on the outskirts of the village, Jon had not bothered to track him down to explain the whole situation in person but had merely sent him a text message asking him to serve on *VJO* for the day. Boli had assumed Ote was going to wield the harpoons.

"I am," Jon answered.

Boli sat down on the sand, as if a great weight had suddenly crashed onto his shoulders, and fingered his mustache.

"Salés has given me the right to wield the harpoons of this ship," Jon said. He acknowledged that he would miss sometimes. Even the great lamafa, like Ote, still failed on occasion. "But I can do this," he insisted.

Boli remained sitting, avoiding eye contact. His thoughts probably resembled many Lamalerans': Jon was still in his early twenties and it was not unusual for men to apprentice until their mid-thirties before assuming the hâmmâlollo. Boli himself was thirty-five, the son of a legendary lamafa, and had been striving as a bereung alep to earn a leka for over a decade. Logically, it was he, not Jon, who should have the opportunity to wield the harpoons on *VJO*. The only reason Jon was able to advance himself was the captainship given to him by Salés. Without any proof that Jon could bring home fish, it would be rational for Boli to seek a harpooner with a track record of success: he had two children and a pregnant wife to feed, after all.

Anticipating Boli's reaction, Jon employed the same strategy he had with his fiancée, Honi, and preempted his abandonment for a rival. "If you want to join another jonson," he told Boli, "that's not a problem. It's not my loss. Up to you." But Boli, unlike Honi, called his bluff, standing and walking off without so much as a goodbye.

Jon refused to watch him go. He felt terrible not only because he had botched his chance to become a lamafa but because the three men who had supported him might lose the opportunity to hunt that day, for every jonson but one had already put to sea.

"You can join another jonson too," Jon told his friends.

"Are you coming?" Alo asked, glancing at Jon, then Ika, and then at the final jonson, which had been pushed to the waterline.

"No, I'll stay. There's work to do onshore."

Alo and the two other crew members pulled their water bottles, snacks, and tobacco containers from *VJO* and ran to the departing motorboat. Quietly, Ika slunk away, knowing that Jon would want to be alone — if she bothered him, he was likely to respond with rage. Jon sat in the boat shed and watched the fleet chase rays leaping less than a quarter mile outside the bay, so close he could discern which lamafa were spearing prey. Finally, he turned from the Savu Sea, unscrewed the clamps holding the outboard motor to *VJO,* carried it to a locker built of discarded scraps of roofing metal, and padlocked it inside. (A few clans had built similar structures, but only Salés kept his locked.) Jon told himself he would come back later and put away the ropes and harpoons — *VJO* would be dry-docked until Léfa was finished, as far as he was concerned — but right then he did not have the heart.

AT HIS HOUSE, JON TRADED his lucky outfit for ragged work clothes. Then he blended some sand he had excavated from the beach with water and cement mix, and began shaping bricks using a wooden frame, careful to perfect their rough edges with a spatula, for he knew these bricks would be displayed atop the cliffs for everyone to see. He tried to ignore the coursing fleet, but he kept glancing at it and muttering that if he was with them, he would definitely get something.

Salés telephoned and asked Jon if he had gone to sea that morning.

"There weren't enough crew," Jon told him. "I'm just making bricks." He paused, then suggested that it would be better just to store the harpoons and the ropes in the metal shed. "I'm done harpoon hunting for the season," he said, though he would still have to gillnet to provide flying fish for Salés's sisters.

When Ika and his grandparents asked if he was annoyed about something, Jon bared his rows of square cigarette-yellowed teeth in a grimace and barked, "Who's saying 'annoyed'? I'm not 'annoyed'! That's your word!"

Just then a neighbor's rooster stalked across his rows of bricks drying in the sun, its talons scoring the still-wet concrete. Jon threw a flagstone at it with lethal force, but it leapt away just in time.

That night Jon conjured up in his cell phone a number that he had not thought about for weeks: it was for Salés's older brother, the one who had offered to hire Jon as a guard at his mansion. If the tribe sneered at his attempts to become a lamafa, he might as well strike out on his own. Really, all the elders were hypocrites. They pressured the young hunters to stay so that the whaling traditions would not be lost, but then they never let the young hunters actually do anything. Why were they surprised if young people decided to seek a richer and easier life elsewhere? It was the elders themselves who were dooming Lamalera, not him.

This time Jon did more than stare at the number on his phone screen. Unbeknownst to his family, he placed the call. To his relief, the businessman was true to his word. He would even pay for a plane ticket to Jakarta, he told Jon. The two of them agreed to finalize the details in person during a festival at the end of the hunting season, when the expat would be in Lamalera again. As the weeks passed, Jon kept his plans to leave for Jakarta secret, from his friends as well as his family, fearing "mouths as wide as buckets," as the expression went, but also afraid that the people closest to him might talk him out of his plan. Slowly he began to withdraw from the tribe, avoiding the beach and ceremonies, for though he remained in Lamalera in the flesh, in his heart he was already gone.

Chapter Ten

THE MARRIAGE

May 9, 2015–June 7, 2015

Ben — Ignatius

On the morning of May 9, Ondu, Ignatius's middle son, woke to find his eyes stinging as if scratched, with amoeba-like sunspots drifting across his vision. "Burning eyes," as it is called by the Lamalerans, comes from staring for days at the sea reflecting the sun. Already that season it had disabled Ote and many other hunters — to the extent that those affected could not even focus their gaze. The only true cure for it was rest. Ondu was forced to inform his father that he would be unable to lead *Kanibal* that day. Yosef, meanwhile, had recently sprained his ankle and had been feuding again with Ignatius besides. Technically, Ignatius still owned the leka for the jonson (as he still did for *Demo Sapang*) so it was his choice who would take up his harpoons. In the past, he had always called his cousin Stefanus Sengaji Keraf, an aging freelance lamafa who had led his téna the previous year during his failed negotiations with Ita's parents, but for the first time, he summoned Ben. In truth, he had been looking for an excuse to do this since noticing his youngest son's increased diligence about going to sea and that Stefanus had been missing some easy strikes since his arm healed crooked after being broken by a whale's tail.

With the masculine glow of repressed pride, Ben agreed. It seemed that everything had been going his way ever since Ita's parents had resigned themselves, earlier that month, to the fact that the Bliko-lolongs would never come up with the exorbitant bride price they had set, and had agreed for the two children to marry during this hunting season. Ben, Ignatius, and his crew rowed *Kanibal,* the family jonson, out over the coral gardens. Then, as one of Ben's neighbors powered up the engine, he stood tall on the hâmmâlollo, turned his back to the crew and his father—and Jon, who stared at him jealously from shore, as his attempt to assemble a crew to support his bid to become a lamafa fell apart—and faced the Savu Sea. It was nothing like standing any-where else on the boat. With his toes clutching the tip of the harpoon-er's platform, the only thing before him was the mercury ocean, the supine horizon, and the cloudless dawn. The jonson roared behind him, the wind slapped his cheeks, and it was almost as if he were fly-ing. Unconsciously, he copied the stance he had seen his father adopt hundreds of time in that spot, his fingers interlinked behind him and his brow thrust forward, except that he kept his heels down instead of balancing on the balls of his feet.

Ignatius stood directly behind Ben, as his bereung alep, holding up the wide brim of his floppy fisherman's hat to observe his son. He still maintained that he could man the hâmmâlollo, but during the last year his once trunk-like neck had thinned to a stalk, and his muscles had withered until he seemed a mannequin of the man he once had been. No matter how much care Ita and Ben lavished on him, as they ran the house that Teresea once had, the previously seemingly invinci-ble lamafa only seemed to get older and weaker. Much of his weight loss was owing to his third-to-last tooth having broken; he had to soak his rice and jerky before gingerly gumming it, and even this he found painful. Tremors afflicted his hands and legs whenever he sat for a few minutes. He would pace until exhaustion forced him down, before soon his haywire circuitry would once more spark his weary march. Often, now, he stayed behind without complaint while *Kanibal* hunted, mending nets in the morning and napping in the afternoon beneath a shady tree in his yard, in full view of passersby, for he had come to believe that his legacy was in good hands.

The previous November, when Ben's plan to work as a bemo driver in Bali had fallen through, he had taken a job transporting bricks in a pickup truck around Lewoleba. Though he was still angry at his presumptive in-laws, custom dictated that he sleep at their house, as it had required him to do even during their most combative disagreements right after Ita's first pregnancy, and one evening his father-in-law to be, Carolos Amuntoda, the namesake of Ben's son, asked if he wanted a government job. Carolos had worked as an administrative assistant in the Lembata Forestry Department for thirty-three years and promised he could get Ben a slot. In poor Indonesian communities, snagging a government position is like winning the lottery, because of the relatively high salary, security, and benefits. But Ben answered that he had to consult with his father, and returned to Lamalera to lay out for Ignatius what had happened.

"If you become an office worker," his father said, "who will take care of me? Ondu and Yosef have their own homes."

"If my father wishes it, then I will follow his wishes," Ben replied. "My feelings are the same as my father's."

As the decision sank in, Ben was surprised to discover that his words were actually true. Though he had spent a lifetime lusting after a beer-advertisement lifestyle outside of Lamalera, as he drove construction trucks around Lewoleba during the rainy season, he did not visit the tuak bars or flirt with pretty girls as he had before. Now he saw through the fantasies he had once harbored, for as his high school friends who had pursued the path of hedonism aged, most of them ended up washed-out, impoverished, and isolated. Instead of sneaking out at night to party away the weekends in Lewoleba, Ben made the arduous trip home to attend to Ita, his two children, and his father. Life in Lamalera might be materially poorer, but the people who mattered to him were there. The more disillusioned he became with the modern world, the more he wanted to invest in the traditions of the Ancestors, which, after all, had offered a fulfilling life to his father and other older relatives no matter how little money they had. He wanted to become a lamafa. Carolos, his toddler son, he began to imagine, might become a harpooner as well.

Now, as *Kanibal* escaped the lee of Lembata, the wind whistled with the power that came from having the runway of the whole Savu Sea on which to accelerate, and whitecaps mounted. Ben leaned into the blow at such an angle that it seemed to be supporting him.

Then someone shouted, "Mōku!"

Ben saw it soaring along the underside of the surface, its horns prodding the frothy waves. Because he was blocking the driver's view of the prey and the engine growled too loudly to shout over, he traced the diving, rising, and corkscrewing of the ray with his left hand, as if drawing a holograph in the air of its flight for the driver, while his right hand gripped the harpoon. Like a conductor leading his orchestra, he infused his hand signals with an interpretive quality that said as much as the signal itself—a stiff-wristed wave, for instance, indicated a sharper turn than one with a limp wrist. Abruptly, the whiptail devil ray doubled back and cut across the right side of the bow. Ben brought the harpoon down with both hands, impaling its torso. Ignatius managed the ropes. Another man boat-hooked it through the mouth. Once Ben had finished it with a duri, he looked back at Ignatius. If there was any critique to be made, his father would surely yell it. But Ignatius smiled, showing the wicket of his two remaining teeth. There could be no higher compliment from Ignatius than silence. The whole hunt, the old man's eyes had never left his son. Ben would later describe how at that moment a weight had lifted from his shoulders, a feeling so universal that the same phrase exists in Indonesian just as in English.

That evening, everyone on the beach addressed Ben as "lamafa": the old men with gruff respect; the mothers in jest, to warn him not to let the success swell his head; the young women with a flirtatious trill;

and the young men who were not yet lamafa with the awkwardness of being simultaneously jealous and happy for him. Whenever someone pointed out that all of Ignatius's boys were now lamafa and asked if he was proud, Ignatius only smiled. At dinner, he lectured Ben for missing another ray after catching the first, but Ben did not dwell on it, for he had already proven himself.

Ben led *Kanibal* for a full week, until, after a successful hunt in which he had taken a sunfish, a mōku, and a manta ray, he staggered home, his eyes red as if he were falling-down drunk and watering as if he could no longer hold back some private grief. Ita boiled the oval leaves of a damar tree, and Ben pressed a small bucketful of the spongy mess to his face, making a seal between his cheeks and the plastic with a rag, after which he inhaled the compost-smelling steam for minutes. His whole body slumped with exhaustion — only his arm remained tensed to support the medicine — and his mahogany skin flushed. Finally, he raised his face and rolled his eyes far back into his head as green tears spilled forth.

While Ben recuperated for the usual three-day healing period, Ondu returned to replace him at the prow of *Kanibal*. He stayed there until sun-blinded once more, and then Ben switched with him, and so on. Burning eyes affected whalers of every position, but lamafa were particularly vulnerable to it because it was their job to squint for prey. Thus the eyes of most lamafa, pitted and lumpy rather than smooth, were permanently threaded with burst blood vessels, which contributed to the cataracts that blinded many old men, like Yosef Boko. Ben's eyes constantly stung, and his vision, even in this short time, began to worsen, but he considered it worth it. After all, it was the mark of a lamafa.

NOT LONG BEFORE BEN BECAME a lamafa, Ita's parents had called their daughter and complained that they "had grown thin" waiting for her bride price to be settled. For the past year, the process had been stalled. Ignatius's letter of entreaty to the bishop to resolve the dispute in his favor had gone unanswered. And in the end, the default to the common-law arrangement had continued. But now, Ita's parents, the Amunto-das, told her, they had resigned themselves to accepting Ignatius's previous offer of a thousand dollars. They asked her to hand the phone over to the old lamafa. After exchanging pleasantries, Ita's father told Ignatius, "I've been thinking: it's time for our children to be married. Are you ready?"

"I am ready," Ignatius answered.

Ita was ready too. She had changed greatly since the day, seven years earlier, pregnant and in her mid-teens, that she had ridden an auto with Ben through the upright porpoise skulls lining the road into Lamalera and realized she was leaving the Indonesian middle-class world she knew. No more would she watch soap operas with her mother or go to university off-island. In a single day, she had transitioned from a modern existence to a hunter-gatherer one. She dreamed of going home, but she had been effectively disowned by her parents. After months of despair, however, she had a revelation that though this was not the life she had been expecting, it was God's plan for her. She invested herself in Lamaleran life as if she had never had any other. She learned to forage for firewood rather than using a rice cooker, to carry water from the well instead of turning on a tap, and to barter sperm whale meat rather than shopping at the supermarket. She was from the Kedang ethnic group and thus did not speak Lamaleran at the beginning, but eventually she learned to slur her *f*'s into *v*'s and force consonants through her nose, as well as all the seemingly endless words for the nuances of harpooning. She became close with Teresea, before the old woman passed, and the other Lamaleran women, and slowly her loneliness lessened. She came to love Ben, her children, and Ignatius, and little by little the village felt more like home.

By the time her father offered to formalize the marriage, she no longer hoped to return to Lewoleba: her life in Lamalera was the life God had given her to make the best of. She saw the marriage as a way to cut the last hanging thread of her past and officially become part of the tribe. As she exclaimed to the other women at the well, "I'm excited to put on the white gown!"

On behalf of Ben and Ignatius, Ondu made his ninth ambassadorial trip to the Amuntodas, this in addition to the five visits Ignatius had made over time. With an hour of chitchat, a negotiation that had spanned seven years was settled. Then Ondu returned to Lamalera and announced that the wedding would be held in about a month, on June 5. The only hiccup was that it would occur in Lewoleba, not Lamalera; in one last jab at the Blikololongs, the Amuntodas had insisted they would triple the original bride price if Ita's future in-laws held the wedding at their Spirit House. Though everyone remained somewhat tense, remembering that the nuptials had been canceled at the last minute before, a cheer spread through the Blikololong family. Ben's unsanctified relationship had never bothered him much — in fact he had secretly enjoyed his general infamy for the respect it won him among the other young men — but as the marriage approached, he found himself unexpectedly anticipating making it official. And Ignatius could hardly believe his luck: not only had his youngest son become a lamafa, but he was finally getting married as well, all within weeks of each other.

Ignatius's good fortune inclined him to be generous when, as May ticked away, he found himself in an almost perfect reversal of the situation the Amuntodas had once faced with Ita. His youngest child, Maria "Ela" Blikololong, who had been born the night he was thought lost to the satanic whale, had recently become an unwed mother, while she was over the mountains at nursing-preparatory school. When the chagrined father asked for her hand, Ignatius had to decide how much to ask for the bride price. At first, he simmered with bad thoughts: he would take the offering, whatever it was, and then demand more payment, punishing Ela's lover for derailing her life. But then he remembered Ben and Ita's misery. He could not put Ela through that. In his old age his strength might be melting, his mind dulling, and his vision fogging, but he refused to let his generosity weaken as well. He named a nominal bride price for Ela and did everything he could to accelerate her nuptials.

A WEEK BEFORE THE WEDDING, Ben and Ita traveled to Lewoleba to join the marriage class, a course run by the Catholic Church that instructed the betrothed in the practical and religious duties of marriage, which all couples desiring the diocese's blessing had to take. They were enrolled in a class that exclusively served couples who had had children out of wedlock, under the assumption they needed special moral instruction. Crammed into child-sized desks in a Sunday-school room, the two listened as priests led them through call-and-response lectures on how to use the natural rhythm method of birth control, prepare for a child's baptism, and cope with the stress of being separated if the husband had to work off-island.

On the last day of the course, a priest confessed Ben and Ita, soberly asking if they understood the gravity of their decision. Both solemnly answered yes. Afterwards, they sat side by side on the concrete stairs of the rectory, watching a goat nibble the grass below, and laughed to each other about the priest's seriousness and the class in general. They'd been together so long! Of course they knew what they were doing. Really, the whole thing felt a bit anticlimactic. Then they fell into a comfortable silence, not touching — which would have been inappropriate — but exuding a deep intimacy, their smiles mirroring each other, as if the two of them were sharing a secret only they knew.

THE EVENING BEFORE IGNATIUS LEFT for the wedding in Lewoleba, he climbed the road to the upper village, clutching a box of candles. In the gloaming, he passed his tribespeople with only a "good night," when normally he would have stopped to jaw away hours. Outside the Bliko-lolong Spirit House, he nodded at his clan chieftain, who was burning trash, but did not stop. At the front of the church, he brushed past the giant honeysuckle flowers trumpeting the scent he usually stopped to enjoy, and then navigated the graveyard by memory, for by now the day's light had failed. He knelt at a modest concrete box from which wax drippings hung like a frozen waterfall. White flowers from the frangipani branches above lay strewn across the lid. Beneath lay the bones of his grandfather and grandmother, his father and mother, his sister and brother, even two of his grandchildren, those whom Yosef Tubé had lost, each generation separated by a layer of fraying cloth.

Teresea had not yet been interred with them. For the last year, she had lain in a brick coffin at the foot of the concrete mausoleum, her flesh and soft organs melting away. When her bones were clean, they would be exhumed and placed with the Ancestors'. Ignatius built a small wind wall with loose broken bricks in front of his wife's grave, then lit three candles behind it. He stood and kissed the stone under which her toe bones lay, and then moved up the coffin, pressing his lips first to where her navel had been and then, last, against the brick above her skull. He finished by crossing himself.

With tears dripping from his red eyes, he asked Teresea why she had left him here alone. Ben wanted to marry now, he told her. "We cared for him together from the beginning," he said, "but I alone must see him wed." He told her he resented the harshness of Ita's parents. If they had not wasted years arguing, Teresea could have seen her youngest son marry. "I often think about that," Ignatius acknowledged. "How I wish you were here."

The cheap wax burned quickly, bubbling and hissing, and soon the candlesticks sloughed. He stayed until they smoldered out—and beyond that, as the brightness of the stars intensified and the locusts keened. He could not help but dream of seeing Teresea again.

So say the stories of the Ancestors: When Ignatius passes, his soul will rise from his body and walk the eastern shore of Lembata until it reaches a sea cave on the Ata Dei Peninsula. There, waiting, will be a boat that will ferry him to the Island of the Ancestors. Teresea will sing his welcome, her shiny black hair swaying around her waist as she takes the first inviting steps of the Oa dance. His three children who never reached maturity will rush to embrace his waist. He will be feasted at a table made from the keel of the previous *Demo Sapang*. By day he will hunt, choiring once more with the Ancestors the canticles that have been forgotten in this world.

But his earthly body will still reside in Lamalera. Once time has cleaned his bones, they will be exhumed, rubbed with coconut oil, and laid beside his wife's skeleton, atop his Ancestors'. Eventually, the bones of Yosef and Ondu and Ben will be stacked atop his, and then their children's atop theirs, and then their children's, onward until the very end of all things.

THE NEXT MORNING, WHEN IGNATIUS stepped from the auto onto the dirt patch of Lewoleba's bus terminal, he did not know if Ben would be there because he had no cell phone to coordinate the pickup. But there his son was, straddling a borrowed motorbike. Ben's face fell when he realized his father was crying. Yet neither had to explain his tears to the other. Ben lit a cigarette and they traded it back and forth to the nub.

The following day Ben's brothers and two dozen other Blikololongs arrived in Lewoleba on an auto they had chartered. As Yosef and Ondu led a goat down from the vehicle—the family's contribution to that day's feast—Ben's first question was what they had caught hunting recently, a competitive flare that he had rarely exhibited before becoming a lamafa. The Amuntoda family welcomed the Lamalerans with a lunch at their house. Now Ita's father speechified prettily about the very family he had been feuding with for years, staring at Ignatius with one eye while the other one roamed—like his daughter, he was lazy-eyed. Next to the plump Carolos, who looked as though he were built of spheres, the stringy muscles and driftwood features of Ignatius bespoke a vastly different life. In fact, most of the Amuntodas, whose Kedang tribe had integrated with modern Indonesia several decades before, had double chins, and all of them were rotund and pale skinned. They sported jeans and patent-leather dress shoes, high heels, or knockoff Nike sneakers. In contrast, the Lamalerans' sun-blackened skin and impressive muscles testified to the rigors of their hunter-gatherer life, and though they had dressed up, they looked itchy in their collared shirts and jungle cotton sarongs.

After the speeches, the two groups mingled in the dirt yard. Some of the Kedang men asked Ignatius, in Indonesian, if the whaling season had begun. He replied that normally the tribe would have caught several whales by that time but this year their prey was late. Then he asked Ondu to play a video on his cell phone of Ignatius harpooning a whale. The Amuntodas politely oohed and ahhed, but were not overly shocked. In Indonesia, many middle-aged people had been born into a traditional lifestyle and then later joined an industrial economy, and the fact that the two could rub against each other was a given.

Once the feast was complete, the families, along with all the other couples who had been in the marriage class, bused to the church for the rehearsal ceremony. Once everyone had memorized their places, an aged and dwarfish priest summoned each supplicant, one by one, to an office chair set beneath a life-sized crucifix whose Jesus had flashing green LEDs embedded in his hands and feet in place of nails, and whose European face tilted down as if surveilling the sinners who sat below him. Soon Ita and Ben were one of only two couples who remained. Ita's sins were quickly dispatched, and she hurried back down the aisle without looking at Ben.

Then the diminutive priest beckoned her fiancé. Ben, who was much taller than the priest, knelt and brushed the ringlets from his forehead to make space for the pater to thumb a cross with holy water. As the molten sun dripped toward the horizon, he itemized his transgressions, rubbing a hand over the breast of his black polo shirt branded by Monster Energy drink, with the logo of the three acid-green claw marks slashed above his heart. The golden rays of the lowering sun angled through the holes in the building's cinder-block walls. As the dim church grew brighter, Ben confessed the times that he had cursed out friends and family, and when he had hit others, including his wife and children. He admitted his plans of abandoning his father for Bali and his occasional desire to go drinking, to flirt with girls, and to drive a bemo. He wanted to get it all out now, to truly start anew. He felt better than he had in years. He was ready to finally become a husband.

AT 7:30 THE NEXT MORNING, in front of the steps of the concrete cathedral, Ben helped Ita out of a freshly waxed Mitsubishi pickup truck borrowed from the Amuntodas. A boutonniere of pink orchids bloomed from his suit coat, and he had managed to cover all but the very tip of a Maori-like neck tattoo with the collar of his white shirt. Ita kept a hand up to protect her hairdo against the sharp-edged wind, though hair spray had hardened the twirls of her bangs so much they barely moved. She wore a yellow dress, gold earrings, and a gold chain necklace with a jeweled pendant, which her father had just gifted her. Ben waved her ahead, then Ignatius escorted his son into the church, his expression happy and yet grave.

Inside, the priest led the congregation in chanting: "I have sinned. I have sinned. I have sinned." Then he preached from I Corinthians: "When I was a child, I spake as a child, I understood as a child, I thought as a child: but when I became a man, I put away childish things." Outside, palm fronds scissored one another in the turbulence: *snick, snick, snick.*

Ignatius had shaved his head of its usual white stubble, such that the bones propping up his skin were more apparent and it seemed as if a skull stared out of his face. He knuckled a tear off his cheek. Anger still smoldered in him that the Amuntodas had delayed the marriage until Teresea could no longer join him. How long she had waited for him back in their day!

He tried to be present here, in this moment, for Ben and Ita, but how could he when he was assaulted by memory? He thought of the end to his five-year exile on the island of Flores, when he had sent that letter to Teresea's friends, which they had snuck to her, asking his eventual bride to meet him on his return in Lewuka, a market town in the mountains above Lamalera. He did not receive an answer. Nevertheless he hiked over the jungle passes carrying a sack with all his possessions slung upon his shoulder. Evening fell on Lewuka as he made his way, heavy with doubt, to a house a friend had left empty for them. And then there she was, his Teresea, five years changed, but still *her*. They wept as they approached each other.

"What are you doing here?" Ignatius asked in disbelief.

"Are you crazy?" Teresea said. "You told me to come. I was afraid you'd be mad at me if I wasn't here." She explained that she had pretended to go bartering to escape her parents.

They kissed then. Nothing more needed to be said.

They did not kindle a torch to light the way home, for Ignatius still knew every divot and swerve of the footpath. Near the village, he let Teresea go ahead so they would not be seen together. As he watched her walk into the darkness, he had no idea if he would finally be able to convince her parents to let him marry her. But he knew that she would always wait for him, just as he would always wait for her, for however long it would take them to make their journey together. Now his only comfort was that when he reached the Isle of the Ancestors, Teresea would be there, ready to welcome him once more.

As he watched Ben twist a ring onto Ita's finger at long last, he was returned to the present and flooded with joy. Ignatius crossed his arms against the pew in front of him, pillowed his head on his forearms, and sobbed. Ondu patted his father on the back. Yosef, unable to witness his father cry, had to stand and leave the church.

After the rings were exchanged, there was no kissing or hand-holding. Ben and Ita smiled with closed lips as they posed for photographs at the altar, for the Lamalerans think only crazy people show their teeth when they smile in pictures. Then they returned in solemn exultation to the pews. Now only one more step remained before they would at last be free to forge their own course from their families.

*   *   *

BACK AT THE AMUNTODA COMPOUND, Ita and Ben were ushered onto a stage and enthroned on finely wrought wooden chairs draped with new handwoven sarongs. Behind the stage stretched a banner that declared LOVE IS SACRIFICE: BEN AND ITA. No breeze penetrated the tarpaulin tent, and soon Ita's pancake makeup had begun to melt and her hair to frizz. Perspiring non-family guests approached the dais one by one, offering the couple their congratulations, along with white envelopes fat with cash, an Indonesian custom that was beginning to be practiced in Lamalera and that was featured prominently at this wedding because the Kedang relatives expected it.

Once the newlyweds had finished receiving these guests, the two of them descended their platform to officially part from their parents. They walked toward the Amuntodas trembling, clutching handkerchiefs, their eyes downcast. As Ita approached, Carolos and his wife quaked and covered their eyes. Ita knelt in the dust in her finery, lifted her father's hand, and pressed her forehead to it. She embraced his knees, wailing with a hiccupy rhythm, keening until she ran out of air, then was silent as she refilled her lungs, after which she cried until the limit of her breath again. Her parents chorused with her, all three of them smothering their faces with handkerchiefs. From that moment onward, Ita, a child no longer, would be responsible for her own fate. She bid goodbye to each of her relatives, her grief unabated as she moved down the line, while Ben trailed her, solemnly bowing to his in-laws' knuckles, his face emotionless as each snuffling Kedang embraced him. By the end of the row, Ita's makeup had smeared and her coif unraveled. Dusty handprints chalked the back of Ben's black suit.

As Ben approached his father and the rest of his Blikololong relatives, the young man's face scrunched up in what appeared to be agony, then released into a laugh before settling back into a groove of anguish. He began to cry as if choking, gasping for air between sobs, just as Ita

236

Ita bids goodbye to her family.

had. His new bride knelt before Ignatius first. Once Ignatius had knuckled her forehead, the old man wiped snot from his nose with his wrist and then turned to his son. Unlike the Amuntodas, Ignatius did not use a handkerchief to cover his face, nor did he look away. Instead he fixed a searching gaze on his approaching child. Rather than forcing Ben to kneel, Ignatius lifted his hand to meet his son's forehead. Then Ben pressed his head on his father's shoulder and wrapped his arm around the old man's frame. Father and son clung to each other, weeping. Slowly, Ben detached himself, but Ignatius palmed his son's skull, freezing him. The glimmering stare of each reflected in the eyes of the other.

Ignatius shut his eyes and gave his son's head a soft push.

Ben drifted free.

Ignatius blesses Ben.

Once Ben and Ita had cleaned themselves up, the wedding feast began. The women of each tribe had cooked their respective cuisines in separate kitchens and laid them out on different tables. The Lamalerans and the Kedang ate on opposite sides of the courtyard, the whalers finger-scooping rice and boiled vegetables and local fish, while the Amuntodas and their relatives used forks and knives to eat prepackaged Indonesian noodles doused in bottled sauces. In the aisles, Lamaleran children, including Ben and Ita's, played lamafa, spearing trash with sticks, while Kedang children poked at their parents' cell phones.

During the meal, Carolos approached Ignatius. "Don't worry about anything with my family again," he said. Ignatius knew it was as close to an apology as he would get.

Afterwards, Ignatius and his sons talked about how much they missed Teresea, even Yosef who had not been able to watch his father cry at the church. Such self-revelation was unfamiliar, and long silences passed while they drained a jerrican of the wedding party's particularly stinky and sweet tuak. Only Yosef turned down the coconut-shell cup, with a miserable but self-congratulatory grimace: he had recently announced that he was going to stop drinking as much, and was impressing his family by following through.

Soon Ben was summoned to help with the sound system, which was emitting only a trickle of music. He investigated the dozen or so speakers stacked atop each other to form an eight-foot-tall wall, and spliced together a red-and-blue wire. Instantly a static boom of Indonesian pop music set the tarp roof undulating. The chairs and tables were cleared. Amuntodas and Blikololongs rushed onto the dirt patch and began to dance. Before long, most of the Kedang tribespeople had collapsed into chairs, prying open the buttons of their suits or fanning themselves with paper plates. The Lamalerans, however, were just getting started, stamping their bare calloused feet on the topsoil in rhythm, tearing up roots so they stood like withered grass. Sparks scattered like fireworks as they tossed their cigarettes into the air. Women spit betel onto the earth like a fertility rite, so that the whole bloodred mess stained the Lamalerans' toes, making them look wounded. Sweat rained down and turned the ground to mud.

As Ondu and his wife danced, they kept stepping back to admire each other's physique, then closing in once more to feel the other's muscles; their mutual love and attraction were widely known and admired in Lamalera. Yosef squatted, gyrating his hips, one hand scratching letters in the dirt and the other whirling an imaginary lasso in the air. His wife bird-called beside him. And all the while Ben controlled the soundboard, exulting in this chance to deejay a Lewoleba party again after so many years. A rabble of young Lamaleran men had hitchhiked to Lewoleba to crash the party, and they mobbed and howled their way into the jiving now too. Then a xylophone trilled, a gong whipped out a frenetic beat: Ben had put on a *dolo,* a modernized version of the Oa, the ancient Lamaleran courting dance. His tribespeople linked hands across the dirt dance floor. Because the tent was too small to accommodate one big dolo ring, the dancers engineered themselves into concentric spinning circles, stamping and yawping. Only a few grandmothers — and Ignatius — refrained.

The father of the groom sat outside the circle with his head bowed, remembering. Once, he and Teresea had danced the Oa, and he had scratched her lifeline with his fingernail as a promise. Now, if his wife was not dancing, he did not see the point. His work was mostly done — Ben a lamafa and married too. Ignatius had recently publicized his will: his sons and daughters would receive equal shares in the téna, *Demo Sapang,* and Ben would be entrusted with the house. Most of his old hunting buddies were already Oa-ing on the Isle of the Ancestors, Ignatius told himself, and his wife was there too, sitting patiently beneath the candelabrum of the banyan tree until her partner appeared. If she was waiting for him, then he would not dance until he was with her once more.

And yet, though it had been decades since the Oa ended, somehow a version of that dance spun on right in front of him, propelled by his children, nephews, nieces, and soon his grandchildren. Wasn't that marvelous? He felt heavy with the sense of an ending, but there were beginnings in endings too. A Blikololong cousin appeared, bug-eyed with drink, his mustache dripping with perspiration and tuak, waving a yellow scarf. The man draped the fabric over Ignatius's neck and bridled him with it, yanking him toward the center of the dolo ring. At first Ignatius waved his hands in resistance. But his cousin kept pulling. The whole tribe yelled at Ignatius to join. He let himself be led into the center of the ring. His hands fumbled at the knot of his sarong to loosen it and free his legs. Then he snatched the yellow scarf from his cousin and shook it, whooping with laughter. For a moment, all of Lamalera revolved around him.

THE PARTY TUMBLED ON INTO the morning, until the hungover Blikololongs flinched at the faint dawn. Ignatius whispered for his niece to fetch him water. Yosef used a knife to clean the grit encrusted beneath his fingernails from writing in the dirt while he danced. The coils of

Ben's mullet had lost their spring. And still the stereo speakers, blown out hours earlier, croaked their tinny Indo pop.

As Ben nibbled rice cakes and bananas, Carolos asked him if he really wanted to work himself to death as a fisherman. "If you stay in Lewoleba," his new father-in-law said, "I'll get you a job in an office with air-conditioning." Or he could drive a bus for government workers. Either way, it would be less work, safer work, and a higher salary, Carolos promised.

Ben thanked him, but said that he wanted to return home. Along with Ondu and Yosef, it was his responsibility to feed his father. If he needed to earn money, he said, he might drive a truck for a few months in Lewoleba, but his wife and children would remain in Lamalera.

Ita was still wearing the golden earrings and necklace her father had given her for the wedding when she and Ben climbed into the auto a short time later. During the weeks that followed, she did not take them off — not while axing firewood, not while butchering mako sharks, and not while scrubbing bloody laundry with a stone and a wooden board. Their luster dimmed as they became nicked and battered, though she polished them until they regained some of their shine. But eventually, when it became clear that they would be destroyed if she wore them constantly, she put them away. She returned only once that year to Lewoleba, for there was just too much work to do at home, and her parents never visited her in Lamalera, disdaining its dirt and lack of electricity. But when she did manage to sneak away for three days at her childhood home, she put on her jewelry again, briefly.

Chapter Eleven

IN THE MIDDLE OF THE TYPHOON OF LIFE

June 13, 2015–September 10, 2015

Jon

As the weeks of Léfa passed, and Jon mulled over his secret plan to leave for Jakarta and the night-watchman job at the mansion of Salés's older brother, he avoided the hunt. Occasionally, he might crew for a jonson other than *VJO,* but mostly he gillnetted alone in his sampan and worked on his half-renovated house. He was biding his time until August, when Salés's older brother would return to the tribe for a special festival, and they would arrange Jon's departure. It would be a clean break with Lamalera and, perhaps, with Honi, though he waffled on that point, depending on whether they were arguing or not. While plucking flying fish from his nets, Jon dreamed of taking cute girls to bars and visiting near mythical movie theaters, never having fully accepted Honi's insistence that big-city living was not as nice as it appeared on TV.

Sure, at first it would be lonely not knowing anyone in the metropolis, especially after living his whole life in the bosom of the tribe, but part of him yearned for solitude. He wanted to live for himself. He was tired of supporting other people—whether his sisters and grandparents or his tribesmen. His and Ika's kiosk had gone bankrupt after giving away too many goods on credit, for the Ancestors had directed their descendants never to turn away any Lamaleran asking for help. Every afternoon, when he pulled his sampan ashore, the men who had spent all day napping in the boat sheds would announce their families were hungry, and he would let them raid his buckets, until there was barely enough left for his own dependents. At times like this, he would wonder if the Ways of the Ancestors were helping or hindering him.

The previous month Jon had strained his lumbar hauling in nets. The pain was such that even Frans's ministrations had not helped, and one Saturday in mid-June, he awoke in too much discomfort to put to sea. All day, he lay on his bamboo pallet, thinking about how he always slaved for everyone, but no one helped him. He tried calling Honi, but she did not pick up. Though he knew that her job as a live-in maid approached domestic slavery, as she worked from dawn to dusk, had only two Sundays off a month, and was not even allowed to leave the grounds of her employer's four-story mansion without permission, at moments like this it was hard not to fantasize that she was living a version of his Jakarta dreams. Meanwhile, Honi was idealizing the farming life back in her native village. Their mutual resentment over the other's supposedly idyllic existence had strained a relationship whose foundation had been shaky to begin with: little more than a week's in-person romance and nearly two years of long-distance effort. Jon missed Honi, and he knew that she missed him, but because their longing had become tainted with frustration, he was never quite sure if she was the source of his unhappiness or the cure for it. Still, he kept ringing her, and grew increasingly agitated when she did not answer.

In the late afternoon, hearing Ika thresh rice in the kitchen, Jon yelled for her to get him a glass of water. No response. He called again. The rattle of the unhusked grains stopped, but she remained silent. They had already fought that morning when Jon ordered her to the well because their jerricans were empty. "The well's dry anyway," she had snapped, "so what's the point?" It was mostly true: the dry season had reduced its usually clear water to silty dregs. And she, like Jon, was overwhelmed by work and feeling underappreciated. But in the end, she had done his bidding.

Jon called a third time, his voice low with anger, and Ika finally descended from the kitchen with a glass of murky water. When she got to his pallet, Jon had a cigarette cocked in his lips. "Get me a lighter too," he said.

Without answering, Ika presented him with the dirty drink. She looked totally different than she had a few months earlier. The plumpness of her cheeks had deflated to reveal cliffs of cheekbones, and exhaustion had puffed up the bags under her eyes. The laughter that had always buoyed her had been usurped by a grimness. Recently, instead of bowing to Jon's bad humor, she had been arguing back. As life had grown tougher with Jon, her relationship with Alo had been deepening, until it seemed they spent every moment together, cackling at secret jokes, the only time she seemed to laugh anymore. Alo had made himself a welcome part of the family, selflessly helping to split firewood or butcher fish after laboring all day on village construction projects or at sea. His silliness was often the only thing lightening the otherwise dark mood in the house. But the couple's concern for propriety had been slipping: it was not unusual for Alo to stay at their house until late into the night. "Ika wants to get married fast," many of the elders said, with a knowing sneer, an insinuation that she and Alo were sleeping together. A wedding to Alo would mean that she would have her own house and family: Jon and her grandparents would be each other's responsibility rather than hers.

Jon pretended not to see the water. "Get me a lighter," he repeated.

Ika pushed the cup toward his face.

Jon snatched it from her and hurled it over the terrace. Glass tinkled on the rocks below.

Ika retreated to the kitchen. The half-finished walls barely separated the house's inhabitants from the elements, let alone each other, and Jon could clearly hear the plangent croon that followed:

Tenang-tenang mendayung,	Row calmly, row tranquilly,
Didalam ombak selepas pantai.	As the waves are loosed upon the shore.
Tenang-tenang merenung,	Daydream calmly, daydream tranquilly,
Ditengah taufan hidup yang ramai,	In the middle of the typhoon of life,
Ditengah taufan hidup yang ramai.	In the middle of the typhoon of life.
Bila terbawa arus didalam doa.	If you are swept away by the currents: Pray.
Laut terenang.	You can swim this ocean.
Sabda penguat doa.	Let the Word brace you.
Resapkanlah didasar hatimu	Let it soak into the depths of your heart
Sedalam laut medan hidupmu.	And your life will be as deep and wide as the ocean.

Jon gave no indication that he heard the song. Instead he called down from the terraces to a girl walking home on the road below to bring him a bottle of water, the kind kept stocked for the occasional tourists, from the rival kiosk he and Ika had once competed against. When the girl did, he paid her a ten-thousand rupiah note, and drank the extravagant waste, as Ika started the hymn over, *In the middle of the typhoon of life*...

That evening Jon refused to eat the rice and corn Ika had cooked, the ultimate sign of opprobrium in Lamalera. His grandparents tried to convince him to join their meal, but both had become fully blinded by cataracts, and now that they were totally dependent on Jon, he rarely listened to their directions anymore. Instead, he dined at his friend Narek's home. Just as he was about to return home to sleep, he received a call from Salés. His patron had returned from his travels, and he ordered Jon to make the trek to his dwelling, in one of Lower

Lamalera's outlying settlements. As Jon descended to the main road, he passed two teenage girls huddled beneath a tamarind tree. One girl was comforting her weeping friend. That afternoon the despondent one had learned that she had failed the admissions test to high school in Lewoleba, meaning she would likely spend the rest of her life in Lamalera. Her friend, who had passed the same test, would be leaving.

AT SALÉS'S TWO-STORY CONCRETE-WALLED HOUSE — a structure the businessman had actually made more modest than his means allowed, so as not to offend his tribesmen, but which still looked like a mansion compared to the single-story brick homes around it — Jon's boss asked for help in organizing a festival to honor his eldest brother Peter's twenty-fifth anniversary as a Catholic priest. This was the celebration for which his second-eldest brother, Josef, Jon's prospective employer, would be returning to Lamalera. Jon was tasked with organizing a group of young men to roll thousands of palm-leaf cigarettes to distribute during the merrymaking. Then Salés swore him to secrecy about an announcement he would make at the celebration: that August, he planned to open a fish-processing company in Lewoleba. The business would buy tuna and marlin from the fishermen of Lembata and export the fish. Salés could hardly contain himself at the achievement of this decadelong quest.

While Salés worked as a manager at a water-bottling company in Jakarta during his mid-twenties, after graduating seminary but failing to receive a pastorship, the descendant of the Lika Telo had observed the thousands of dollars being paid at the docks for the very same tuna that his tribe turned into jerky every year. That realization had inspired him to return home, in 2003, to enrich both himself and his people. He built *VJO* and was the first to experiment with drift nets, proving with the rich hauls he and Jon brought in that a viable fishery existed. But his ambitions went beyond running a single craft. Four years later, when he was elected mayor, he enticed government officials and businessmen to travel all the way from Jakarta to Lamalera—a journey of more than a thousand miles, which at the time took around four days by plane and ferry—to see the bounty the tribe was wasting. Everyone agreed that a treasure trove was being squandered, but investors could not figure out a way to monetize the catch: there was no ice to be had in Lamalera, nor was there sufficient electricity to run an ice machine if one could be procured, for all the generators in the region were too small to meet such power requirements. The fish would spoil even before it reached Lewoleba, which was a dead end itself, without an efficient way to ship tuna onward.

Even after stepping down as mayor after a year, Salés continued meeting with investors and government officials during trips to Kupang and Jakarta. Then, in 2014, Jokowi won the presidency partly by promising huge investments in eastern Indonesia, and outsider businessmen immediately began searching for local partners to cash in on the coming mining and fishing booms. Salés was happy to help. At the beginning of May 2015, Salés once more ushered Jakartan officials along the beach as the jonson unloaded their catch. Then the delegation and the current mayor took less than five minutes to agree to support Salés's business. That night, Salés feasted the dignitaries on whale stew and gifted them with rings carved from orca teeth.

By the time Salés summoned Jon to tell him of these developments, the construction of an ice-making plant and an international-standard fish-processing factory had almost been completed under his supervision, and he had already pre-hired twenty-one employees, none of them Lamaleran because he wanted workers with at least a high school education. There had been no choice but to erect the facilities near Lewoleba because it would have been impossible to truck all the building materials over the mountains, so he had also outfitted a dump truck with a huge icebox to transport the fish from Lamalera and other rural fishing villages to the city. On trips out, the vehicle would carry a mountain of ice, which it would then swap for fish in the villages, so that the inhabitants could preserve their new catch in specially built concrete bunkers until the next run, though it retained a bit of ice for the return trip to keep its load unspoiled. Meanwhile, in western Indonesia, he was having a thousand-ton freighter built to ferry the processed fish onward to Jakarta. His goal was to have everything ready in the next few months, so that when Léfa ended and the Lamalerans started driftnetting again, he could purchase their catch. He was finally harnessing the power of global capitalism that he had long marveled at.

Salés was aware, of course, that his fishing business would encourage the tribe to give up harpoon hunting and that the cash he paid them would speed the end of Lamalera's barter economy. But to close friends, he advanced a rosy prophecy. In a decade, he predicted, every family in Lamalera would own a car. The whalers would primarily be employed in drift-net fishing — the prohibition on their doing so during Léfa having been rescinded — and the tribe would be getting rich off his payments for their fish. With the constant electricity that was bound to be available by then, many tourists would come to stay in an international-class hotel built at the beach, and in time his tribesmen might even prefer guiding them on tours to hunting. Yes, many of the Ways of the Ancestors would inevitably be lost, but he felt that as long as the tribe still hallooed the baleo and hunted sperm whales with téna, the core of what it meant to be Lamaleran would endure. It was not necessary for their entire existence to be contingent on the capriciousness of the chase. Besides, modernity was no longer something they could keep at bay. It would soon overtake the tribe whether he opened this business or not. He was merely preventing the tribe from being left behind, or, worse, being taken advantage of by someone with less honorable intentions. They could surf the tsunami of change, like he was doing, or they could be drowned by it.

However, while Salés shared these plans with Jon in exchange for his silence, he knew it was best to keep the rest of his thoughts to himself, at least until the factory was up and running. After all, it was no secret that he had not relinquished his brief mayoralty of his own accord. The last time he had tried to modernize the tribe, seven years earlier, the effort had ended in disaster, with him stripped of his position and run out of town by death threats. But Salés had faith that this time the tribe would finally be ready to embrace the outside world.

As June slouched into July and then August, it seemed that the whole tribe was stuck waiting. Jon, still ostensibly mad at Ika for failing to honor him, but really frustrated with his whole life, supped at Narek's and bided his time until he could go to Jakarta. Salés impatiently monitored the slow completion of his fish-processing factory. Ika, desperate to be relieved of Jon and her grandparents, held her breath for Alo to ask his clan chief to begin the series of rituals that would lead to their marriage, even though they had promised Jon to wait until after Honi returned. At the same time, she worried that a pregnancy from their trysts might force the issue. She wanted the marriage to be his desire and not his obligation. And though everyone anxiously anticipated the arrival of the sperm whales, for no spouts had yet been sighted during Léfa, Ben and Ignatius felt the absence most keenly, for both father and son hoped that Ben, as a newly minted lamafa, might take a whale. When Frans, at the tribe's behest, asked the Wujons to summon the whales again, the Lords of the Land demanded the surrendering of their outboard motors, an injunction that was rebuffed. The Lamalerans did not starve, as they might have in days of old, but many grew gaunt as their diets were reduced mainly to flying fish, the needlelike ribs of which constantly jammed between their teeth. Men crowbarred giant barnacles off tidal rocks and slurped the navel of pink flesh right out of the shell.

In mid-August, the celebration that Salés and Jon had been waiting for arrived, briefly relieving the tensions permeating the tribe. A banner honoring Father Peter Bataona's twenty-fifth anniversary as a Catholic priest was hung above the piled orca skulls at the entrance to the village, and strangely familiar people, dressed in Benetton hoodies and Zara jeans, walked beneath it, chattering in Bahasa, embarrassed about how much Lamaleran they had forgotten. A total of nine pigs were slaughtered for the feast. Then three hours of speeches were endured, interrupted only by a group of old men in the back of the crowd arguing loudly about why the whales were not appearing. When the chairs were cleared, people began kicking up sand in the three dolo rings with an exuberance so contagious that even visiting nuns joined in, tanning the hems of their white robes with soil. On the sidelines of the dance, Josef, Salés's businessman brother, fell into deep conversation with Jon about the young man's potential move to Jakarta.

But instead of announcing his business or enjoying the party, Salés strapped on a dust mask and zipped back toward Lewoleba on his motorbike. The stated reason for his early departure was that the next day, August 17 — Indonesian Independence Day and the anniversary of the end of the Wulandoni barter market — his incomplete fish-processing factory in Lewoleba would host a celebration attended by three hundred people, including the governor of the province, meant to usher in a new economic era for Lembata. In truth, however, the building was not yet finished and the business was weeks away from launching, an embarrassment he was not keen to discuss. But there was also a second, perhaps more important, reason for Salés's brief stay and early departure. Despite the large house he maintained in the village, ever since his ouster from the mayoralty he had tried to spend as few nights as possible there, instead staying in a villa in Lewoleba whenever he was back on the island. His swift fall from grace had been no ordinary small-town politician's descent. In fact, his tribespeople had attempted to murder him with sorcery.

AT FIRST, GIVEN SALÉS's SUCCESS with the drift nets and his Lika Telo blood, he had seemed the perfect candidate to guide the tribe through these new days of balancing tradition and innovation. But soon representatives of the Indonesian branch of the World Wildlife Fund (WWF) opened an office in Lewoleba and began visiting the tribe as part of an effort by a consortium of NGOs to have the entire region designated a marine national park. Based on a contentious experience with Greenpeace about two decades earlier, the tribe feared that WWF also sought to end the hunt, though it promised it wanted only to help the Lamalerans establish tuna fishing and ecotourism businesses such as whale watching. When Salés learned that WWF and the other NGOs had the backing of the Indonesian government, he decided to encourage his people to cooperate with them to enrich the village.

The trouble began when, in February 2009, a newspaper quoted a government official contradicting WWF by saying that the reserve was being created to protect sperm whales from the Lamalerans. Suddenly, the developmental aid seemed merely a tactic to trick the tribe into replacing whale hunting with whale watching. The tribe sailed a fleet of téna to Lewoleba, pushed one of the ships through the streets on log rollers to the island's legislative center, and protested to the governor. Lamalerans living abroad, including some, like Salés's older brother, who had become successful politicians or businessmen, waged a pro-whaling publicity campaign in the national media. With Salés as intermediary, WWF held a meeting with the Lamalerans in Kupang to reiterate that, notwithstanding the quote in the newspaper, the marine reserve would not limit the Lamalerans' hunting as long as whale populations remained stable. When the Lamalerans remained unconvinced, WWF dispatched a PR team to Lamalera, but as their trucks approached the village, they were blocked by about fifty whalers, who tore open the doors of the vehicles, screamed at the conservationists to leave, and declared they would die before giving up whaling. The organization soon closed its office in Lewoleba, and when the Savu Sea Marine Protected Area formally became the largest such reserve in Indonesia several months later, its boundaries detoured around Lamalera.

Internal WWF documents that were later uncovered showed that the Lamalerans were correct that the organization had not been forthright. Although WWF's end goal was indeed to enrich the Lamalerans and protect their environment, they had also seen whale watching and other development projects as a way to phase out harpoon hunting. As WWF's head of the Lewoleba office emailed other conservationists, "What the people of Lamalera need is improvement to their economy and restrictions on whaling so that their culture can still exist and be diverted for ecotourism." He concluded, "This is what WWF is doing in the region!"

Soon after the WWF representatives had been driven off, the Lamalerans who had collaborated with the NGO, including Salés, were lined up in front of the whole tribe at the Blikololong Spirit House. In Javanese-accented Lamaleran, Salés apologized for welcoming the outsiders, explaining that he had not known their true intentions. But the tribe was not satisfied.

The Lika Telo sent an envoy to a distant volcano on Lembata to purchase a sheep from the flocks tended there by a herding people. A Lamaleran shaman then sacrificed the animal to perform a deadlier version of the Curse of the Black Goat — calling on the Ancestors to visit misfortune and sickness unto death on the quislings — for in Lamaleran sorcery the most powerful fuel for magic, even more than a goat, is a sheep. To escape his people's wrath, Salés resigned as mayor and moved to Lewoleba, where he suffered a nervous breakdown and other health problems, which the Lamalerans attributed to their voodoo. The less wealthy men and women who had done low-level administrative jobs for WWF in the village could not afford to leave and endured being ostracized for years, as their tribespeople avoided talking to them and inviting them to rituals. Time eventually allowed the transgressors to rejoin the community. But they were never totally forgiven: when one of the cursed men died six years later of what was likely a heart attack, some people whispered that the Curse of the Sheep was working.

Even once Salés recovered from his breakdown, he never felt truly at home in Lamalera. He continued to mourn the conflict between the whalers and the conservationists because he suspected that the extra protections provided by a marine park could have curtailed nearby dynamite fishing and illegal long-lining, and that the developmental aid might have improved people's lives. It would have been to everyone's profit, he was sure, if they could have found a way to work together. But he had come to see that the two sides' worldviews were just too different to be reconciled and that the clash between them would continue until the hunt ended or the foreigners gave up.

The confrontation between the Lamalerans and the conservationists was not unique, as the creation of most of the earth's six thousand national parks has been accomplished by curtailing indigenous tribes' traditional livelihoods or by forcing them from those territories — usually so their lands can generate ecotourism revenue, the majority of which often ends up in the pockets of local officials and businessmen, and not with the displaced tribes. As the UN special rapporteur on the rights of indigenous peoples says, "The world's most vulnerable people are paying the price for today's conservation."

At the heart of this conflict are contradictory ways of looking at how natural resources should be utilized. For the Lamalerans, the very idea of conservation is foreign: after all, if whales are gifts from the Ancestors, the only way to exhaust them is by using up the spirits' goodwill, and to decline to hunt a proffered animal is to insult their forebears. Besides, the Lamalerans feel, their hunt has been sustainable for centuries — it is primarily pollution, overfishing, and climate change caused by the conservationists' very own societies that are damaging their ecosystem. Why are the conservationists targeting them rather than more influential bad actors? Furthermore, the Lamalerans are not wrong to fear that ending the hunt could destroy them. History has shown time and again that depriving indigenous people of their livelihoods often leads directly to their end, as they lose their identities within a generation. After all, who are whalers who do not whale?

Conservationists in turn argue that the Lamalerans and other indigenous people are harvesting resources at an accelerated pace with the help of new tools like drift nets and outboard motors (or chain saws and guns in the case of jungle-dwelling tribes) and thereby causing significant ecological damage. Now that foragers have more modern ways to survive, some conservationists suggest, they should try those rather than impacting fragile ecosystems. Of course, the belief that usually goes unstated in all of this is that for many activists it is immoral to hunt whales, with their human-like brains, even if doing so is essential for sustaining an ancient culture.

It is a conflict that can appear intractable, or one that will inevitably be resolved by traditional cultures being overwhelmed by globalization. But analyses by the World Bank and others have shown that when indigenous peoples partner with governments to manage their territories, they protect them more efficiently and cost-effectively than outsiders can. Such partnerships can strengthen fragile ecosystems and traditional cultures. But that takes buy-in from both sides. And after the Lamalerans' experience with WWF, Western-style conservation is still spoken of in the tribe with anger, fear, and disgust.

NOT LONG AFTER SALÉS LEFT EARLY from his brother's festival, Jon stumbled out of the dolo, brushing dust from a collared shirt embroidered across the back with a skull. As he wound his way through the crowd, he was pulled aside by an old man who possessed the stunted frame of someone who had endured starvation as a child but who now had the belly of a rich man. It was Josef, Salés's older brother.

"Why aren't you in Jakarta yet?" Josef joked. He told Jon that his only job would be to guard the mansion. He would not have to do women's work like cleaning—a maid did that.

But Jon admitted that he was actually not quite ready to move to the capital. He asked if it would be possible to start work at the beginning of the monsoon season, explaining that he needed the extra time to arrange a few things for his family. Josef said it would not be a problem.

Even though Jon was still furious at Ika—and at his grandparents for siding with her — he had decided to stockpile dried fish to tide his family over until he could start sending wages from Jakarta. He also wanted to finish construction of the house as a parting gift. The progress he had made on it was the one positive consequence of the lean whaling season. Because even the gillnetting had been poor, Jon spent most days at home, pounding out concrete bricks one week and then mortaring them to the foundation the next, so that the walls grew as if in stop-motion. Meanwhile, bit by bit, he jigsawed the pieces of the roof together.

Having alienated his friends with his black moods, Jon worked all alone now. Only his grandfather kept trying to assist. Still bearing a grudge over the row with Ika, Jon had spoken roughly to him at first, letting him know that with his sight hemmed in by cataracts he was more worry than help. But Yosef Boko seemed oblivious to his grandson's displeasure. He spent hours sorting different lengths of nails by feel or laboring to carry one brick at a time to Jon, shuffling his feet to avoid tripping over anything, the skin hanging from his skeletal arms like a loose sweatshirt. In the end, Jon gave up trying to shoo his grandfather away, for he knew the septuagenarian was only following to the end the Ancestors' prime directive for a Lamaleran man: to provide food and shelter.

When Yosef Boko had courted Grandmother Fransiska, almost five decades ago, the town's priest had required couples to own a house before he would marry them. But since every inch of flat land had already been claimed, Yosef Boko had to conjure a new space. He spent his Sundays stacking large stones at the base of the loose dirt cliffs to make a sixty-foot-long retaining wall, which he then backfilled with earth. Over the course of a year, he formed a ziggurat with three more terraces on top of the first, creating about five hundred square feet of Lamalera for himself and his bride-to-be. He and Grandmother Fransiska wove a bamboo house on it, alternating dark and light slats to design motifs of whales into its walls. Beneath its grass thatch they had one son and two daughters, the eldest of whom was Jon's mother.

Eventually, in the late 1980s, the house was updated with brick and concrete, and it was in this structure Jon was born.

When Jon was a teenager, he had badgered Yosef Boko into retirement, afraid that people would say he could not support the family on his own. Now, though, after he had gotten in his digs about Yosef Boko's eyesight, he held his tongue, for he saw that his grandfather was trying to mitigate his shame at having to be cared for. Where once the taciturn hunter had ruled his family with drill-sergeant imperiousness, the same way he bossed around his crews at sea, in his dotage he had become voluble. He chattered as if to himself while they worked, though he knew that Jon was listening. To Jon's surprise, his grandfather apologized for his younger, cruder self. He admitted that he had been wrong to impede Lusia's marriage to Jon's father. He regretted criticizing his son, Jon's uncle, for his shaky seamanship until the young man fled to Kupang, where he died without ever seeing his father again. There were so many things that had seemed to be what the Ancestors wanted at the time, but now he thought they were mistakes. How grateful he was for Ika and Jon's nurturing. He found an almost divine grace in it, as if God was strengthening his grandchildren to transcend the failures of their forebears by providing better care than they had ever been given. How he wished there was more he could do than carry one handmade fragment of home at a time to Jon. And yet, he comforted himself, he had built the land the new house would stand on. He would always be their foundation.

Through all his grandfather's talking, Jon never answered him because he did not know how to respond to the raw emotions raised by the old man's reckoning with his life. He had learned from his stints working in Lewoleba that no matter how much his family frustrated him, the moment he left he would desperately miss them. Back then, his grandparents would order Ika to call him and in tears they would ask for the date of his return, even though often the three of them could barely carry on a civil conversation. He felt trapped by the paradox that if he stayed in Lamalera, he would fight with Ika and his grandparents, but if he went to Jakarta, he would yearn for them. Above all, he understood that, given his grandparents' failing health, to leave would mean to say goodbye to them forever. Grandmother Fransiska was doing even worse than Yosef Boko, spending all day triple-cocooned in sarongs despite the equatorial heat, shivering with malarial chills, occasionally hallucinating.

Jon's plan to stockpile food for them, however, was not succeeding. Still not a single Gift of the Ancestors had been sighted. Because the whaling and gillnetting had been so bad during that Léfa, driftnetting began early, with Jon and many other Lamalerans breaking the moratorium in August, more than a month before what should have been the official end, in late September. As if in punishment, the Ancestors did not favor them with bountiful catches, and Jon drove himself all the harder: driftnetting at night, butchering the meager catch in the morning, then delivering Salés's portion to his sisters before napping briefly with blood and scales pasted to him, then making more bricks for the house throughout the afternoon, and finally piloting *VJO* toward the sunset to begin it all again. His lower back ached constantly.

He tried not to dwell too much on the future. A relentless focus on the present was a coping mechanism he had learned over his years. If he worried too much about how many fish he needed to net that night or how many days remained until he left for Jakarta, the worry sapped his energy. *There is no use in thinking right now,* he repeated to himself like a mantra, *only working.* He seemed uncharacteristically subdued, his strut having vanished, as if he had at last given up on proving himself a true Lamaleran and not a kefela. For the first time he was willing to acknowledge that he had flouted propriety by pushing to become a lamafa earlier that year. Yet his rage was ever more coiled. He got in two fistfights with other young men, and he began having long verbal brawls over the telephone with Honi. Behind his back the elders tut-tutted that the promise he had shown early in the hunting season was being lost. Whatever his private feelings, however, publicly Jon said he did not care that he was no longer harpoon hunting.

And yet despite his constant threats to put *VJO*'s harpoons into storage, Jon never had. Even after a harpoon head was stolen, its empty leash loop cast on the deck like a taunt, Jon did not store away the weapons for the season. Instead, he kept the harpoon heads atop their piles of ropes in the prow, resembling compass arrows pointing out to sea, ready to launch at a moment's notice. And once driftnetting resumed, and he began launching the jonson again, he always shaded his eyes with a hand and surveilled the horizon as he steered, waiting for his luck to finally turn.

EARLY ONE MORNING NEAR THE end of August, the Lamalerans finally shouted, *Baleo! Baleo!* for the first time in about five months. After being dragged out by waddling jonson freighted with drift nets, the fleet of téna harried a breeding school of whales along the sea cliffs while the women spectated from the heights. One whale, on being attacked, hurled its many tons clear of the water and then slammed down, creating a mini tsunami that pushed the assailants back. As a few of the older and more seasoned harpooners had recently retired, several téna were being led by new lamafa, who drove their crews recklessly, to the point that ships kept inadvertently ramming one another, with the result that the fleet managed to land only a single juvenile kotekělema. The rest escaped by submarining underneath the cordon the hunters had established. But after so many months bereft, the whalers were happy to have at least a slight blessing from the Ancestors.

Jon had joined *Demo Sapang* on the hunt, but the Blikololongs' téna was not among the four that had taken the whale, meaning he shared in Ignatius and Ben's disappointment at coming home empty-handed. (*Boli Sapang,* the Harionas' téna, had not launched that year because of a dispute between Krispin, the clan chieftain, and the owner of the jonson that towed it.) Frans and *Kéna Pukā* were similarly unlucky. So as the whale was butchered, all four men were forced to wait to see if they would be fed by the běfãnã, the gift portions.

This year, perhaps exacerbated by the poor harpoon-hunting season, there had been widespread complaints about unfair distribution of meat — and creeping changes to the system of umã and bĕfãnã. Many elders blamed the jonson. While organized into corporations just like téna, jonson are generally not owned by a whole clan. Instead, their umã are held privately, usually by five or six men wealthy enough to pool their money to buy an outboard engine for several thousand dollars. Thus, unlike with téna, the benefits of jonson often accrue to a small rich group rather than to everyone. As jonson expeditions had gradually replaced téna ones during the 2000s, the families who relied solely on téna umã had suffered. Even when whales were caught, there was less meat to go around, because the jonson that had towed the victorious téna would claim two umã, one for the tow and one for the gas.

Ultimately, it was the poorest Lamalerans who were most hurt by the diminishment of the communal téna benefits. That August afternoon, many of the families who had received an umã found themselves approached by old women bearing plates of corn kernels or fried dough balls. This was the *pafã lama,* in which women traded token offerings for a load of meat — an unequal exchange that was effectively charity. In the Days of the Ancestors, only a few women had resorted to the pafã lama, but in recent years the practice had grown more common, as many people who had counted on the umã no longer found it reliable. And with everyone's larders so bare and needing whale meat, no one knew if they would be lucky enough to receive a bĕfãnã.

Jon, however, was lucky enough to receive a bĕfãnã platter of whale steaks and organs from a second cousin, which he shared with Ika and his grandparents. Though no apologies had been exchanged on either side, he was now eating meals again with them, which he insisted was because it was impractical to make others cook for him, though in reality he had simply missed his family. He knifed his grandparents' steak into tiny gummable portions but ate his whole, gnawing through the vascular tubes threading the gamy seared meat, which tasted like beef that had been brining for years, pausing his chewing only to declare that surely now the Ancestors would favor them with more prey.

The next dawn, Ika queued with the tribe's other women as the Lords of the Land sawed into the head of the whale, which had been left whole the previous day, though the body had been stripped to the spine. As an almond-scented yellow liquid gushed forth from the punctures in the blubber, Ika filled her bucket. This spermaceti oil was the very thing that had enticed nineteenth-century European and American whalers on years-long voyages around the world, for when burned it provided a smokeless steady light that had been the best illumination before electricity — a use Lamalerans still put it to, though they more often employ it for cooking and medicinal remedies. After the head had been drained and the blubber and flesh chiseled away, the Wujons piled the naked skull with the remnants of other whales at the end of the beach to summon more Gifts of the Ancestors.

But after the landing of one more small whale, the next two times the fleet launched in pursuit of distant spouts, the whales disappeared before the Lamalerans had an opportunity to strike. Hunters squinted at the horizon through their binoculars until the end of the dry season, but their luck had ended. The tribe's total count for the year would be just six whales.

WHEREAS THE PREVIOUS MONTHS OF Jon's life had felt like a loop, suddenly time's spiral seemed hammered into a line, with unprecedented happenings almost monthly. The Ministry of Fisheries counted all the tribe's vessels and whalers, and soon the téna were listed alongside long-liners in a national database. The wharf of the Wulandoni Port was finally completed, but the still-unresolved conflict between the Nualela and the Luki meant the passenger terminal remained to be built, and the opening date had been pushed back to the next year. Meanwhile, to take advantage of the new asphalt on the track over the mountain, the Scrooge of Lamalera, an old relative of Frans's, imported a fifteen-seat Mitsubishi van with air-conditioning to compete with the auto, and paid a shaman to baptize his "téna of the road" by decapitating a rooster and smearing the white vehicle with its blood.

As the dry eastern winds of Léfa gave way to the wet western winds of the monsoon season, Jon could have finally left for Jakarta: he had saved up enough flying fish that his family could survive until he remitted a portion of his salary. And yet when Salés's older brother called, Jon asked for just a little more time to finish the house for his family. Although the eastern wall had not yet quite reached the roof, the rest of the structure was in good shape. But Jon was no longer working with the feverish intensity he once had; what were meant as guide wires had long ago begun to be used as clotheslines. Sometimes it seemed that he was not even trying to finish, only futzing around in order to delay making a decision.

A number of recent developments argued for him to stay home. He had yet to talk with his family about his plan to go to Jakarta, but when he had finally told Honi, she had thrown a crying jag, threatening to end the engagement. At first, he had thought she was afraid he would find a new girlfriend there, and had been disappointed, for things had been going well lately, and he had hoped she would no longer question his loyalty. But when he reiterated his undying love for her, she surprised him by explaining that it eased her homesickness to know he was in Lembata and to think of returning to him there. On the one hand, he thought this a bit silly, as they were still separated whether he was in Lamalera or Jakarta, but he was also touched that he represented her most powerful link to home. Their spat even had a silver lining in that it prompted Honi to start talking about breaking her contract and coming home a year early — another incentive for him to stay.

Meanwhile, Alo's mother had shown up one morning to inform him that Ika was pregnant. (The couple, fearing his wrath, had been too shy to tell him themselves.) Jon was disappointed that Ika had followed in their mother's footsteps, and he was angry that Alo had led her down that path. But they were his two best friends, and he could see they loved each other, and the baby was coming with or without his approval. He asked for them to delay their marriage until after he and Honi were wed, and once they agreed, there was never another tense word about the pregnancy. In fact, the impending birth drew everyone closer together, as Jon began to anticipate having a niece, and he and Alo further bonded over dividing up the labor, such as fetching water from the well, that Ika had begun to struggle with.

Even more, with his grandparents continuing to senesce, now it was all the clearer that the family would need extra support while his sister was laid up. And though he had not become a lamafa this year, there was always next hunting season to try again. More than all of this, however, he hesitated because the Lamalerans were his people. Here the tribe's reciprocal altruism meant he never lacked for help, whether it was a free meal or a fishing partner. Jakartans, he had heard, were ruthless. He was not even sure if the Ancestors would be able to watch over him in the city. And without the guidance of their Ways, how else would he know how to live?

And yet the material advantages of the outside world were undeniable. Soon he would have to choose once and for all which life he wanted.

Without reading a single paper on the subject, Jon could intuit what the scientific evidence shows, which is that traditional people feel more fulfilled in many ways than citizens of industrialized nations. Because traditional societies are more egalitarian and inclusive, with everyone playing a role in the group's life, their members are less likely to report feeling lonely or depressed, or to suffer from post-traumatic stress disorder or other socially based mental-health problems. Hunter-gatherers also work much less than the modern forty-hour workweek. How much less depends on a forager's lifestyle, season, and other considerations—an Inuit has a very different routine from a Kalahari Bushman—but in general, hunter-gatherers work about twenty hours a week, though there are obviously exceptions, like Ika's near constant labor. The rest of the time foragers devote to art, leisure, socializing, and especially religious practices, a balance that contributes to anthropologists' observations that foragers have much richer spiritual lives than modern citizens.

That said, there are distinct advantages to industrial societies, which have enticed countless traditional people to join them. Even a poor citizen of a Western nation has access to conveniences — air-conditioning, supermarkets, etc. — that are unimaginable to hunter-gatherers. Tools like engines, chain saws, guns, and telephones allow a single person to accomplish feats that once would have taken a lot of manpower. State societies are much safer than traditional ones, as without a police force each person has to take justice into his own hands, leading to events like the conflict between the Luki and the Nualela over the Wulandoni Port. Women and minorities, such as people who identify as gay or lesbian, often enjoy significantly more freedoms in modern societies than in traditional ones. Perhaps most important, despite the greater health and fitness of hunter-gatherers while they are in their primes, their infant mortality rates are many times higher than those of industrial nations, and in old age they diminish quicker than Western citizens, who live on average a decade longer. It can escape no person, traditional or modern, which lifestyle is amassing more followers and will dominate the future.

It was these merits of both ways of life that Jon was debating as the first rains began to fall. Sometimes he would stare at Salés's brother's number in his cell phone for whole minutes.

NOT LONG AFTERWARDS, ONE MORNING in the still-dark hours, a yellow dump truck with a refrigerated box welded to its bed jounced over the volcano from Lewoleba to Lamalera. As dawn broke, a pair of dread-locked men, both of them Salés's employees, wandered past the devil rays piled on the beach without a second glance. But when they spied a small pair of tuna, they handed out laminated papers listing the week's prices. The fishermen grumbled that their payment should be higher, but they accepted two blue bills of 50,000 rupiah each, or about ten dollars, for the tuna.

The next night, after picking up fish from other rural tribes, the yellow dump truck rumbled through a humble brick village to Salés's hundred-meter-long refrigerated factory, which looked futuristic with its huge exhaust fans and exterior metal ventilation tubes. Despite the late hour, outside the warehouse, sparks jetted from rotary saws splitting rebar, as construction workers raced to finish a second such building. When the dump truck backed into the receiving bay, several dozen workers with smocks over their jeans rushed from the dormitories to meet it.

As the masked workers slid three huge swordfish down a tin chute into the heart of the factory, a Jakartan overseer in a purple batik dress shirt and fancy leather sandals asked Salés in horror, "The Lamalerans just dry these swordfish out?" Salés confirmed it. They both used the English word "swordfish," as they called all export fish by their English names. They knew the fish were worth several thousand dollars apiece, and began speculating about how many hundreds of dollars of profit they would make off them. Soon Salés planned to lease a plane to rush prime specimens like these from Lembata to Jakarta's international airport, so they could be on a plate in Tokyo or New York in twenty-four hours. Once the factory was fully operational, he expected to process more than one hundred twenty tons of fish a month.

Now, through Salés, the last link in the chain between Lamalera and the global marketplace had been completed. The whole time Jon had been scheming about how to escape his tribe for the outside world, it had already been careening toward him.

PART THREE

2016

Chapter Twelve

THE NEW *KÉNA PUKÃ*

April 2016

Frans — Bena

One Sunday in April, Frans sat on his front porch mending drift nets while keeping his ear cocked for the rumbling approach of the auto, straining to hear over the pulsating drone of the locusts, which still numbered in their rainy-season hordes. His wife, Maria, stroked the margins of their dirt yard with a straw broom, an excuse to linger near the road. Occasionally, she bent to pluck a stray blade of grass, for to the Lamalerans, bare earth rather than lush lawn is a sign of respectability, evidence that civilization has been carved out of the aggressive jungle, all the more fecund now from the monsoons. Frans grunted at Maria not to work too hard: in February she had fallen off a motorbike en route to the market and badly cut her head. The injury had baffled his healing powers, and they had spent nearly a week at the Lewoleba hospital. Though she had mostly recovered, he worried about her constantly. As Frans intuited that the aches of his fifties would soon transform into permanent disabilities, this same man who had treated his own whale-broken arm with a sprinkling of holy water and an immediate return to work was becoming almost a hypochondriac.

A foghorn honk echoed down the hill. His daughter, newly graduated from university, had arrived. He and Maria had not seen her in over a year, since her last visit. He hoped that her return and the coming Léfa would enable a fresh start, for tragedy had hamstrung the Mikulangu Bedionas, Frans's branch of the clan, at the end of the previous hunting season when their téna had been destroyed. It was a loss so great that it could be salved only by the happiness that came from his most beloved child moving back home. Maria rushed down the alley to the road, laughing joyfully. But Frans remained sitting on the brick porch, from where he could not see the auto pull up, frowning as he listened to the exclamatory greetings. Then his desire to glimpse his daughter overcame his stoicism. He stood and leaned off the porch so that he could see the gathering crowd. There was his cherub, Bena, surrounded by Maria and seven of his family members competing to carry her cardboard boxes tied with string. A smile opened his face. He hustled back to his seat and recomposed his stern mask before they saw him.

Bena sprinted up the steps and pressed her forehead to Frans's right hand. He nodded, his dour mouth twitching toward a grin. Bena had left home more than a decade earlier. Her parents could not afford the high school in Lewoleba, and had asked if she wanted to end her education with middle school, as no high school had yet been built in the village, or take up the offer of an uncle to live with him in the city of Sintang, on a distant island, and complete her schooling on his dime. Tearfully, she had bid her parents goodbye, promising to move back, for even at twelve she had known it was her responsibility as their youngest to care for them in their old age. Her sojourn had extended five years longer than expected when the uncle had gotten her a university scholarship to study to become a teacher. Now, despite her degrees, she was keeping her childhood promise.

"Welcome home, my child!" Frans said in formal Lamaleran. "Welcome home!"

As the rest of the party settled on benches, Bena, though she was in her early twenties, plopped onto her father's lap—not uncommon behavior in Lamalera, as even grown children act young with their parents. While everyone asked Bena about life in Sintang and she chattered happily about internet cafés, social media, and pizza, Frans remained silent and scrutinized her with gleaming eyes. Meanwhile, Maria kept her hand on her daughter's thigh. Except for weeklong trips every few years, they had not seen their daughter for about a decade.

Frans felt that he would always know his daughter, and yet it was clear that she had become someone new. Indoor life had made her plump and fair, and her skin was rendered even more ghostly with whitening powder. She wore tight jeans, a zebra-striped blouse, Mickey Mouse earring studs, and pink fingernail polish. She looked, as other Lamalerans would later say, "city."

As evening dusted the afternoon, Frans dismissed the rest of the guests and reminded Bena that, having returned, she needed to light the candles. They climbed to the church graveyard in Upper Lamalera, where, nearly three years after Teresea's death, Ignatius still went most evenings to kindle a flame for his wife. Bena knelt by the crypts of her Ancestors and set three candles burning. In Indonesian, the word used to describe what she was doing was "pairing": fire with bone, living with dead, present with past. On the way home, Frans detoured them off the main road and down onto the beach. With no lights to illuminate the boat shed, Bena could see only the outlines of the newest member of the clan, a téna. The chemical odor of fresh paint and the comforting scent of sawdust powdered the air. Frans had spent the entire rainy season rebuilding the ship. Bena set her hand on the prow, tentatively, as if it were a large, jumpy animal, and they prayed.

After a dinner of fried flying fish, moringa leaf soup, and red rice, Bena ducked into her old room and closed the door. She unpacked: several pairs of high heels, including pink ones with lacy frills; makeup kits and a Hello Kitty handbag; a sound system with three large speakers; and a laptop computer. Soon she was chattering on her cell phone, the singsong rhythms of Lamaleran replaced by tumbling Indonesian with a Sintang accent. Once the call finished, Katy Perry's "Last Friday

Night" boomed from her sound system, sending geckos fleeing for crannies in the brick walls. Without understanding the words, Bena karaoked the American party anthem, flexing a voice that had been trained in the Sintang Catholic choir: "It's all a blacked-out blur, but I'm pretty sure it ruled...last Friday night!"

Everyone in the otherwise silent neighborhood could hear her. Once, Frans would have been apoplectic, but now he lay back beside Maria, and they both listened to their daughter sing. Though he believed that following the Ways of the Ancestors should be enough to make any Lamaleran happy, he privately worried that after her experiences abroad, Bena might find life with the tribe unsatisfying. He knew that while she would never complain about coming home to tend to her parents, she was sacrificing a bright future in Sintang. Her disproportionately advanced education guaranteed her a job teaching at the elementary school, so she would not want for money, but could she find everything else she needed in the village?

If Frans or anyone else asked her, Bena was adamant that she was glad to be home: family and tradition came first. But as the weeks passed, and he watched her closely, he could tell that things in Lamalera were harsher than she had remembered. She picked at the pimples broken out on her forehead and tried to cover them with makeup. Having become accustomed to air-conditioning, she sweated constantly. Treks up the volcano that once had been easy exhausted her. Though she enjoyed playing with the babies of her friends from the old days, these young women were mothers first now, and could not spend much time with her. Even the few who did not have children quite yet, like Ika (though she was pregnant), still had so many chores that hanging out was not an option. And then there was the obvious — the worrying lack of educated bachelors. Frans wondered: Would Bena be satisfied with a lamafa, even? On most nights, after eating dinner with him and Maria, she would retreat to her room, where she burned through phone credits texting, calling, and using Facebook, and every few days she would badger relatives and friends abroad to refill her account for her.

More than two decades before, while adrift after the devil whale had crippled *Kéna Pukã,* disoriented by the featureless sea, Frans had looked up to see the clouds part to reveal the Pointer, the Southern Cross, the Lamalerans' guide home. Turning in that direction, he had prayed to live so he could see Bena grow up. Now he was sure the Ancestors and God had preserved him so he could prepare the future for Bena and her generation. For most of his adult life he had taken the lead in steering the tribe in its reckoning with the modern world, helping negotiate the settlement that legalized jonson towing téna and repeatedly mollifying the Wujons. He was determined to make sure there was a place for people like Bena in the tribe. But what did he know about keeping a city girl happy? And could the Ways of the Ancestors provide a modern woman with a rewarding life? Even as he struggled to forge ahead, the undertow of the past drew at him, especially as he had rebuilt *Kéna Pukã* to the specifications of the Ancestors. Now, as he faced his most personal challenge yet in syncretizing the new and the old, he could not help but worry that his long-stated belief that the two could coexist might be proven wrong.

THE FINAL VOYAGE OF THE previous *Kéna Pukã* had been the last hunt of 2015, when a bulldozer wind and the resulting waves prevented the fleet from chasing down a school of breeding whales. By the time the téna returned to shore, the tide had dropped and the swell intensified, so that the petrified lava chute leading between an outcropping of boulders and the eastern headlands, which was usually covered with water, was exposed between waves. As there was no other way for the téna to access the boat sheds on that side of the beach, and staying at sea was too dangerous, the fleet queued, each ship waiting for an exceptionally large wave that could be surfed all the way to the sand. Frans, who had missed the baleo, watched from shore as one by one the téna rode a wave as far as possible up the chute before its men leapt out and pushed the boat the rest of the way to safety.

At last only *Kéna Pukā* remained. It was impossible to know whether Frans would have been able to guide them in had he been captaining the téna, but from the shore, he could immediately see that the crew of *Kéna Pukā* had miscalculated. Their wave broke before the beach and dropped the téna onto the rocks so hard that the groaning of wood echoed across the bay. The crew leapt out and tried to push the boat landward, but their feet scrabbled on the slippery algae. They had only seconds now until the narrow confines funneled the next wave toward them. Frans watched helplessly as the sea flooded into the chute and the crew scrambled to escape the onrushing water. Ote was the only man who stayed with the vessel. He crouched on the hâm-mâlollo, trying to brace the boat with a harpoon shaft, but as the new wave arced over his head, he dropped to his knees and clutched the platform. The wall of water scraped the téna along the volcanic hard-pan and then, with a cracking of timber, slammed it against a trio of boulders. And still the sea was not finished. The backwash dragged *Kéna Pukā* into the chute again, just as an even larger wave reared. Once more the téna was hurled against the rocks, and then drawn back into the danger zone. By the third wave, water no longer flowed around the ship but through it.

In a lull between waves, everyone on the beach rushed to haul the wreck to safety — except for Frans, who stood paralyzed. When he examined the shattered téna on the beach, he felt as if his heart had been similarly ravaged. The keel had been split and boards peeled away, leaving a hole wider than his spread arms. Ignatius confirmed that the wounds were fatal. For Frans and his clansmen, it was like the death of a family member had occurred on their watch. For weeks Anso, Jon's driftnetting friend and one of the téna's materos, would weep at night and have trouble sleeping.

Rather than move on, as those in the West might say, Frans instead tried to re-create in every detail what had been lost. He salvaged all the boards he could, wrapped them in tarps, and laid them on the runners where the ship had once rested. The planks he could not save he stacked atop the rotting timbers of previous *Kéna Pukā*s, which lay in the back of the boat shed like the skeletal strata of the Ancestors in their sepulchers, for about once a generation a téna is rebuilt. In December, Frans sailed with his clansmen around the Ata Dei Peninsula and spent three days felling thirteen trees in the virgin jungles of that remote coast. He chose water-resistant Burmese rosewood for the lower hull, while for the top of the téna he cut softer kapok trunks. He searched through dozens of Chinese chaste trees to find one already bent in the shape of the all-important keel. Then, while January and February rains dripped off the thatch of the boat shed, Frans supervised the construction of the new *Kéna Pukā,* following exactly the blueprint laid out by *Kebako Pukā,* the original téna of the tribe and the one on which the construction of all others was based.

This was perhaps the most important work Frans would undertake as a clan leader and a shipwright. The date of the last time *Kéna Pukā* had been rebuilt was scratched in charcoal on the rafters of the boat shed: "1989." That téna had been the sole survivor of the odyssey with the devil whale, in 1994, as on its return, Frans had studied under a senior shipwright to fix its damaged hull, so that he would be ready now, twenty-two years later, for the task at hand. About seven years had passed in the village since any clan had built a new téna, and children who had never seen the process before watched in fascination, and older men dropped by to help and to revel in the ancient practice.

First, Frans and his clansmen sculpted the thirty-two boards of the hull not with chain saws or other modern tools but with hand adzes, as the Ancestors had, until they had all the pieces of the boat ready to assemble. Week by week, they then snapped the hull boards onto the keel, their ends carved into lap-jointed hooks, so that the wood jigsawed together for strength. Throughout the process, Frans was severe in making sure his men followed the Ways of the Ancestors in their work. If he observed even a tiny imperfection in the shaping of a board, he ordered it redone. In all the construction, not a single nail or screw was used, for the Ancestors had not employed them, and the building materials were totally sourced from the jungle. The only concession to modern tools that Frans made was electric drills, as they made cleaner holes and were many times faster than the mallets and conical-shell bores used in the Days of the Ancestors.

In the end, to force all the pieces tight, the builders wrapped the boat in rattan ropes and then torqued the lines around staves, pressuring the joints and the internal dowels pegged between them for days, until they fused. This lashed-lug method was developed in Asia and Europe during the Bronze Age, but by the time of European colonial expansion, it had already been mostly superseded. Today the Lamalerans are the last known people to use it on a large scale. To make sure that the tradition continued, Frans paid extra attention to instructing Anso, for some said the thirty-five-year-old was being cultivated as the next chief and clan shipwright, and it would be up to him to rebuild the téna decades hence, once Frans was gone.

Frans regulated not only his men's actions on the building site but also the attendance of ceremonies honoring their Ancestors, and worked to resolve interpersonal disputes in his clan, for the Lamalerans believe that any dissension can disturb an embryonic téna's gestation. Far more than a merely physical exercise, the building of the new *Kéna Pukā* was a spiritual one, as divine and holy as the birth of a child. After the old *Kéna Pukā* was shattered, Frans had carried some of the splintered boards to his Spirit House and performed a shamanistic ceremony to allow the vessel's soul to convalesce there until a new body could be built. As the boat developed, it gained human characteristics. Holes were bored on either side of the prow to represent its ears. A groove was chiseled into the center of its bowsprit to provide a mouth. Eyes were painted on the cutwater. In the womb of the boat shed, a new life was taking shape.

As the typhoons dwindled to drizzles and Léfa drew near, Frans carried the old *Kéna Pukā*'s planks from the Spirit House to its successor and transferred the téna's ancestral spirit to its new body. He had already incorporated several of the former ship's unbroken planks, so that the spirit would find a familiar home. But the infant ship was not quite ready to be born yet. Just before the hunting season, the clan would hold a village-wide festival, at the end of which the boat would slide down a birth canal made of logs into the Savu Sea. Despite this impending rebirth, Frans would never call the téna "new." For him it was not novel, but a reincarnation of its predecessor. Even more, it was an embodiment of his covenant with the past. If he was forced to bow to modern transformations in other ways, the téna was proof that even in these volatile times some things would never change.

For recently the young Bediona men had badgered Frans into building a jonson so they could go driftnetting, as he had held out until now the Mikulangu Bedionas were one of the last clans lacking a motorboat. Recognizing the ascendancy of driftnetting, Frans finally gave in, and they constructed the jonson at about the same time as the new téna, employing the screws and chain saws he had forbidden in crafting the sacred ship. Once the new jonson was complete, the Bedionas faced a fresh challenge: where to put it. Across the beach, whalers were joking about "jonson gridlock," as the tribe now owned thirty-five, and there was barely any space to dry-dock new ones, leading to disputes over space like the one between the Harionas and Nudeks. To widen the boat shed to accommodate the new vessel, the Bediona men spent a backbreaking week relocating pillars and restacking rock retaining walls. Even with the changes, the structure was too narrow for the téna and the jonson to rest side by side. Given that the motorboat would be used much more often than the téna, Frans was forced to make a hard but practical decision, the symbolism of which was not lost on him: *Kéna Pukā* was slotted into the back, while the jonson was parked at the front.

ONE MIDNIGHT A FEW DAYS before the start of Léfa, Frans woke to the susurration of water sluicing through the pipe beside his house: the mountain tribes had unexpectedly opened the cisterns in the hills above, providing a rare spurt of liquid to the Lamaleran public faucets, which were almost always dry, forcing the villagers to rely instead on the distant and inconvenient wells. Despite the fact that in just a few hours he would have to lead the festival to mark the completion of the new *Kéna Pukā,* it was his duty to provide, and Frans carried a dozen plastic jerricans outside. With the water pressure so low, drops plinked into his containers at such an agonizing pace that it would take until morning to fill all of them. Soon Maria sat on a stone next to him, a sarong shawled around her shoulders. This was her silent offer to stay awake and fill the cans for him so he could be rested for the ceremonies.

"Go to sleep," he told her.

"I will, in a little bit."

Five minutes later, he repeated, "Go to sleep."

"In a little bit," she answered.

It took them until nearly five o'clock to finish filling all twelve jerricans. They did not speak or touch as the radiant full moon declined, yet they exuded the hard-won contentment of a couple who have everything they need from each other and seek only more shared time.

Once the containers were at last full, Frans dressed in his best sarong and paced his front porch in the predawn darkness. He kept cocking his ear for the chatter of his clansmen gathering on the beach, but heard only roosters shrilling. The night was graying when he ordered Bena, just awakened, to fetch a bucket of seawater. She smirked at him to show that she understood — her father did not want to appear too eager to his men — then sauntered down to the beach on his behalf. A few minutes later, a shriek echoed through the alley, followed by the patter of bare feet running. Bena burst into the yard, dripping, trailed by a grinning young man with a bucket hefted over his head. When the young man saw Frans glowering, he froze. Water sloshed over the lip of the bucket onto him. The young man's face formed into an expression halfway between a shit-eating grin and a horrified grimace, then he sprinted away.

In the old days, a téna festival would have been inaugurated by a melee between young men from Upper and Lower Lamalera, to inspire the téna with boldness, but the church had outlawed such violence. Nowadays fistfights had been replaced with water fights: anyone from the host clan was a target, especially its young women, whom men doused as a sign of their affections. Bena twisted water from her frizzy hair and confirmed with a pout that Frans's men awaited him on the beach. When she stepped inside and out of her father's sight, though, she was all smiles.

After Bena had changed her clothes, Frans descended with her to the beach, where the Mikulangu Bediona men surrounded *Kéna Pukã* like bodyguards. The téna's name blazed in freshly painted tiger-stripe lettering on the bow. Frans blessed the ship with holy water, then the men toddled the téna forward on log rollers onto the beach. Soon the Wujons arrived. Because Marsianus was away on a monthlong fishing trip, it was his son who toted a baby pig bound with vines. This was the *fafi koteķělema,* the whale pig, which represented a sperm whale caught to honor the téna. Once Frans had approved the sacrifice, the Lords of the Land knifed it in the heart, then rubbed flaming palm fronds across its carcass to sear off its hairs. Next, a dozen or so shipwrights, including Ignatius, chopped the singed corpse into umã shares, as if it were a Gift of the Ancestors, after which they handed the meat over to Bena and the other Bediona women, who roasted it. From the ruined téna Frans had managed to salvage the cracked *néfi* board — the longest and most important plank — and it had been laid atop logs to create a banquet table. After the feast was concluded, Frans announced to the shipwrights of the other clans, "I have tried to follow the model of the Ancestors. If there are any mistakes, correct me."

Jogo, leader of the Nudeks, was the first man to tap the téna with his chisel, for even though he had never become a shipwright himself, he was one of the few remaining descendants of the original ata mola. Then the shipwrights mobbed the boat, some climbing on top, some wriggling underneath. Ignatius punched the hull and stuck his clawlike fingernails into the cracks between the boards to test their flushness. A few shipwrights went so far as to shave wood off a board with their adzes, less to fix any structural flaw than to assert their claim on the ship.

Frans stood back from the scrum, his arms folded, his face grim. Ignatius completed his examination and smiled at Frans. Once all the other shipwrights had also certified that Frans had faithfully reproduced the past, they congratulated him one by one with a solemn nod. But everyone knew that the real judgment would come from the sperm whales, for the Lamalerans believe that those emissaries of the Ancestors will break a téna at any point it differs from *Kebako Pukā*.

With the past honored, it was time to celebrate the future. The Bediona men and women handed out tubs of fata biti, smashed popcorn, to all the tribe's children. Meanwhile, young men scooped up buckets of surf and doused Bediona girls, who squealed with laughter. Bena ambushed her distant uncle, one of the bawdiest men in Lamalera, a father of ten children, as if she were courting him, inspiring such hilarity in the crowd that people fell over laughing. Frans faked that he did not see a gang of young men sneaking up on him, and put up only a token fight when they grabbed his arms and legs. The young men lugged him over the headlands and did not so much as throw him into the Savu Sea as collapse into it along with him, spluttering and laughing in the waves. Then this same drunken, merry band hunted down and dunked the rest of the male members of the Mikulangu Bediona clan.

As the tribe continued to celebrate, Frans sat apart, smoking a cigarette and dripping, tired in a good way. *Kéna Pukā* would carry a fresh generation of Mikulangu Bediona hunters to sea. He could be proud that his téna would not soon become like one, just a few boat sheds down, spattered with chicken poop and blotted with moss. Looking back over his nearly six decades, Frans could trace how the transformations that had left that téna in disrepair had accrued, each one seemingly unimportant, though in the end they had changed a great

Lamaleran men drag Bediona clan members to the sea to celebrate the new Kéna Pukã.

deal. He marveled that transformations that once would have seemed catastrophic now struck him as inevitable and, if not necessarily good, then at least acceptable. For despite what the Wujons and other die-hard conservatives said, change had always been happening in Lamalera. What was it if not change when the Ancestors learned to forge metal harpoon heads from a neighboring tribe, allowing them to replace the ones fashioned from brazilwood? Even the religion of Lera Wulan, which Father Bode refined with Christianity, had not proven immutable.

For centuries, the Lamalerans' line of reasoning—"This is correct because it has always been this way"—was a survival strategy. In demanding environments like Lembata, societies have evolved to be conservative because people have a strong incentive not to change what has worked, as even a small mistake can result in the loss of crucial food, leading to severe hardship or even starvation. As a child, Frans had endured a famine. With the line between life and death so thin, it was logical for each téna to adhere exactly to the blueprint of *Kebako Pukā*.

But the advantages of conservatism for societies vanish when a static environment begins to rapidly transform: in these cases, adaptation rather than rigidity is the key to survival. Frans had accepted that no amount of effort could resurrect the past or freeze the present. The only choice, then, was how much to evolve. For if change was inevitable, he wanted to co-opt what was beneficial about the outside world while rejecting its bad influences. It was possible: the tribe's negotiations around the ratification of the jonson in 2001 had modeled such an approach. Institutions like the Council on the Beach would allow the whalers to continue collaborating to synthesize the past and the future.

Frans had come to see the Ways of the Ancestors would endure only as long as the Lamalerans invested in them while also balancing them with the realities of the modern world. It was for this reason that Frans had taught Anso and the other young Bediona men everything they would need to reconstruct *Kéna Pukā* once he was gone, but had also consented to the jonson. Ultimately, though, the choice about how the tribe should modernize would soon be out of his hands. It would be up to Bena, Anso, and the rest of their generation to make sure the Ways of the Ancestors continued as best they could.

Because of that, there was something about completing the new *Kéna Pukā* that sated a restlessness within Frans. He had discharged one of his major responsibilities in passing on the Ways of the Ancestors. He did not stop putting to sea altogether, but in the days to come, he increasingly stayed ashore, claiming he had clan matters to arrange. Inevitably, though, he would tend his grandnephew, rocking the infant while chanting a prayer for the wind to blow or for a thrashing whale shark to surrender. It was the only time the old songs were sung anymore. Though the child would forget he had ever heard it by the time he matured, the music of the Ancestors would echo somewhere in his subconscious forever.

*   *   *

LATE THE NIGHT OF THE festival for *Kéna Pukã,* while Mars burned like an ember to the east, Frans and Bena returned to the boat shed. A naked bulb hung from the rafters over the new *Kéna Pukã,* a power cord snaking away to the nearest house, for the Lamalerans believed that the new téna, like a young child, might be scared of the dark. During its first hunt, the whalers would seek small prey like whiptail devil rays — as the ship's immature stomach could not handle larger food — before working their way up to a sperm whale. Frans shooed away dogs nosing the sand for leftovers from the feast, and he and his daughter sat on the dark beach as the tide swished toward them. The artificial light of Bena's phone illuminated the two of them, and Frans watched her silently as she fired off text messages to friends spread across the Indonesian Archipelago, immersed in a world foreign to him.

Like many other older Lamalerans, Frans often wondered if modernity and its tools had transformed the very beings of the youth. Certainly, he could feel their effects on him. When he was young, he had focused his attention on his tribespeople and the Ways of the Ancestors, enjoying a sense of unity with the spiritual and natural world, and rarely felt hurried. Now, though, he worried constantly about the future and felt his connection both to nature and to the Ancestors weakened. The simplicity of a life defined by feeding himself and his family had been replaced by a welter of demands from taxes, motorboats, and more. It was too much. Meanwhile he could see that the youth were becoming ever more affected by cell phones, TVs, and other gadgets. He believed it possible that their brains had come to work differently than his own.

Bena, too, had recently been questioning the chasm between her experience and her father's, for on returning to her childhood home, it had been hard for her to tell if she had changed or if Lamalera had. She missed Sintang's supermarkets, 24/7 electricity, plumbing, TV, and internet, as well as the friends she had made in her classes. The heat and dirt of the village felt like a physical assault, and the yearning for her previous life was almost overwhelming.

But as the weeks had spun on, she adjusted. She got used to physical labor once more, and her body hardened to the stress of the village. The other Lamalerans deciphered her city slang, and her shirts decorated with anime characters no longer attracted stares. Bartering at the market, she remembered how to count in munga rather than in Western math. And though she got a job teaching at the elementary school, she also threw herself into preparing the festival for the new *Kéna Pu_kā,_* managing her female relatives as they cooked hundreds of treats. It was possible, she saw, to live both a modern and a traditional life. Eventually, she would forget that she had ever seen any clash between the two at all. As with most people, Bena was sure that however she was living was natural. She had instinctively fused the past and the future into her present.

These days, she spread ebullience wherever she went. With a favorite daughter's insouciance, she pinched her mother's cheeks while Maria cooked and sat on her father's lap as he tried to mend nets. With the same relish she had picked out a goat to be awarded to the winner of a traditional contest of strength at *Kéna Pu_kā_*'s festival, she perused different shades of nail polish online for one of her cousins to mail her. She was at home.

While the tide crept closer and Bena toyed with her cell phone, Frans fixed on her an almost awed stare, as if he needed nothing more in life than just to watch his daughter. Then Bena glanced up at the stars. They were nothing like the cheap sequins over Sintang. Instead, it was as if a trove of diamonds had been spilled across the sky. She put her head on her father's shoulder and asked him to tell the Ancestors' stories of the constellations, as he had when she was a child. "What's that one?" she asked. "And that one?"

Frans's crooked arm worked its way down the sky until it aimed at the Southern Cross. "That's the Pointer," he said. It was the same constellation he had fixated on while adrift at sea more than twenty years ago, after the failed pursuit of the devil whale—at first so it could pilot him home to his family, to his infant Bena, and then, once he was convinced that he would die, just so he would know where they were, as distant as they might have been. "Those," he told his daughter, "are the stars that show us where we belong."

As Frans recounted the stories of the Ancestors, his clanspeople bedded down on bamboo mats laid atop the sand or circled around a jerrican of tuak. When the moon rose, its light streaked like a golden spotlight across the Savu Sea, revealing Bena asleep with her head on her father's belly.

Around midnight, the clan was awakened by the hiss of the encroaching tide. The women lit torches of bamboo wrapped in whale oil–soaked rags and formed a fiery alley to the water. The men heaved and hoed, *Jo-hé! Jo-hé! Kéna Pukã* coasted down the log track. The slope was so steep that the hâmmâlollo dipped and the stern rose, levering Frans, who clung to it, into the air. Then the téna slid comfortably into the Savu Sea, as if returning home, its rebirth completed.

As far as the Lamalerans were concerned, this was not its first journey but rather a continuation of an odyssey that had brought it from Lepan Batan, to Lamalera, to Kupang, and back. It was a voyage that would now continue into the future. Frans raised the sackcloth flag of his Ancestors. Then he and his clansmen rowed *Kéna Pukã* into the darkness.

Chapter Thirteen

AGAINST THE LEVIATHAN

April 21, 2016–May 2, 2016

Jon — Ben — Ignatius

In the end, Jon had not left Lamalera, not even to work construction in Lewoleba. Instead, he had raced to finish his house, screwing down the last metal roofing just before the clouds burst, and then had driftnetted through the blustery months. Despite the allure of Jakarta, he was never able to bring himself to abandon his grandparents and Ika, for as he was about to leave, everything good about life in the tribe — the community, the traditions, even his maddening clanspeople — suddenly seemed too precious to give up. And becoming a lamafa this year had begun to seem more achievable. As an incentive for Jon to remain, Salés had built a new *VJO,* which Jon had been badgering him about for years, given that the previous jonson was nearly a decade old, and its warped boards were stained with the stigmata of rust from nails. But Salés's motivation was twofold. In addition to placating Jon, and thereby avoiding having to recruit a replacement to oversee his affairs in town, he also wanted to test a theory. Soon, he believed, the Lamalerans would harpoon hunt and net fish at the same time, a development for which his new jonson would be ideally suited.

Every detail of the new boat, *Little VJO,* had been specified by Salés. At twenty feet long and four feet wide, it was about a third shorter and skinnier than its predecessor. The more hydrodynamic frame meant both that it would be better able to chase the dolphins the Lamalerans had begun to focus on as ray populations diminished and that it would devour less gas. Salés had modified his old joke about Jon for the new craft, calling it "small, but hot, like its captain." What most excited Jon, however, was that, with its compact size, *Little VJO* required only three men to crew it. Before, the lack of just one man had scuttled his bid to become a harpooner, but the new boat would be easier to staff.

About two weeks before the coming Léfa, Jon, Alo, and another friend, Cornelius Tapoonā, launched *Little VJO* as the sun separated from the horizon. Alo cranked the motor and Jon crouched on the hâmmâlollo and scanned the sea, his hands forming a brim over his eyes. Finally, he had his chance to become a lamafa. Once he had made the decision to stay, his drinking and other misbehavior had diminished, and he had returned to his old workhorse ways. The elders had noticed, and Frans went so far as to suggest to Jon that he would earn his chance as a bereung alep on a téna soon. Some elders even started addressing him with the pronoun for a married man, a mark of respect, which Jon felt he needed to live up to, but also deserved, as he now considered himself basically wedded, for at the end of that year's hunting season, he planned to cross the archipelago and bring Honi home. During the rainy season, he seemed to have gained gravitas, though he had not put on any physical weight, as if the inner lightness of youth had solidified into the burden of adulthood.

As *Little VJO* slashed across the polished sea, it kicked up what appeared to be water droplets, but instead of falling in arcs, the droplets — actually baby flying fish — arrowed away in straight lines. The powdery blue sea blended with the powdery blue sky, creating the illusion that the distant volcanoes floated in the atmosphere or were submerged in the ocean. About two miles offshore, they dressed the surface in a lace of white gill nets. Meanwhile, the three men surveyed the expanse for larger prey.

Until this moment, with Salés's modifications of *Little VJO,* there had been a strict division between one-man sampans, which used gill nets to catch flying fish, and jonson, which were intended for harpoon hunting. Fueling a jonson was too expensive for gillnetting, with its more limited returns, to make sense, and even if driftnetting had not been banned during Léfa, it happened at night, when harpoon hunting was impossible. But with *Little VJO,* Jon could set a net on a buoy, go harpoon hunting, and, even if he did not spear anything, collect the net later and return home with flying fish. And any sushi-grade catch, whether speared or netted, could be sold to Salés for his new factory.

Jon glared at the sea with a manic intensity, as though willing a devil ray to jump or a dorsal fin to chop a wave. Translucent jellyfish pulsed past, their organs visible as four concentric circles, as green and fuzzy as algae. Then a sea turtle's head periscoped *Little VJO.* Jon snatched his harpoon and Alo rip-corded the engine, but the turtle dove and did not resurface.

The morning's flat seas had rucked up into rollers when Jon finally spotted a dozen or so spinner dolphins charging toward their nets. Within seconds, he armed himself, Alo kindled the engine, and Cornelius unclipped the nets from the boat, so that they floated free, visible among the whiteheads only by the buoy that held them aloft. The three sailors scared the pod of dolphins out of their raid, then chased them up and down the hills of water.

A seasoned lamafa makes riding a hâmmâlollo look effortless, adjusting fluently to the pitch and yaw of the jonson as it thuds through the waves. Jon lacked this grace, though in fairness he was hampered by difficult conditions. One thing that Salés had not anticipated was that because *Little VJO* lacked the mass of a larger jonson, it was less stable in chop, which made balancing on its hâmmâlollo more difficult. When the ship plowed into a particularly tall roller, Jon pitched forward and almost fell off the platform.

The dolphins swung north, chasing a school of mackerel, and as *Little VJO* turned and put its back to the rollers from the south, everything changed. Now, rather than fighting against the jonson, the waves propelled it toward the prey. Jon stood resolute. Tiny muscles spasmed up and down his calves and veins flickered in his ankles, but his feet did not shift. The mackerel, trapped against the roof of the ocean as the dolphins swirled beneath them, hurled themselves into the air. Distracted by their own prey, the dolphins did not notice that they themselves were being hunted. Jon was close enough now that he could discern their black button eyes and puckered blowholes. A dolphin corkscrewed skyward, releasing a helix of spray. Jon spread his feet wide, squatted, and slid his right hand under the butt of the harpoon, copying Ote's throwing stance. The swell, the wind, the waves, were at his back, as if even nature blessed him. Alo and Cornelius yelled for him to strike. But he was just a few inches too far away.

Suddenly the dolphins swerved, following the juking mackerel. *Little VJO* spun with them — back into the headwinds and against the swell. When the boat rammed the first roller, Jon had to brace the butt of his harpoon against the hâmmâlollo to keep from pitching overboard. Amid the contrary spindrift the gray dorsal fins outdistanced them and disappeared.

Jon kept *Little VJO* searching long past his friends' objections. Eventually, however, Alo returned them to the net. Flying fish hung in it, unmoving and glittering as dragonflies trapped in a spiderweb. As Cornelius reeled in the net, Jon drew the snake-bodied fish one by one through the mesh, in the process ripping away their only beauty, the delicate, iridescent wings. Occasionally, Jon would pause, bite out an eye, and chew it like a wad of gum while surveying the deserted sea. A few hours later, their second draw of the net brought in another full load of flying fish, but they had not glimpsed any larger prey since the dolphins. In six hours of work, though, they had landed about three hundred flying fish, more than enough to make their time worthwhile.

As the afternoon grew dusky, Alo piloted *Little VJO* along the edge of Lembata, riding the homeward current just beyond the surges that chewed the petrified lava cliffs. Even in that violent zone, where few sea animals ventured, Jon maintained his watch on the hâmmâlollo. Only when Lamalera's church towered above the jungle did Jon finally unscrew his harpoon head from its shaft.

But as he was coiling the rope, he spotted something, and yelled, "Over there! Over there!" He grabbed the bamboo he had just racked and frantically pounded the spearhead back into it with the heel of his hand. Alo gassed the engine. Jon aimed the harpoon at a glistening dorsal fin bobbing in the white fray — then let the weapon droop.

Only a knotted, rot-darkened log twisted there in the surf.

"You're harpooning wood now, Jon?" Alo laughed.

Jon managed a faltering toothy smile.

"You need these glasses?" Cornelius said, chuckling, and offered his knockoff Ray-Bans.

But Jon was already staring back out to sea.

On a Saturday afternoon, Ika rose from a nap, one hand under her pregnant stomach, which had swollen so much that it stretched out the *o* of her Hello Kitty T-shirt and embossed her popped-out belly button into the fabric. She was at least seven months pregnant, though without effective medical care she could not tell the baby's exact age. As Ika's stomach had grown, the rest of her had withered, her once chubby cheeks becoming gaunt and her arms thinning until the knobs of her elbows seemed as sharp as spikes. Deep circles were engraved beneath her eyes, and her movements were lethargic. But no matter her exhaustion, dinner had to be made.

With evident reluctance, Ika carried her belly through the new house, supporting herself against the wall with her free hand as she shuffled across the dirt floor in her bare feet, stirring up dust. While some work remained before the structure would be complete, including laying concrete floors, Jon had finished the walls and the new galvanized tin roof. But he had made no improvements to the bamboo shack that served as the kitchen. All he had done was to lift it with the help of several other men and walk it twenty feet east, to make room for the expanding house.

Inside the kitchen shack, Ika shooed wandering, clucking chicks into the corners. She stooped, using one arm to prop up her belly, and built a teepee of wood scraps and trash. With a lighter, she set a foot-long shard of green plastic aflame, then let the molten plastic drip onto the kindling like napalm. As she watched the jade-colored fire, she thought about her friend Lindsay, the American.

Three years earlier, Ika had been carrying her goods to the Wulandoni Market when a stout young white woman had asked in Indonesian if she could accompany her. Lindsay, a student from Alaska, had taken a semester off university to travel. During the long walk to the market, they traded stories, and Ika was delighted to learn of the similarities in their lives: whereas Ika cut firewood each morning, Lindsay chain-sawed brush around her home; Ika cured flying fish, while Lindsay smoked salmon. For the rest of the week, Lindsay would show up each morning at Ika's house and give her a small juice box of condensed milk, a treat Ika loved and could rarely afford, and then help Ika with her chores, such as foraging for wood and butchering rays, all the while taking photos that she would post on Facebook. But the longer they were together, and the more Ika listened to Lindsay's plans of getting a university degree and traveling the world, the more she realized how different their lives actually were.

Weeks after Lindsay had left, a battered envelope addressed to Ika arrived at the village mayor's house. (Lamalera had no post office.) Inside was a Christmas card and a photo: Ika and Lindsay laughing, the American towering over her and bearing a load of her firewood. Ika had safeguarded it between the pages of her Bible, but eventually its cheap ink would fade, like her memories, until the interiors of the two figures had smudged and only their outlines remained distinct.

As Ika stared at the witchy fire, she wondered how her and Lindsay's fortunes had diverged — how her and everyone else's fortunes had diverged, for that matter. If Mari had been born before her, then her younger sister would be supporting her while she went to high school. And now her old friend Bena was a schoolteacher and being pursued by the tribe's most eligible bachelors. Ika told herself that the pregnancy was God's will. Although at first she had viewed it as a path toward her own family, house, and freedom, she now regretted that she had followed her mother in having a child out of wedlock, and worried that she would pass her profligacy on to her baby. She did not even have a formal wedding to look forward to, as her second uncle, Jogo, the chieftain of the Lama Nudek clan and closest matrilineal relative, and thus the person responsible for setting her bride price, had chosen an extremely high one on the reasoning that just because Alo and Ika were in love did not mean that Jogo and her older relatives should not profit. How had her life come to this?

Since Ika had begun to show, she hid in the house as much as possible. When she had to collect Jon's fish on the beach, she did not stop to gossip with the other women but rushed home. She avoided church, afraid of what Father Romo would say, even though she yearned to take Communion and rejoin the choir. No longer would she so much as sing alone, and her neighbors missed the hymns that had echoed through the alleyways. She rarely laughed anymore either, and when she did, it seemed as if she was mocking herself or the world. An infected cavity had made it painful for her even to smile. When the pregnancy plagued her with cramps and dizziness, Jon and Alo stepped up to do some of her work, like fetching water from the well, but her responsibilities still seemed endless, especially as her ever-frailer grandparents required more care each day. On becoming fed up with them, she tried to remind herself that one day she too would be old, and that her granddaughter would take care of her only as well as she was taking care of them, but she often spontaneously burst into tears, and then her grandparents would start crying too.

Ika feared the future. After getting pregnant, she had gone to the social services office in Lewoleba. There she learned that her mother had never registered her birth. Technically, then, she did not exist, meaning that although she was trying to race through an involved, confusing, and expensive citizenship process, she would likely be unable to give birth in Lewoleba's public hospital. Instead, her only option was Lamalera, with its part-time nurse, who had few medicines to offer. Ika was not sure of the sex of her baby: a doctor had told her it was a girl, but his nurse had palpated her belly and announced a boy because the fetus favored the right side of the uterus. But Ika figured that in some ways its sex did not matter, for its fate had already been decided. In the Age of Song, when a baby was born, the men of the clan would point to the sea if it was a boy, and intone, "That is your place." If it was a girl, her aunts would point to the land, and declare, "This is your place." Even though the ritual was now mostly defunct, Ika planned to make sure that neither she nor Alo assigned their baby to the land or the sea. Perhaps if Lamalera kept changing, her child would be able to choose its own future.

DURING THE RAINY SEASON, Salés's business had been a moderate success, but even during peak catches, he had not assembled enough tuna or swordfish to make exporting them to Japan profitable. Instead, he had sold them to hip restaurateurs in Jakarta. His biggest moneymaker had turned out to be sardines, caught via purse seine by fishermen in Lewoleba — in April alone he claimed to have processed two hundred fifty tons of them, shipping some of that to America. Since opening the business at the end of the previous summer, he had already doubled his staff, to about seventy men, and more than a hundred fishermen regularly supplied him. He planned to purchase his own thirty-ton longliner soon. Then maybe he could get enough tuna to make his business international.

In the last six months, Salés had become even more certain that his prophecy of Lamalera's inevitable modernization was correct. The Wulandoni Port was nearly complete. The governor of the province was set to announce a drive to bring more tourists to Lamalera, declaring that it could become one of the most popular destinations in the country, a push that would cause officials to resume their efforts for the Lamaler-ans to offer whale-watching tours instead of hunting. Salés also knew from inside sources that in August the government would begin supply-ing Lamalera with 24/7 electricity. By early 2017, internet-equipped computers at the elementary school would follow.

Sometimes, to escape the pressures of his businesses, Salés would join Jon on *Little VJO,* for despite everything else he had become, he was at heart a fisherman. The salt spray would pat his cheeks as it had when he was a child sailing with his father, and feeling the wind pivot, he still remembered how the great sheet of palm leaf should be reori-ented. If asked to sing the old songs, he would pause, then the music would waver forth. For all his worldliness, he too mourned the passage of the Ways of the Ancestors, but he did not think their diminishment was the end of Lamalera. No, as long as the whales were still hunted, Lamalera could not die, it could only change.

Salés lacked a male heir. But all those years when he had made sure the fatherless Jon learned how to driftnet and run an outboard motor, he had been preparing for the boy a place in the Lamalera he was creating.

Two DAYS BEFORE LÉFA, as the sun edged toward noon, Jon was again fixing his tapestry of nets, a daily chore, biting the top line and using his toes to stretch out the mesh so he could restitch the tasseled holes into clean diamonds. He had tucked his cell phone into the collar of his shirt so he could talk to Honi while he was working. Since her boss had agreed to allow her to break her contract at the end of that year, their fights had evanesced and they spent hours making plans for Jon to take a weeklong ferry ride across the archipelago and fetch his bride home. Once they ran out of things to say, they left their phones on, and Jon simply listened as she swept or cooked, as if she were in the next room.

Just then a baleo boomed out. Jon bid Honi goodbye and hastily untangled himself from the nets. He sprinted across the clifftops to

Narek's house and borrowed his binoculars. When he glassed the Savu Sea, he spotted a geyser. Narek's wife asked him how many whales there were.

"Just one," Jon answered. "But it's big." Indeed, it was as large a bull as any he had ever seen, leaving a battleship wake as it swam east.

Jon sprinted home, pulled on a shirt, stuffed tobacco confetti into a battered pill bottle, and filled a jerrican with water. When he ran onto the beach, Ben called to him to help launch the jonson *Kanibal*. (*Boli Sapang,* the Harionas' téna, was still dry-docked because of an ongoing intra-clan dispute from the previous year.) Jon assisted Ben in getting the jonson into the water, but he turned down his friend's request to board the boat. Instead, he helped Ignatius slide *Demo Sapang* down its track of logs and claimed the left befaje oar at the prow, the same position where his leg had been crushed two years earlier. Ignatius had given the harpoons to Stefanus Sengaji Keraf, his aging lamafa cousin, who was known to have missed several easy strikes during the last few Léfa. If Stefanus failed, Jon reasoned, he might get a chance. Across from him sat Gabriel Oleona, a Blikololong clansman who pulled the right befaje oar as the official bereung alep.

Kanibal lugged *Demo Sapang* east. The Blikololongs had been quick to respond to the baleo, and only one téna juddered through the Savu Sea ahead of them. The rest chased. While every other whaler aboard the téna, including Stefanus, was seated, Jon remained standing. As they approached the whale, everyone murmured at the height of its spouts. Its size was intimidating: over seventy feet from nose to tail, twice as long as a téna. The fleet hounded the old bull into Labala Bay, managing to pin it in shallow water about half a mile from the cliffs. One by one the téna detached from their tugboats. Then it was as it had been for centuries—just the Lamalerans, the téna, the kotekělema, and the Ancestors. Jon braced his feet against the hull and pulled the befaje oar with his whole body to the rhythm called out by Ignatius. The whale, however, swerved away from *Demo Sapang* and into another pack of téna that had since caught up.

By now a total of nine boats had joined the hunt. When *Horo Téna* was close enough, its lamafa drove his harpoon into the bull with such violence that the shaft splintered and a cartwheeling shard slashed open his chin. The whale responded by hammering the sea with its flukes, just missing the ship but raising waves that nearly swamped it anyway. The next téna to strike was *Téti Heri,* and the answering blow from the tail of the enraged bull would have killed its bereung alep had he not leapt off the hâmmâlollo just in time. The colossus battered the two téna while the hunters curled up beneath the thwarts. Abruptly the animal tried to flee, only to find itself boxed in by the fleet. Too breathless to dive, it kept spy-hopping, poking its head above the surface while keeping the rest of its body underwater.

The head, with its helmet of spermaceti, was impenetrable, and so the phalanx of téna jostled for a position to strike its submerged body. *Kelulus,* with Ote balanced on the hâmmâlollo, raced toward the whale from its right while *Demo Sapang* approached from the left. Jon hauled on his oar, but *Kelulus* beat *Demo Sapang* to the whale by about twenty feet. As Ote plunged his harpoon into the whale, the crew of *Demo Sapang* screamed at Stefanus, *Adok! Adok!*—"Jump and spear it before it's too late!" Stefanus crouched, but just as he was about to push off, a wave smacked the prow and the vessel wobbled. Stefanus lost purchase. His feet windmilled in the air, and his arms strained to force the spearhead to its target. But the harpoon head arrowed into the

Stefanus slips and misses the sperm whale.

water inches short. When Stefanus surfaced, the harpoon shaft floated beside him with the spearhead still in it.

With the full harpoon floating in the soup of froth, Jon abandoned his oar and beat Gabriel, the bereung alep, to the top of the hâm-mâlollo. He began reeling in the harpoon rope hand over hand, passing the coils back to Gabriel, who hesitated before helping, stunned at Jon's audacity. So much rope had paid out that no matter how many coils Jon took in, the harpoon floated unmoving.

As Stefanus swam back to the boat, the oarsmen yelled at him: "There are so many boats! How will we get another shot?"

"Of course we'll get another shot!" Ignatius swore at his men.

Aboard *Kelulus,* meanwhile, Ote was leaning his whole weight down on his harpoon shaft, his feet braced against the hâmmâlollo, trying to drive the iron farther into the flesh, when the whale finally gathered enough breath to dive. The hunters were left peering into the depths of the Savu Sea. Jon frantically continued to pass coils of rope back to Gabriel. He was nearing the end of the rope when the bull erupted out of the water beneath *Kelulus,* sending the téna spinning and almost knocking Ote from the harpooner's platform.

Finally, Jon felt the weight of the harpoon on the rope. He gave a last pull and the spear stood up out of the water and he grabbed the iron tip. The whale was less than two meters away, thrashing in exhaustion, its head pointed toward another téna. Its back, hashed with white scar tissue, spread before Jon. He focused on the vulnerable dimple of flesh two handbreadths below the dorsal fin, inches from where the harpoon of *Horo Téna* was already lodged, blood bubbling around it. He hesitated. The challenge with harpooning a whale was not hitting it, but striking the right spot with enough force to penetrate its foot-thick skin. Did everyone else think he was waiting too long?

Ignatius broke Jon's reverie. *Segêt!* he yelled — "Stand and stab it!"

Instead, Jon jumped, putting his entire bodyweight behind the harpoon. The spear tip pierced blubber. But then his grip slipped and his hands shot down the sea-slicked length of the bamboo. When he smashed into the water, he could feel that little of his force had trans-ferred into the weapon. He yanked himself aboard *Demo Sapang* and Gabriel yelled to ask whether the harpoon had entered.

"It didn't go in!" Jon said. "My hands were slippery!" (Later, Igna-tius would explain to Jon that he had been too close to the whale to jump on it, because that meant all his momentum had been down-ward, whereas ideally a lamafa struck at a perpendicular angle, so his forward momentum could drive the spearhead into the whale. In that situation, Jon had needed to segêt, stand and stab.)

Gabriel had readied another harpoon, but Stefanus regained the hâmmâlollo before his assistant could strike. The bereung alep surren-dered the weapon to his lamafa and again took up the rope. While the rest of the crew focused on rowing Stefanus back into position through the scrum of boats, Jon assembled the *nodah puka* harpoon, a smaller weapon normally used for devil rays, because the great harpoons had already been used. This time, as *Demo Sapang* neared the whale, the bull stopped swimming suddenly, and the téna nearly ran aground atop it. Stefanus choked up his grip on his harpoon. Jon skipped across the téna's railing to the base of the hâmmâlollo, where he squatted and raised his weapon.

The immensity of the whale emphasized Jon's frailness. He weighed only a hundred ten pounds. Was it sheer madness to think he could defeat a creature thousands of times heavier? He had only one thought: to make sure the harpoon entered, for himself and for his tribe.

Stefanus hurled himself off the hâmmâlollo once more, going fully horizontal. Half a second later, Jon followed, legs tucked up beneath him, the pale hourglasses of his bare soles flashing at the crew. The head of his harpoon punched in. When he saw blood spurt, joy shook him: the iron had penetrated through the blubber to the flesh. He was not a lamafa yet, but he had just taken the most important step to becoming one in full view of the tribe.

Jon (left) harpoons his first whale.

Jon cut desperate strokes through the water back to the boat, trying to outdistance the whale's gnashing jaw and thrashing tail. Once he pulled himself aboard, he realized that his part in the battle was over. Other téna had engaged the whale. *Demo Sapang* was now just weight towed behind it. Jon could rest. He had nothing left to prove.

The whale fought through the afternoon. It managed to flip *Kebako Pukā,* the ur-téna, by swimming underneath it and shrugging the boat over. Eventually, all nine téna that had launched were attached to it, but the leviathan hauled the whole fleet as if they were nothing; at nearly seventy tons, it probably outweighed all of the ships put together. In time the Lamalerans' teamwork began to overwhelm it. The boats acted like anchors, creating drag, and the whale became too tired to dive. More than a hundred men harried it in concert, lancing it from afar or swimming in close to slash it with their duri, attacking it from its weak side whenever it turned to attack a téna. The sea turned purple. By the end, the Lamalerans were sitting on top of the whale, knifing into it until

297

their arms disappeared up to the elbows. In one last burst of strength, the animal shook off the men atop it, and tried to bite its tormentors, but they swam away through the slick of blood and by now it was too weak to catch any of them. Soon it stilled forever.

No matter how modern pressures might be splintering the tribe, in the hunt the Lamalerans are still unified. The only way they can defeat a whale is together, as the Ancestors did: *Talé tou, kemui tou, onã tou, mata tou*. One family, one heart, one action, one goal. Elsewhere, in the industrialized world, as the relentless onslaught of globalization continues and tribal identities are overwritten with national or international ones, the intense bonds that once linked humans, that once gave them their sense of purpose and helped them survive, have weakened, leaving citizens increasingly isolated — both rootless and lonely — with a concomitant rise in mental-health disorders, all of which are well documented in scientific literature.

In the Days of the Ancestors, humans had no option but to rely on each other. To harvest a rice paddy, to construct a cathedral, to vanquish a sperm whale, the solution was cumulative strength. In their decades of resisting the outside world, in defending the Ways of the Ancestors, the Lamalerans had, more than anything, been trying to defend this shared humanity. For the moment, as they towed home the defeated leviathan, they had succeeded.

ONCE *DEMO SAPANG* WAS DRY-DOCKED, Ignatius and Ben braced their backs against the wooden pillars of their boat shed and slumped to the sand.

"Tired," Ignatius said, with a loopy grin, like a child who had played himself to exhaustion.

Ben had rarely heard his father admit to fatigue before. The rest of the crew passed around cigarettes and began complaining about Stefanus missing his first strike, for the aging lamafa had already gone home in shame.

Ignatius cleared his throat and everyone fell silent. It had been his intention, he said, to choose Ben for the hâmmâlollo, for he still owned the leka for *Demo Sapang*. But when Stefanus presented himself, Ignatius thought it was inappropriate for a younger man to take his place. However, he assured the crew that next time, Ben would take up the harpoon.

Ben tried to suppress his smile. He wanted nothing more than for his father to see him land his first whale. He was confident it would happen soon. Over the last year, aboard the jonson *Kanibal,* he had become one of the most renowned of the young harpooners. No longer did the shadow of his father and brothers fall on him. He had even developed his own style of harpooning, built off the judo moves his father and brothers used to compensate for their smaller bodies, but adding a physicist's calculation as he computed the overlapping vectors of the prey and his harpoon until the perfect opportunity arrived. Jon and other aspiring lamafa were already studying his tricks.

Instead of interpreting Ignatius passing over him for the hâmmâlollo as a slight, the way he once might have, Ben understood his father's hesitation to be a sign of love. As his son had progressed as a lamafa, Ignatius's advice to him had transformed from exhortations to cautionary tales. He warned Ben never to jump on a manta ray's back, for its enormous wings could enwrap him, and then the animal might drag him into the depths and drown him. And he should never strike the impenetrable forehead of a kotekĕlema, because the shock could break his arm. It was as if the danger into which Ignatius had inducted his son by encouraging his development as a lamafa had suddenly become real. For his part, Ben understood that his father was just trying to keep his boy safe a little longer.

THAT EVENING, AS THE WESTERN SKY blazed saffron and parents called for their children to come home from watersliding down the whale's corpse, the Lamaleran elders paraded to the Council on the Beach. Although two years earlier the crowd had filled the whole beach, now only about thirty old men were assembled before Sipri and Marsianus.

Frans and a few other whitebeards kept glancing back, searching for latecomers. In murmurs they blamed the low turnout on everyone's exhaustion from the hunt that day. Frans and his clansmen had not joined the chase because they had rowed *Kéna Pukā* to bring gifts to the Wulandoni tribes, a symbolic gesture meant to recall the original exchange with the warrior Dato that led to the creation of the market, and to indicate that the new téna would serve the whole region. Later that year *Kéna Pukā* would harpoon its first whale without suffering a single crack, proof from the Ancestors that it was perfectly built.

Eventually, Sipri shuffled to the head of the circle, kicked off his flip-flops, sat cross-legged, and wrapped a wispy sarong around his neck like a scarf, as if he was cold. Marsianus had effectively become the chief of the clan now, and would perform the Calling of the Whales the next day, but in deference to his father was allowing the old man to lead this ceremony. An air of grief shadowed Sipri, for his long-enfeebled wife "no longer felt the bites of ants," as the Lamaler-ans say, meaning she had recently died. Sipri asked his people to unburden themselves of their cares, so that he could bring them to the Ancestors. The usual complaints about whalers stealing one another's prey followed, but also concerns about the dwindling number of rays and sharks. A resolution to expand the driftnetting season into Léfa was again rejected. But the Council did resolve that cell phones could be used at sea, though only to communicate with other boats or people onshore about the location of prey, and never to play songs or videos for entertainment.

Then Sipri waved his hand to silence everyone. The elders strained to catch his hoarse voice over the shushing of the waves. Why, he asked them plaintively, had they not returned to sailing and rowing as he had ordered? But there was no threat in his voice, only exhaustion and defeat.

Jepo, the Bataona representative of the Lika Telo, asked the assem-bly if anyone wanted to answer the Lord of the Land. When no one raised their bowed head, Jepo apologized to Sipri, saying the Lamalerans would do their best to hunt more with the téna that year, but everyone knew it was an empty promise.

The old argument of téna against jonson restarted as evening finished strangling the day. An unshaded lightbulb flickered on in the chapel and revealed the statue of Saint Peter glaring at the assembly, gripping a real harpoon, with the desiccated organs of whales and dolphins scattered around his concrete feet. Soon stars dewed the sky, and everyone had lost his individuality to the darkness. The voices could have risen from anywhere and anyone, as if even the Ancestors might have joined the ceremony. The never-ending argument rattled on. Whalers kept walking away into the darkness, until only a small band continued to dispute the old questions. Down the beach, crumbling waves swished the tail of the slain whale back and forth, making it appear still alive. The children had all gone home.

After forty minutes of debate, Sipri's phlegmy voice echoed with surprising strength. "Lamalera is famous across the world because of our culture," he said. "We must not lose that. The hunt must never end. But jonson are only tools." The tribe could use them without losing their culture, he finally allowed, as long as they were careful. He had accepted that they could not entirely reject the modern world, but they could control how it affected their lives. And with that, Sipri, the Lord of the Land and the Guardian of the Ancestors, who had railed against the jonson for more than two decades, ended his formal opposition. In his heart, he still felt the Lamalerans would be better off without the motorboats, but he remembered the Ancestors' primary directive: *Talé tou, kemui tou, onã tou, mata tou.* The tribe's harmony was more important than fighting a battle he had already lost. Even if the way the Ancestors had hunted were to vanish, at least their unity would remain. Besides, there was nothing more he could do. Now that the power in the Wujon clan had formally passed to Marsianus, Sipri was aware that he was the Lord of the Land in name only.

The next day, Sipri waited by the Whale Stone, trying to scrub away the tears that forced themselves out, unbidden, while his son led his younger relatives up through the jungle to call the Ancestors. His body could no longer make the trek. Unbeknownst to Sipri, Marsianus began the Ige Gerek ceremony at the lower Nuba Nara stone, the same place his father had been forced to launch it the year before, when the late departure from the village had made it impossible for him to reach the traditional starting point a few miles higher. Marsianus had no such excuses, but he did not want to make the sweaty climb and justified to himself that the ceremony had worked the previous year anyway. Of course, what Sipri would say, had he known, was that this was how the Ways of the Ancestors had slowly diminished, withering in proportion to the fidelity of their defenders, incrementally pared of their inessentials in the name of expediency, until there was almost nothing left.

THE MODERN INDUSTRIAL LIFESTYLE did not colonize the world because it was best at fulfilling the emotional and spiritual needs of human beings. No, it conquered everywhere because advanced societies were stronger than traditional ones, and those in power rapaciously sought peoples, territories, and resources to further enrich themselves. Once industrialism had established itself, it offered enough significant advancements in material wealth, education, and healthcare to ensure that there was no going back. The benefits of modern states still prove irresistible to indigenous peoples in the contemporary world, often luring them away from their traditional lifestyles. After all, what person would prefer to scrub clothes on a board as opposed to dropping them in a washing machine? There is no citizen of, say, the United States or Japan who would ever want to return to the high levels of infant mortality, shortened life spans, food insecurity, and the ever-present threat of violence that hunter-gatherers have historically endured. And some disadvantaged individuals in traditional communities, from women to low-caste groups like the Kĕrofa clan, would unsurprisingly prefer to overturn the social order that keeps them down.

Even in positive scenarios, however, not all development is beneficial. Progress also means that something is left behind. At least half of change is always loss. The craze in advanced societies to reconnect to our past selves — from paleo diets, to New Age spiritualism, to wilderness retreats, to the many ways in which we romanticize indigenous peoples — suggests that citizens of those nations intuit that they are missing something. The worst forms of modernity look a lot like an addiction, and perhaps the Ways of the Ancestors are an antidote.

The debate about the benefits of a hunter-gatherer lifestyle versus a modern one is often framed as a determination of which one is absolutely better. But that approach misses the point: both lifestyles have advantages and disadvantages. Instead, we should be asking what each type of society can learn from the other. For though people of all cultures like to declare their way of life the natural one, no modern or traditional lifestyle is inevitable. It is possible for us to pick what is best from one while rejecting what is bad from the other. This is what the Lamalerans are doing at the Council on the Beach. Their great heroism is that they are striving, despite overwhelming odds, to control the process that has hijacked all of humanity.

Our ability to determine how technology and globalization shape us may turn out to be essential to human happiness and even survival. So far, modernity has not been a well-thought-out process. Rather, it has been a series of impulsive leaps at each new technological advance — a process that has *happened* to us instead of one that we have controlled. Is it possible for modern societies to implement their own Council on the Beach?

No matter what, it is an ethical imperative to preserve traditional cultures and thereby to protect the earth's most vulnerable peoples. Even the most casual observer is aware that globalization has been an immensely inequitable process, with its greatest rewards flowing to the elites capable of capturing them, while vast swaths of the 370 million indigenous people worldwide have emerged worse off — deprived of their ancestral livelihoods and support networks in exchange for the lethal poverty of urban slums or plantations. Nations and corporations, which are often the ones harming traditional groups thinking they know what is best for them, must empower them to make their own choices.

By making it possible for each person to choose his or her own path, we may be making it possible for us to save ourselves in the future. After all, each traditional culture represents a centuries-long natural experiment in determining the best way to survive in a particular environment, often guarding knowledge that Western science has not even guessed at. Just as ecological diversity is important for the health of an ecosystem, so cultural diversity may prove essential for the resilience of humanity, should a fatal weakness in the monoculture of globalization ever be revealed. And when a traditional culture like the Lamalerans' vanishes, it is a tangible diminishment in the number of ways to be human: a contraction in the possibilities inherent in our species, and therefore in each of us. To protect traditional societies is to guarantee each person's right to live the way that is most spiritually rewarding to him or her, a right every human deserves.

The upheaval that Jon and Ben and Frans and the rest of the Lamalerans are experiencing is a process every modern citizen's ancestors underwent, at a slower speed, and one that has led to an unprecedented moment in human history, when we are on the verge of completely wiping out the foraging cultures from which we all descended. Our bodies, minds, and hearts are still calibrated by tens of thousands of years of evolution and our hunter-gatherer past, no matter the disorienting demands of the present. Shouldn't we at least try to shape our contemporary lives to honor our original nature? What happens next is unclear, but if we forget our Ancestors, we will lose an essential part of our future.

THE NEXT DAY, THE LAMALERANS butchered the Gift of the Ancestors. Pugilist waves splashed its leaking oil into the men's eyes, irritating them until they blazed. When the time came to divide the meat, a duty usually reserved for the man considered responsible for taking the whale, the crew of *Demo Sapang* chose Jon. He stepped into the center of the circle of men and, with sincere gravity, picked up a gigantic steak with both hands and carried it to Ignatius, bending forward with its weight. Then he apportioned the rest of the gory bricks, ensuring that each man was awarded an equal share, while also stacking a bloody cairn for himself.

Because Ika was too weak from the pregnancy to help Jon carry the bounty, he bore the flesh up the cliff by himself and laid it on the oil-blackened wooden table behind the house. Yosef Boko, despite his near blindness, tried to help, painstakingly slicing off ribbons of meat by feel, but it was Jon who did the real work. With a machete he hacked steaks into strips and draped them on the bamboo poles. His complaints of the previous year were gone. After spearing the whale, he felt strong enough to support his family alone, no matter how much of a burden they became. Meanwhile, the umā were being divided into běfānā and spreading through the tribe, until the whale fed almost everyone.

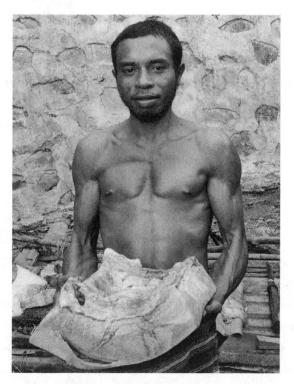

Jon with a piece of the whale he harpooned

Tonight was Misa Arwah, the annual Mass for Lost Souls. After a bucket shower, Jon descended to the beach by himself, for Ika refused to expose her embarrassing belly and his grandparents could no longer climb the stairs. As they did every year, the choir sang: "Row calmly, row tranquilly, / As the waves are loosed upon the shore. / Daydream calmly, daydream tranquilly, / In the middle of the typhoon of life, / In the middle of the typhoon of life." Jon lit his candles in an isolated corner of the beach and prayed to become a lamafa, to marry Honi, to live in his house on the cliffs, and to have many children who would continue the Ways of the Ancestors.

Bena asked that the spirits continue to welcome her back into the tribe. Frans requested that his forebears bless his new téna. Ben prayed to take a sperm whale, and Ignatius sought that his son should be kept safe doing it. Their entreaties mingled with those of the other Lamalerans to form a single choir — unheard by all but the Ancestors — one that has been singing as long as the tribe has existed and that will continue until it goes silent, for the human heart will never stop desiring.

The sea was calm that evening, and the miniature armada that was launched for the lost souls paraded around the western cliffs like envoys rushing to meet the outside world. A few candles sank, but most of the Lamalerans' wishes escaped the island this year — though only each man and woman knew what private desires flickered in those flames.

ALMOST ALL OF HUNTING IS WAITING. Staring intently but emptily at the loop of the horizon, yearning for the gift of prey. But when spouts are sighted, when the sun sparks on the freshly whetstoned edge of a harpoon, when the Ancestors return to hunt at a whaler's side, when each moment resonates with the gravity of life and death, that makes everything else worth it. For a Lamaleran, the hunt never gets old.

On the morning of May 1, in front of the whale's skeleton, the Lamalerans celebrated Misa Léfa. Because it was a Sunday, they waited until the next dawn to launch *Praso Sapang*. As the téna rowed out, the crew did not sing. Once, the tribe had choired together. Once, every facet of Lamaleran life had been accompanied by a song. But the Age of Song was over. And yet when the crew of *Praso Sapang* unrolled their palm-leaf sail, from afar it appeared that the Ancestors hunted again. As the Lamalerans onshore went about their tasks, they kept an eye on the sea, for the success of the téna would be an omen for the year ahead.

In the late morning, Ote was monitoring *Praso Sapang* with binoculars when he spied pilot whales. According to the Ancestors, only *Praso Sapang* should have hunted that first day, but Ote raised the alarm. Eight jonson rushed out, their engines screeching. Incensed at the violation, Frans forbade the Bedionas' jonson to join. The fleet zipped past *Praso Sapang* and caught the pod. Ote's strikes were usually automatic kills, but today both he and another lamafa failed to embed their spearheads. Then the pilot whales dove and disappeared. The Lamalerans did not know it yet, but the year would be a barren one, just like the year before, with only six sperm whales caught and a marked dearth of other prey, especially manta rays.

Normally, once Léfa commenced, the weather blew in from the east. This day, though, after the pilot whales disappeared, all the way home a west wind howled in the Lamalerans' faces and clawed the clouds heaped atop the volcano into streamers. But the whalers never took their eyes from the horizon. Whatever was coming would arrive from beyond it. They could do nothing but wait, ready for whatever the future swept toward them.

EPILOGUE

May 2016–May 2018

Over the next two years, in many respects the most dangerous threats to the Ways of the Ancestors seemed to be defused. Although the Wulandoni Port was finally completed in mid-2017, no ferries were yet scheduled. Newly sworn-in bureaucrats saw little commercial potential in the impoverished region and did not want to deal with the still-feuding Nualela and Luki tribes. These politicians disparaged the whole project as a boondoggle for the opposing party. Salés, meanwhile, was unable to procure enough tuna from the Lamalerans and other coastal tribes to make exporting sport fish profitable, and pivoted instead to buying baitfish by the ton from commercial trawlers in Lewoleba and grinding it into animal feed, some of which he claimed to ship to America. And though some young Lamalerans were still moving away, a core group had committed to life in the village.

When Honi's contract concluded, near the end of 2016, Jon crossed the archipelago to escort her home, and experiencing western Indonesia's polluted megalopolises on that trip snuffed any vestige of interest in ever living in one. Honi moved into his house and helped him care for his grandparents, who by then were in grave decline. During Léfa 2017, Jon earned the léka of a jonson, and was even called to lead several téna. Though he was unable to take his first sperm whale during those hunts, it was clear that no one would ever again call him a kefela.

In late 2017, he and Honi welcomed a son, Yosef Boko Jr., who carried on the name of his great-grandfather. The birth, ironically, delayed their formal marriage indefinitely, as they would have to refile paperwork with the Catholic Church to acknowledge the out-of-wedlock child, and they decided they had more pressing duties. When the following year's Léfa opened, sometimes Jon tested the wobbly-legged toddler on the harpooner's platform of his jonson. It seemed to him that Yosef Boko Jr. was destined to become a lamafa.

Alo and Ika were happily married, and their toddler daughter laughed with the same sweet abandon as her mother. For though Ika had experienced depression during her pregnancy, she eventually regained much of her old vim. She enjoyed being a mother, and after Honi arrived in Lamalera, she and Alo moved into his parents' house, a situation she found much less stressful than caretaking her grandparents and Jon. Like most of her contemporaries, Ika had never learned to weave, since she and other young Lamalerans primarily wore factory-made clothes instead of the traditional sarongs spun from jungle cotton. Recently, however, she had asked Alo's mother to teach her, for though she had accepted that high school was now out of reach, she realized there was fascinating knowledge about her own people that she had yet to master. As for Alo, after working as a bereung alep for Jon, he was on the cusp of becoming a respected lamafa in his own right, often being called to the hâmmâlollo of various jonson.

As age burdened Frans, he gave up everyday whaling, though he still occasionally joined the baleo. Much of his time was now spent passing on his shipbuilding and shamanistic knowledge to younger members of his clan, especially Jon's friend Anso. Though his daughter Bena had not yet settled on a suitor, she had happily reintegrated into the tribe. But she could still sing every English word of Katy Perry's "Last Friday Night."

Though at Ige Gerek of 2016, Sipri had appeared to be on his last legs, as the months passed his health dramatically improved; this may have been because he no longer had to endure the stresses of caring for his stroke-crippled wife, who had passed shortly before the ceremony. Soon enough, Sipri retook control of the Wujon clan from Marsianus, though this caused some tension between father and son, and he began making frequent trips from Lewoleba to the tribe to perform all manner of arcane rituals, now that he was freed from his bedside ministrations.

Given all this and more, as the tribe released their candle-bearing miniature fleet at the Misa Arwah of 2018, everyone assumed the Ancestors were happy. The next day brought more good omens, for during the inaugural solo hunt of *Praso Sapang* at Misa Léfa, Yosef Tubé harpooned a large devil ray for the téna. Throughout the next week the whole fleet enjoyed extraordinary success, capturing dozens of rays and a whale.

Not every story, however, has the ending we would wish for it. At the end of the second week of Léfa, Ben led forth *Kanibal,* the Blikololong jonson, at dawn. When the hunters saw the darkness sliding across the sea, at first they thought it was the shadow of a cloud on the otherwise sunny day, for the manta ray had such a wingspan. As Ben lifted one of his father's harpoons, none of the crew suspected that the colossal animal was beyond his abilities. Since becoming a lamafa three years earlier, he had taken every type of prey except a sperm whale, and many in the tribe already considered him the greatest harpooner of his generation.

Though Ben had found attaining this stature satisfying, it had been even more rewarding to master the Way of the Lamafa that pertained to how a man achieved harmony with his tribespeople. His and Ita's love was halcyon. Ignatius, who had officially retired from the hunt, dwelt happily in his house. In the mornings, the old man chose which of his ships Ben would captain, usually *Kanibal,* though if whales appeared, sometimes he would select Ben over his older brothers to lead *Demo Sapang.* After helping the ship to sea, Ignatius would nap on the sand until his son returned with the day's catch. In the late afternoons, Ben coached his young son, Carolos, on how to spear driftwood in the surf, and then Carolos and the other boys would pre-tend to be him as they practiced.

When Ben leapt to spear the manta, then, he was at his apogee. The sun flashed around him as he descended, spear point leading. The strike was true. The rope yanked taut as the ray rebelled. Ben swam furiously back toward *Kanibal*. But when he was just a few strokes away, he screamed out. Then he was yanked underwater, leaving only evaporating froth and fading ripples in his place.

The crew of *Kanibal* tug-of-warred with the manta ray, knowing that Ben's foot was likely ensnared in the harpoon line or that the ani-mal had abducted him in its wings. But the rope went limp, and they reeled in only its broken end. The water was exceptionally clear that day, with beams of sunlight illuminating its empty upper reaches, but though they waited, nothing rose out of the unfathomable darkness below.

They raced home, as if Ben was merely holding his breath and every second counted. Like a tragic baleo, the entire fleet scrambled to launch at their news. For a whole week téna and jonson scoured the Savu Sea, for if the lamafa's body was not buried with honors, his dis-pleased spirit might wreak vengeance. But the sea had swallowed him and would not relinquish his corpse. The fate that Jon Hariona had nar-rowly escaped several years earlier had now claimed Ben Blikololong.

THE ELDERS CONVENED NIGHTLY UNDER the banyan tree, debating why the Ancestors had stolen Ben. Many answers were proffered, but the one to which the council returned again and again was that they were being punished for failing to adequately defend the Ways of the Ances-tors. For though some threats to the Ways had been mitigated, like the Wulandoni Port and Salés's business, new perils threatened a crisis point. There was the usual straying of the Lamalerans themselves, for as smartphone prices had cheapened and the cell phone tower's signal was upgraded, many Lamalerans had become enmeshed in the World

Wide Web and social media. And bartering was becoming rare at the Lamaleran market, as the mountain tribes increasingly adopted cash.

Even more hazardous, a coalition of Western conservationists, including the Nature Conservancy and the Dolphin Project, was pushing the Indonesian government to severely regulate the hunt. Until then, several readings of the relevant Indonesian laws had suggested that the Lamaleran sperm whale hunt was legal, as indigenous groups are guaranteed the right to continue traditional subsistence activities. The International Convention for the Regulation of Whaling, which Indonesia has not signed, allows for sustainable subsistence hunting by indigenous groups. But the conservationists argued that laws banning whaling superseded those defending indigenous rights, and which have primacy has never been tested in court.

And though the legality of the sperm whale hunt was debatable, it was certain that the Lamalerans' poaching of manta rays was not, as in 2014 the Indonesian government banned such killing. Few Lamalerans were aware of this legislation, however, until late 2016, when a conservation NGO worked with the Indonesian police to set up a sting operation in which a Lamaleran elder was arrested for selling manta ray gills, shocking the tribe. The goal of the arrest, a representative of the NGO explained, was to discourage the capture not only of those animals but also of whales.

By the following year, the Nature Conservancy was publicly arguing that the Lamalerans had given up their culture when they chose the jonson over the téna, and so should be encouraged to stop hunting. Together with the Indonesian government, conservation NGOs drafted regulations in 2018 aimed at limiting the tribe to taking at most a handful of whales each year — or even none — with the intent to implement the rules in 2019. Though in the past the Lamalerans had united to defy such measures, this time most of the tribe were not even cognizant of the threat because the elders who were in the know about the incipient laws disagreed about how much to inform and involve them.

*　　　*　　　*

BEN'S BODY WAS NEVER FOUND. Hunting stalled for weeks, as Jon and many of the other young lamafa were spooked by the sense that the Ancestors were displeased with the tribe. They worried about their own deaths. It seemed as if almost every Lamaleran grew out their hair and nails during the forty-day mourning period, for Ben was related to so many people, like Frans's wife, Maria, who was Ignatius's sister, and he had been close friends with many others, like Jon. In the end, Ignatius, Ita, and Ben's two children buried a nautilus shell in his place. A minuscule, fragile token to stand in for such a monumental presence. Where there had been a son, a husband, a father, and a true lamafa, now there was only longing. Where there had been a future full of possible joy, now his family faced a grief that would last as long as their lives and be as large as their hearts.

The loss of a culture is as permanent as the loss of a life, but rather than one star darkening, it is a whole constellation burning out. It is the disappearance of every soul that has constituted it. It is the end of a past and a future.

And yet, for the Blikololong family and the other mourning Lamalerans, the Ways of the Ancestors mean that Ben will not vanish. When the roll call of whalers lost at sea is read at Misa Léfa each year, he will be spoken of first, for a time. As an Ancestor, he will continue to bless and curse their lives. He will remain a vital member of the tribe.

But the Ancestors have such potency only as long as their descendants honor them. Every day the Lamalerans still choose to follow the Ways of the Ancestors, and every day that choice is getting harder. Their story is not yet finished.

About This Project

When I first visited Lamalera, in 2011, I was amazed to find that the Ways of the Ancestors still defined the tribe's life. I had just spent almost a year working on a nearby island, watching as several other traditional cultures rapidly succumbed to the stresses of globalization, and as I sailed with the téna, witnessed prey be ritually shared, and joined the ancestral ceremonies, I knew that I was experiencing something important and yet endangered. After I left, I missed the friends I had made and worried about their future.

The dominant story line about globalization is that it is making countless people wealthier, healthier, and better educated. This is true and in many important ways a blessing, but such a narrative overlooks the experiences of the millions of indigenous people for whom the encounter with the industrial world has been traumatic or even deadly. What does modernization look like from their side? What if instead of ignoring their stories because those individuals are "primitive" and the upheaval in their lives is "progress," we valued their experiences as seriously as our own? Surely, it seemed to me, the Lamalerans have a great deal to show citizens of so-called advanced societies about who we once were, how we became who we are today, and who we could be in the future.

In 2014, I returned to Lamalera, this time to stay for several months. Many things had already changed. But the Lamalerans had not forgotten me and heartily welcomed me back.

In total, I spent about a year with the Lamalerans while writing this book, spread over six visits from 2014 through 2017, with a three-week follow-up in 2018. During that time, I tried to immerse myself as deeply as possible in the tribe. I participated in dozens of hunts, despite a tendency to "bait the fishes," as the Lamalerans laughingly referred to my seasick vomiting. I was the first foreigner to attend the full Ige Gerek ceremony. I cooked and ate manta brains. I wove ropes. I spearfished. I slept in the Lamalerans' houses. I bartered at the market. Day after day, I recorded the stories of the living Lamalerans and the stories of the Ancestors.

There is a tendency among people writing about their time in foreign cultures to hype how beloved they were, obscuring the messiness of everyday life in order to seem a more perfect observer of it. While I was lucky enough that right after the youth dunked Frans during the festival for the new *Kéna Pukā,* they "baptized" me as a clansman too, there were just as many times I felt isolated and ignorant in Lamalera. Ultimately, I had a thoroughly human experience in the tribe, with all the friendships, squabbles, rapprochements, and social highs and lows of living in any group. I thought of this as striving as much as possible to be a part of — rather than above or separate from — the Lamalerans.

While my blindness and biases as an outsider can never be fully overcome, I endeavored to minimize them through dedicated, careful reporting. Writing this book, I interviewed more than 100 Lamalerans, many of them dozens of times. My research notes exceeded 600,000 words. I shot more than 20,000 photographs. My audio and video recordings stretched for dozens of hours. I am one of the few outsiders ever to become proficient in Lamaleran, though I also communicated in Bahasa, Indonesia's national language, which I speak fluently. During a visit to Lamalera in 2017, I fact-checked most of this book by summarizing its contents to the individuals depicted in these pages. When appropriate, I incorporated their suggestions and corrections. I foreground all of this to say that I have labored to earn the privilege to write about lives far different from my own.

To anchor the facts in this work, I was able to lean on a rich set of records. To confirm dates, I perused the baptismal and burial lists kept by the church. Local administrators, from the villages' mayors to school principals, were kind enough to open their archives to me. I also consulted two different whaling annals, a public one compiled by a Lamaleran named Fransiskus Keraf, and a more complete private one kept by a benefactor who wishes to remain anonymous. To understand the interactions between the tribe and the initial missionaries, the UN Food and Agriculture Organization, and the World Wildlife Fund, I consulted their own reports. Many Indonesian bureaucrats and NGO workers generously let me interview them about their experiences with the Lamalerans. Reams of newspaper articles and several film documentaries also informed this book. And the trove of academic research proved especially invaluable, most notably the work of Robert H. Barnes, David Nolin, Michael Alvard, Kotaro Kojima, Tomoko Egami, and Anita Lundberg. Finally, I was lucky enough to read what the Lamalerans wrote about themselves, especially Gregorious Keraf's dissertation *Morfologi Dialek Lamalera* (*Morphology of the Lamaleran Dialect*), the in-progress monograph of Jacobus Blikololong, and the works of Bona Beding.

Reporting in Lamalera presented several unique challenges. The inequity of my disproportionate wealth as an American was never far from my mind. However, the Lamalerans were gracious or indifferent enough to rarely emphasize it. The realities of living with the tribe necessitated a more interwoven economic relationship than usual for a journalist and his subjects. As can be imagined for one staying with a tribe whose culture places importance on reciprocal giving, I exchanged many items with the Lamalerans, including cigarettes, knives, diving masks, fishing hooks, and other sundries, as well as modest sums of money. In return, I was given rice, whale jerky, and other daily necessities, plus several non-essential items, such as nautilus shells, weavings, and miniature téna, like those used in the Misa Arwah ceremonies. I provided the Lamalerans in whose homes I boarded the same fee tourists paid at homestays. I did my best to keep my expenditures consistent with my daily needs to avoid unduly influencing anyone's life. The exception is that several times I paid for families to bring a loved one over the mountains for urgently needed medical care. The recipients of these gifts were not the individuals primarily portrayed in this book. In these cases, I chose to prioritize being a human before being a journalist.

The Lamalerans who participated in this project did so with the knowledge that they would not be paid and that they might not like the things I wrote about them. This makes the uncountable hours they gave me all the more generous. They endured my incessant questions out of a belief that sharing their stories could create a record of their culture and show an increasingly inhospitable world the richness of their way of life and why they should be allowed to continue to live as they choose. In these pages, I endeavored to remain in the background as much as possible in the hope that when readers remember this book, they will think of Jon, Ika, Frans, Ignatius, Ben, the rest of the Lamalerans, and the millions of other indigenous people who are enduring similar turmoil. I hope people will listen to their story. It has been a great honor to tell it.

Sharing so much life with people of another culture, anyone will find himself adopting their mannerisms, thoughts, and feelings — an unnerving but important experience because it reinforces that one's way of life is not inevitable and that no single culture has a monopoly on the correct way to live. I hope that after finishing this book, readers will be a little less American, or any other tribal identity, and just a bit more human, alive to the myriad possibilities that dwell within us all and the need to esteem each of them. Certainly, I harbor the residue of this blessed estrangement. Since I have returned to America, Lamaleran words echo in my brain, a constant reminder that the only other people who can understand them are half a world away and that there are many more ways to be human than I encounter in my everyday life.

Whenever I depart Lamalera, the Lamalerans always tell me to come "home" soon. That word "home," *balik,* is a special verb, condensing into a single word a sentiment that takes a full phrase to express in English — "to come home" — for the tribe uses it so often and the idea has such great resonance with them. *Goé bera balik,* I always answer: "I will come home as soon as possible."

Acknowledgments

My list of debts is long, as it should be for a book about how it takes a community to overwhelm a leviathan, whether literal or metaphorical.

Foremost, I am deeply grateful to the Lamalerans depicted in this book, whose bigheartedness in sharing their lives knew few limits. Many Lamalerans who are not described in these pages also assisted me. To name each one would be impossible — seemingly all fifteen hundred members of the tribe living in the village aided me at some point. However, I would like to offer special thanks to the village mayors Jeffery Bataona, Thomas Sabon Kĕrofa, and Yakobus Dasion for their support. And Aloysius Gnesser Tapoonã was the best possible instructor in the Way of the Lamafa, for few have embodied it as well as him, and his precise memory was invaluable when writing about Lamalera's history.

I've been blessed to have the incomparable Ben George help conceive, edit, and launch this project. My editor, my friend, it's been an honor working with you. This book is immeasurably better for the spirit you have lavished on it, and my life has been similarly enriched by the time we've spent together.

Cynthia Saad also offered incisive editorial help and steered the book's production.

The excellent Little, Brown and Company team — Reagan Arthur, Craig Young, Maggie Southard, Sarah Haugen, Betsy Uhrig, Dianna Stirpe, and everyone else — have gone above and beyond the call of duty.

Jim Rutman is the Steve Nash of agents. I've also appreciated the assists from Brian Egan.

David Nolin deserves special thanks for discussing Lamalera for hours, perceptively commenting on a draft, and reparsing some of his data for me. I'm also grateful for his belief in this project when I doubted.

I am indebted to Robert H. Barnes for our interview and access to his archive of photographs. His *Sea Hunters of Indonesia* has been an inspiring touchstone for all work on Lamalera, including mine. The small number of times when I've differed on details about Lamaleran culture should only highlight how perfect the vast majority of his ethnography remains decades later.

Jacobus Belida Blikololong generously shared his reminiscences and in-progress research.

I am still grateful that the Fulbright Program sent me to Indonesia — and thus Lamalera — in the first place, and for the guidance and friendship of Astrid Lim, then and afterwards.

Oscar Hijuelos, Reynolds Price, Darin Strauss, and Joseph Ashby Porter first encouraged me as a writer. I hope this has lived up to their teachings.

Ben Vatterot, Liana Engie, Brian Kraft, Rick Ferrera, Gordon LaForge, and Elena Fanjul-Debnam were kind enough to show me hospitality when I darkened their Jakartan doorsteps with only whale jerky to recompense them.

This work has benefited from perceptive reads by Julie Miesionczek, Boyce Upholt, and my wife. Liana Engie provided an early and especially essential edit.

I owe more to my parents than can ever be summarized in writing, but regarding this book, I am especially thankful to them for teaching me to always relentlessly *try* no matter how quixotic the quest and for their unwavering love, which has cushioned my many stumbles.

And lastly, but also firstly, I am indebted most of all to my primary reader, my wife, for co-adventuring with me near and far, through the good and the bad, on this voyage and the greater one called life. Wherever you are, that's home, always.

NOTES

Blind notes for sources can be found on the following pages. Additional material, including the Lamalerans' suggestions for how tourists should act while visiting, further readings on indigenous rights, and information about how readers can help the tribe, awaits on my website: dougbockclark.com.

Prologue

p. 3   *Baleo! Baleo!...* In Lamaleran, "The hunt is on!" The Lamalerans speak a dialect of Lamaholot, a language confined to the islands surrounding Lembata, which I have termed "Lamaleran" in this book. Lamaholot has about 200,000 speakers divided among an unknown number of dialects—likely dozens. Gary F. Smith and Charles D. Fennig, eds., *Ethnologue: Languages of the Word,* online edition, http://www.ethnologue.com/language/slp. Many of these dialects are mutually unintelligible. As Hanna Fricke of Leiden University, the only scholar researching Lamaholot on Lembata, said, "Lamaholot is a dialectical continuum in which many of the dialects are nearly as different as languages, so the Lamalerans may not be able to understand someone who grew up just a few villages away" (interview, May 9, 2016). Certainly, this was my experience with the language, and the reason I have dignified the Lamalerans' dialect as "Lamaleran" in this book and not Lamaholot.

p. 3   **all fifteen hundred souls...** There were 1,503 individuals living in Lamalera in July 2017 according to the village records of Lamalera A and B. This total excludes the population of the nearby mountain hamlet of Lamamanu, which is administratively included in Lamalera, but which has a different livelihood and culture. Of the population, 303 men were listed as fishermen.

p. 4   **Although the leviathan measured only about the same length as the téna...** When providing the lengths of sperm whales, I have relied on the public records kept by Fransiskus Keraf, a Lamaleran teacher, who uses a tape measure to size them. I also had access to a set of private records kept by another Lamaleran, who has asked to remain anonymous. As it is impossible to load a sperm whale onto a scale, whalers from ancient to modern times have used the formula that one foot of length equals a ton of weight, which I have subscribed to as well.

Chapter 1: The Lamaleran Odyssey

p. 11 **The Lamaleran Odyssey...** This chapter is based on interviews with the expedition members. It also draws on an article by anthropologist Anita Lundberg, who was working in Lamalera at the time: "Being Lost at Sea: Ontology, Epistemology, and a Whale Hunt," *Ethnography* 2, no. 4 (2001): 533–56.

p. 11 **even one of the sperm whales schooling just offshore...** See the discussion in the notes to chapter 4 about how much meat each whale provides the tribe.

p. 11 **hunter-gatherer societies remaining in existence...** Hunter-gatherers are people who primarily rely on wild foods for subsistence. The Lamalerans derive most of their food from the wild, though they also do a limited amount of farming and recently have purchased a small but growing amount of supplies from outside the tribe. Contrary to popular belief, most hunter-gatherers today have some access to modern tools and many have engaged in some agriculture for centuries to supplement their foraging. Richard B. Lee and Richard Daly, eds., *The Cambridge Encyclopedia of Hunters and Gatherers* (New York: Cambridge University Press, 2004). Today, anthropologists such as David Nolin and Michael Alvard study the Lamalerans as a model for how hunter-gatherer societies work.

p. 11 **The tribe's three hundred hunters...** The use of "tribe" as a descriptor for indigenous peoples has a fraught history because it was applied pejoratively by colonialists, often to justify abusing them by suggesting they were primitive. However, in this case, I use "tribe" in the anthropological sense, in which it describes an ethnic group that shares a self-name and territory, defines itself against other neighboring groups, is composed of smaller bands (in the Lamalerans' case, clans), and works together in essential activities, such as hunting, trade, agriculture, and cultural ceremonies. This description fits the Lamalerans. Additionally, the Lamalerans call themselves *lefo* in Lamaleran or *suku* in Bahasa Indonesia, both of which translate as "tribe."

p. 12 **making the Lamalerans the world's last true subsistence whalers...** A few indigenous peoples still hunt small numbers of whales in Canada, Greenland, the United States, and elsewhere, using a mix of traditional and modern technology. However, the hunt is generally more important for cultural than dietary reasons, as the people derive most of their calories from other sources. Industrial whaling is mostly confined to Russian and Japanese fleets, which use exploding harpoons to slaughter scores of whales in arctic waters under the auspices of "research" exemptions granted under the International Convention for the Regulation of Whaling, though really much of the meat is consumed. No other indigenous group relies nearly as much on whaling as the Lamalerans, for whom sperm whales are still the most important source of food and the core of their cultural identity.

p. 12　**meaning the tribe has little impact on the animal's global population...** The exact number of sperm whales in the world is difficult to determine as the animals are tough to track. The best guess, however, is that there are around 360,000. Hal Whitehead, "Estimates of the Current Global Population Size and Historical Trajectory for Sperm Whales," *Marine Ecology Progress Series* 242 (2002): 295–304. Other estimates have put their population as high as one million. The International Union for Conservation of Nature, whose Red List is the scientific authority on the population status of animals worldwide, describes the sperm whale as "vulnerable." The Endangered Species Act, however, defines it as "endangered" to activate legal protections needed for its conservation.

p. 13　**In 2009, the United Nations reported that many of humanity's 370 million indigenous people...** As estimated by the UN Department of Economic and Social Affairs, *The State of the World's Indigenous Peoples* (New York: United Nations, Secretariat of the Permanent Forum on Indigenous Issues, 2009), 8.

p. 13　**all people, whether in industrialized or traditional societies...** When I use the term "traditional societies" in this book, I mean past and present societies with anywhere from a dozen to several thousand people, who survive by hunting and gathering, farming, or herding, and have been little influenced by industrialized societies. There are probably no groups on earth that have not been affected at least to some degree by the modern world—flyovers of uncontacted Amazonian tribes suggest that they have imported non-native banana trees—so it may be best to think of "traditional" societies as "transitional" societies. Western or modern societies, in contrast, are those run by state governments, whose primary economy is industrial.

p. 15　**There were different songs for each kind of prey...** I have built off Barnes's translations for songs included in this book, occasionally tweaking them to highlight certain elements I feel were underemphasized in the translations.

p. 21　**they were the *leo*...** Each téna actually carries two types of leo: the major leo, a thick hawser for whales and manta rays, and the thinner minor leo, for smaller game.

p. 21　**with the souls of each clan's Spirit House...** For this reason, in the Days of the Ancestors, the leo were brought home each night. Thus, the term *baleo*— a contraction of *ba*, "to bring," and *leo*, "Spirit Rope"—which literally means "bring the leo" from the Spirit House to hunt the whales. Today, however, they are left in the téna.

p. 21　**pull tiger sharks ashore by their tails, and club them to death...** Robert H. Barnes, *Sea Hunters of Indonesia* (Oxford: Oxford University Press, 1996), 170.

p. 23 *Talé tou, kemui tou, onã tou, mata tou* — One family, one heart, one action, one goal... Literally, the phrase means: "One rope, one knot, one unity, one action." Barnes presents the archaic version: *Onã tou, mata tou, kemui tou, k̄a tou.* However, most contemporary Lamalerans only remember their grandparents using that version of the phrase occasionally and that the current formulation was more popular even then.

Chapter 2: At Play in the Graveyard of Whales

p. 41 **got his hands on an enormous severed penis...** Boys are boys the world over. When the anthropologist David Nolin was researching how much meat the tribe consumed in 1999, a group of boys dragged a penis over to his scales while the rest of tribe was butchering an especially large whale, yelling, "Weigh this! Weigh this!" He remembers it registering at around forty-five pounds.

p. 42 **Even when the Southeast Asian financial crisis ravaged the region's economies...** Adam Schwarz provides an in-depth description of the effects of the Southeast Asian financial crisis on Indonesia in *A Nation in Waiting: Indonesia's Search for Stability* (Boulder, CO: Westview Press, 2000).

p. 42 **When Jon enrolled in first grade...** As recorded in the elementary school registry of Lamalera A (Upper Lamalera).

p. 45 **Lower Lamalera... Upper Lamalera...** Upper and Lower Lamalera are actually different villages as defined by the Indonesian government, with parallel administrations, though physically they are contiguous. They are sometimes also referred to respectively as Lamalera A and Lamalera B; this is not an alphabetical reference but a nod to their Indonesian names, in which *atas* means "upper" and *bawah* means "lower."

p. 50 **for anthropologists have estimated that back then...** Michael S. Alvard and David A. Nolin, "Rousseau's Whale Hunt? Coordination Among Big-Game Hunters," *Current Anthropology* 43, no. 4 (August–October 2002): 533–59. Supplemented with additional data from David Nolin, personal communication, January 17, 2018.

p. 53 **But Jon, at seventeen — though he told everyone he was nineteen...** He would realize his error later when I asked him to count out his birthdays.

p. 58 **13,000 islands that make up Indonesia...** Estimates of the number of islands in Indonesia vary widely, with low figures starting at 13,000 and high ones reaching more than 17,000. At the time of this writing, Indonesia was still conducting a census to determine the number definitively.

Chapter 3: The Child-Eating Eel and the Curse of the Black Goat

p. 66 **but the date would probably have been not long after January 1522...** Jacobus Belida Blikololong, a native son of Lamalera and a lecturer at Gunadarma

University, has suggested these dates in his excellent paper "Masyarakat Lamalera" (publication pending). The argument for the date of the Lamalerans' arrival on Lembata is circumstantial, but strong. In short, when Magellan's party passed Lepan Batan on its circumnavigation of the world in January 1522, they recorded the island as inhabited, suggesting the tsunami had not yet forced the Lamalerans and other societies on it to relocate. However, records show that in 1525, when the king of Larantuka called his vassals to help him attack a neighboring kingdom, he enlisted a "bloody and bold" group that had recently settled in Lembata after fleeing a tsunami to the east—which was likely the Lamalerans, as they would continue an alliance with the king of Larantuka for centuries to come.

p. 66 **a childless crone...** There are various interpretations of the old widow's name. Most Lamalerans give it as Somi Bola Deran, though others claim she was nameless. However, all my sources agree that Korohama's wife was also named Somi Bola Deran (which Barnes records as well), so it is possible that both had the same name or that the two names have become conflated.

p. 67 **they left only one thing behind: the crone...** According to the Lamalerans, the crone eventually escaped Lepan Batan and tried to rejoin her people, following them until her flesh petrified mid-step at the Ata Dei Peninsula. Today, the human-shaped boulder can still be seen, trapped halfway between her tribe's future and past, and it gives the Ata Dei Peninsula its name in Lamaholot: Standing Person Peninsula.

p. 67 **Along the way, they weathered storms...** A longer and more detailed description of the Lamaleran hegira from Lepan Batan to Lembata can be found in Robert H. Barnes's *Sea Hunters of Indonesia* and Ambrosius Oleonâ's *Masyarakat Nelayan Lamalera dan Tradisi Penangkapan Ikan Paus* (Bogor, Indonesia: Lembaga Galekat Lefo Tanah, 2001).

p. 67 **their idyll was shattered when a son...** My understanding of the Lamaleran origin story matches Barnes's, except for concerning the transfer of power from Tana Kĕrofa to Korohama. Barnes writes that the conflict between the Lamalerans and the tribe whose land they settled on was started when one of the women of Tana Kĕrofa's clan was pestling maize, but inadvertently missed the mortar with the pestle and smashed a baby chicken owned by the natives. Several Lamalerans chortlingly informed me that this was an example of their forefathers practicing *teka teke,* or inventing a story to cover up a fault. They explained that the pestle failing to enter the mortar symbolized a sexual infraction: thus, one of Tana Kĕrofa's sons had relations with the daughter of the neighboring chieftain. In this version, the demands for the dowry-like ransom and the violent reaction of the other tribe make significantly more sense than in Barnes's version, in which the locals were just reacting to a chick that was killed.

p. 68 **the Wujons and the Tapoonãs lived on the volcanic ridges above…**In those times, the human geography of Lembata looked significantly different. Today, there are relatively few settlements in the mountains and most of the population lives along the coast. But when Europeans first sailed into eastern Indonesia, explorers wondered why natives favored out-of-the-way ridges over the Edenic bays below—until they realized that highland villages were secluded and easily protected. Slavers periodically pillaged the region; the Iranun Kingdom of the Philippines would dispatch fleets of warships on raids across Indonesia that could last years. Neighboring tribes attacked each other to acquire material and human loot, from child thralls to brides. The widespread practice of headhunting required that families revenge the murder of a relative by taking the killer's skull, resulting in interminable cyclical wars. The Dutch and Portuguese did not calm the situation when they arrived, fighting some tribes directly, enlisting others in proxy battles, and slaving into the 1800s.

Consequently, back then the inhabitants of Lamalera mostly lived in what is today the village of Upper Lamalera and the even more removed hamlet of Futung Lolo. These sanctuaries were accessed by a staircase called Géripé, cut into the cliffs, which is likely what Korohama climbed. The vertiginous steps were an integral part of the town's defenses, and visiting missionaries would later describe climbing them as terrifying. However, as the Dutch pacified the region, the need for Géripé diminished. In 1917, the Dutch dynamited Géripé and transformed it into a more comfortable set of stairs to help their administrators better access the village. In early 2000, a team of Javanese stone breakers spent a month weakening the rocks of the Dutch path with sledgehammers and hand chisels, so that when the bulldozer arrived, it took the machine less than a week to grade a ramp across the cliff to connect the two villages. In 2017, there were still a few remnants of Géripé and other ancient trails winding through the hills, but there were plans in 2018 to convert them into concrete paths.

p. 68 ***dpa*…**Barnes records this unit of measurement as *ƙesebō* (*Sea Hunters of Indonesia,* 105), but people today use the word *dpa*.

p. 68 **The formulation of "older brother"…**The distinction is so important that the Lamaleran language and Indonesian both use different terms of address depending on whether the speaker is talking to an older or a younger family member.

p. 70 **a monstrous seventy-foot-long schoolmaster sperm whale…**Doubts are often raised as to whether contemporary sperm whales grow much over sixty feet. The Lamalerans' experience provides evidence that a few whales outsize modern scientific estimates. The whale that killed Gregorious was measured at seventy feet by the town's elementary school teacher and keeper of the whaling records by moving a ten-meter rope along the giant corpse. Men stood on ladders to butcher it. In April 2016, I watched the Lamalerans measure a landed bull sperm whale at twenty-two meters, or seventy-two feet, an animal they considered large but not remarkably so. In February 2016, they had caught another whale of comparable size. In 2007, the Lamalerans took a bull whale they recorded as measuring twenty-five meters, or eighty-two feet. I have also seen the skull of the largest whale they ever caught, which was likely bigger than any of those animals, and which has been kept for ceremonial purposes. When they killed it in the 1970s they failed to record its length, but village elders remember it as being larger than the twenty-five-meter whale taken in 2007. I can attest that the skull far outsized that of the twenty-two-meter male caught in April 2016. There is also evidence that in the past whales grew this large—the Nantucket Whaling Museum has an eighteen-foot-long jawbone that it suggests belonged to a whale exceeding eighty feet.

p. 73 **Sickness and accidents stalked the clan until they went extinct...** Barnes provides a slightly different version of these events from that provided by my sources, on page 71 of *Sea Hunters of Indonesia*.

p. 75 **the Lamaleran system of orientation draws its locus from the Blikololong Spirit Houses...** Barnes, *Sea Hunters of Indonesia,* 74, 165.

p. 77 **Lera Wulan was a double-faced god who divided men into factions...** "Demon" here is a proper name and has no relation to the English word "devil."

p. 77 **Lamalera and Paji groups as each side sought blood...** A description of the Demon and Paji divide can be found in Robert H. Barnes's article "Construction Sacrifice, Kidnapping, and Head-Hunting Rumors on Flores and Elsewhere in Indonesia," *Oceania* 64, no. 2 (December 1993): 146–58.

p. 77 **In his letters, he described hearing that Lamaleran warriors had killed twelve Paji men...** My description of Bode's time in Lamalera is drawn from Barnes's *Sea Hunters of Indonesia* and articles, with additional details added by the Wujons. The descriptions of Lamaleran headhunting and Lera Wulan are drawn from Barnes's article "Construction Sacrifice, Kidnapping, and Head-Hunting Rumors on Flores and Elsewhere in Indonesia."

p. 79 **The best part of Sipri's year...** Previous descriptions of Ige Gerek, including Barnes's and even native Lamalerans', have been incomplete or erroneous when describing the ritual hidden on the upper reaches of Ile Labalekang. My account is based on accompanying the Wujons as the first foreigner to ever see the ritual. I also drew from extensive interviews with them and a step-by-step write-up provided by Sipri. Previous descriptions of the second half of the ceremony, from the Fato Kotekĕlema onward, are generally more accurate, as it takes place close to the village. Readers curious about the historical context of the ritual can find an accounting in Barnes's *Sea Hunters of Indonesia,* 26.

p. 80 **Tobo Nama Fata, the Council on the Beach...** Tobo Nama Fata literally translates as "to sit in the maize field," a metaphor that implies that the beach and the sea are as productive for the Lamalerans as the farms in the mountains above are for the agriculturalists dwelling there.

p. 81 **a sorcerous incantation, entreating the spirits onward...** "We bring the food to the widows and the orphans at the beach who are hungry and thirsty. Let's go! Let's go! Let's go!" Which is followed by mimicking the sound of the three barnyard animals, as Sipri does at the Whale Stone.

p. 81 **the next Spirit House, Pau Lera...** Barnes glosses Pau Lera as *Pau Lere,* or "low mango." However, the Wujons confirmed to me that in this case, *pau* means "to feed" — though *pau* is also a homonym for mango in Lamaleran. *Lera* means "sun" as in Lera Wulan (or Lama*lera*), with Lera Wulan here standing in for the Ancestors. Thus, "to feed the Ancestors" makes significantly more sense as a name for this step of the ceremony than "low mango."

Interestingly, embedded in Ige Gerek are indications that it may have existed as a harvest ritual before the Lamalerans converted the Wujons from agriculture to fishing. Hints include the three farming animal sounds the Wujons make and the fact that Lamaleran folktales describe Pau Lera as a petrified water buffalo *and* a whale (with an almost Trinitarian seamlessness). Ige Gerek also happens essentially contemporaneously with the harvest rituals of neighboring tribes, meaning it would not have been difficult to convert such a ceremony into a fishing rite once the formerly highlander Wujons joined the Lamalerans to become a coastal people. Thus, instead of just regarding Lamaleran religious practices as Christianity layered over fishermen's worship of Lera Wulan, scholars should consider the possibility of a third ancient agricultural practice underlying them both.

p. 84 **there were about 100,000 languages worldwide...** In my discussions of the contraction of the number of languages in the world, I have drawn from Daniel Nettle and Suzanne Romaine's *Vanishing Voices: The Extinction of the World's Languages* (Oxford: Oxford University Press, 2002) and John McWhorter's *The Power of Babel: A Natural History of Language* (New York: Harper Perennial, 2003), especially chapter 7, "Most of the World's Languages Went Extinct." The "100,000 languages" is drawn from Robert M. W. Dixon's *The Rise and Fall of Languages* (Cambridge, UK: Cambridge University Press, 2006), 68–73, and McWhorter's *The Power of Babel,* 259.

p. 84 **each representing its own culture...** Counting cultures is a difficult task — one so complex even professional anthropological efforts inevitably end in confusion or debate when trying to draw boundaries in the spectrum of difference between peoples. For example, at what point does Hollywood culture become Los Angelean culture become SoCal culture become Californian culture become American culture? Cultures exist as Venn diagrams rather than separate spheres of influence.

But though demarcating exactly where one culture ends and the next begins may be headache inducing, there are inarguably distinct cultural groups throughout the world: peoples with their own traditions, beliefs, self-proclaimed identities—and, often, languages. Because language acts as a hard boundary for a group's identity, it can serve as a crude but useful indexer of cultures, especially because the number of languages in the world—and their decline—has been extensively studied.

p. 84 **as different as English and Mandarin Chinese in valleys only ten miles apart...** Lembata is part of this linguistic treasure trove. Though it has only two unique classified languages, Kedang and Lamaholot, each has many dialects whose differences are so pronounced they may actually be separate languages, including Lamaleran. See previous note for a discussion of the nature of Lamaholot and Lamaleran.

p. 84 **As agriculture developed in several places...** In sketching the shape of world history, I have relied on John Darwin, *After Tamerlane: The Rise and Fall of Global Empires, 1400–2000* (New York: Bloomsbury Press, 2009); Jürgen Osterhammel and Niels P. Petersson, *Globalization: A Short History* (Princeton, NJ: Princeton University Press, 2009); Jared Diamond, *Guns, Germs, and Steel: The Fates of Human Societies* (New York: W. W. Norton, 2005); and Ian Morris, *Why the West Rules—for Now: The Patterns of History, and What They Reveal About the Future* (New York: Farrar, Straus and Giroux, 2010).

p. 85 **As foragers either joined civilizations or were wiped out by them, the number of languages and cultures shrank...** In my summary of the fate of hunter-gatherer societies and their evolution through history, I've relied on *The Cambridge Encyclopedia of Hunters and Gatherers,* edited by Richard B. Lee and Richard Daly; *Guns, Germs, and Steel* by Jared Diamond; and *The Lifeways of Hunter-Gatherers: The Foraging Spectrum* by Robert L. Kelly (New York: Cambridge University Press, 2013).

p. 85 **hunter-gatherers still occupied a third of the world...** *The Cambridge Encyclopedia of Hunters and Gatherers,* 389.

p. 85 **Europeans had little permanent presence in the Solor Archipelago...** In writing the history of the Portuguese colonization of Indonesia, I have drawn on *Nathaniel's Nutmeg* by Giles Milton (New York: Penguin, 2000), as well as Barnes's *Sea Hunters of Indonesia* and *Excursions into Eastern Indonesia: Essays on History and Social Life* (New Haven, CT: Yale Southeast Asia Studies, 2013), especially the chapter "Avarice and Inequity at the Solor Fort."

p. 85 **Westerners began to avoid the islands, fearing their people as cannibals...**
A description of the European fear of the Solor Archipelago can be found in
Barnes's article "Construction Sacrifice, Kidnapping, and Head-Hunting
Rumors on Flores and Elsewhere in Indonesia." The surgeon of one English
ship wrote of Lembata and the surrounding islands that they "are inhabited
by inhuman savages, which in person resemble the natives of Timor but in
nothing else. In disposition as far as is known, they are bloodthirsty and
cruel. They speak a language peculiar to themselves, and they go destitute of
clothing...Ships dare not venture to trade with them." Descriptions of the
Solorese using goat bone arrowheads can be found in Robert H. Barnes's
"Lamakera, Solor: Ethnohistory of a Muslim Whaling Village of Eastern
Indonesia," *Anthropos* 90, nos. 4–6 (1995): 497–509.

p. 86 **a Dutch official noted that the interior of Lembata had still not been visited
by Europeans...**I have relied on Barnes's *Sea Hunters of Indonesia* for the
history of how Christianity arrived in Lamalera and for descriptions of
Dutch bureaucratic communication about Lembata. I also referred to Robert
H. Barnes's "A Catholic Mission and the Purification of Culture: Experiences in an Indonesian Community," *Journal of the Anthropological Society of
Oxford* 23, no. 2 (1992): 169–80.

p. 86 **Though five centuries earlier hunter-gatherers had occupied the entirety
of Australia...** *The Cambridge Encyclopedia of Hunters and Gatherers,* introduction, 2.

p. 86 **7,100 languages remained...**Gary F. Smith and Charles D. Fennig, eds.,
Ethnologue: Languages of the World.

p. 86 **the global population will communicate mostly in English, Mandarin Chinese, and Spanish...**Michael Krauss, "The World's Languages in Crisis,"
Language 68, no. 1 (1992): 4–10.

p. 87 **two entire languages and their accompanying cultures...die every month...**
David Crystal in the *Cambridge Encyclopedia of Language* (Cambridge, UK:
Cambridge University Press, 1987), 287.

Chapter 4: The Cleansing of Harmful Language

p. 107 **The Hariona clan arrived in Lamalera several generations after Korohama...**
The exact reasons the Harionas left Lamakera, their original village, are murky,
even to clan members. Krispin told me that they fled because their neighbors
were denying them hibiscus bark to weave their ropes, though he also suggested
that his ancestors may have used the conflict over the ropes to symbolize a more
serious problem, just as the Lamalerans camouflaged the sexual indiscretion at

Labala with the story of the baby chicken killed by the pestle. Ultimately, the Hariona ancestors successfully concealed the details of what truly drove them from Lamakera—or perhaps the Hariona clan has decided to keep the true story to themselves.

p. 109 **the right side of the boat shed...** The Lamalerans orient themselves toward the sea, so in the nomenclature of their cardinal directions west is right.

p. 110 **the world's most populous Islamic nation...** Indonesia is the largest Muslim country in the world. About 88 percent of its 250 million inhabitants are Muslim and 10 percent are Christian. Badan Pusat Statistik, 2010 Indonesian Census, http://sp2010.bps.go.id.

p. 110 **the country's overpopulated core...** Java is one of the most overpopulated places on earth, with 150 million or so inhabitants crammed onto an island the size of Louisiana. Comparatively, Nusa Tenggara Timor, the province of the Lamalerans, which is many times bigger, has only 5 million inhabitants, of which only 16 percent live in cities. Badan Pusat Statistik, 2010 Indonesian Census.

p. 111 **Lamalerans use a whole different vocabulary...** Robert H. Barnes in *Sea Hunters of Indonesia* deals with this subject at fascinating length in the "Prohibitions" section of chapter 15 (page 295).

p. 116 **This was the foundational Lamaleran ritual: the division of the umā...** The division of the umā is a complex subject that I have been only able to gloss in this book. For those interested in further details, I suggest Michael S. Alvard's work: "Carcass Ownership and Meat Distribution by Big-Game Cooperative Hunters," *Research in Economic Anthropology* 21 (2002): 99–132; "Rousseau's Whale Hunt? Coordination Among Big-Game Hunters" (written with David A. Nolin); and "The Adaptive Nature of Culture," *Evolutionary Anthropology* 12, no. 3 (2003): 136–49. Also see Barnes's description in chapter 10 of *Sea Hunters of Indonesia*. It's also worth consulting Gregorious Keraf's *Morfologi Dialek Lamalera* (Jakarta: University of Indonesia dissertation, 1978) and Ambrosius Oleonâ's *Masyarakat Nelayan Lamalera dan Tradisi Penagkapan Ikan Paus* directly to read how native Lamalerans interpret the division of the shares, though both describe practices they saw in their childhood after decades of living in Indonesian cities. As Barnes notes, every person who has written about the division of prey in Lamalera has come to similar conclusions for general share distributions, though they have differed in the details.

p. 117 **that were most often called the běfānā...** Like the umā, the běfānā is an exceptionally complicated subject that I have been only able to gloss in the main portion of the text. The most in-depth work on the běfānā is by anthropologist David Nolin, who spent months tracking how meat was spread among the community, and was able to quantify how it embodied reciprocal altruism. See "Food-Sharing Networks in Lamalera, Indonesia: Status, Sharing, and Signaling," *Evolution and Human Behavior* 33, no. 4 (2012): 334–45; "Kin Preference and Partner Choice: Patrilineal Descent and Biological Kinship in Lamaleran Cooperative Relationships," *Human Nature* 22, nos. 1–2 (2011): 156–76; and "Food-Sharing Networks in Lamalera, Indonesia: Reciprocity, Kinship, and Distance," *Human Nature* 21, no. 3 (2010): 243–68.

When discussing the bĕfãnã it is important to distinguish the *bĕfãnã bela* and *bĕfãnã ķéni,* which Barnes describes as portions of the whale reserved for a small circle of relatives of the clan, and the bĕfãnã, which are gifts of meat shared widely outside the clan. In my writing about the bĕfãnã, I have understood it as Nolin describes it in "Food-Sharing Networks in Lamalera, Indonesia," as any meat to be shared out among the wider community.

p. 117 **probably around 90 percent of the village had received whale meat...** David Nolin, personal communication, June 9, 2017.

p. 118 **anthropologists asked the Lamalerans to participate in an experiment called the Ultimatum Game...** Interestingly, researchers found that players from industrial countries usually kept 55 to 60 percent of the money for themselves. In contrast, 63 percent of Lamaleran players split the pot evenly, while the rest of the Lamalerans actually gave away as much money as modern citizens usually kept for themselves, offering on average 58 percent of the pot. Michael S. Alvard, "The Ultimatum Game, Fairness, and Cooperation Among Big Game Hunters," chapter 14 in *Foundations of Human Sociality,* ed. J. Henrich, R. Boyd, S. Bowles, C. Camerer, E. Fehr, and H. Gintis (Oxford: Oxford University Press, 2004), 413–35. Also see Joseph Henrich et al., "'Economic Man' in Cross-Cultural Perspective: Behavioral Experiments in 15 Small-Scale Societies," *Behavioral and Brain Sciences* 28 (2005): 795–855.

p. 118 **Researchers have calculated that an average-sized sperm whale yields...** The original number is from "Traditional Whaling Culture and Social Change in Lamalera, Indonesia: An Analysis of the Catch Record of Whaling 1994–2010" by Tomoko Egami and Kotaro Kojima, in *Anthropological Studies of Whaling,* ed. N. Kishigami, H. Hamaguchi, and J. M. Savelle (Osaka, Japan: National Museum of Ethnology, 2013), 169. David Nolin also ran his own calculations for me, which resulted in similar numbers (personal communication, January 17, 2018). The average amount of meat taken from a whale can be found in table 2 of "Rousseau's Whale Hunt? Coordination Among Big-Game Hunters" by Michael S. Alvard and David A. Nolin.

Notes

Chapter 5: This, My Son, Is How You Kill a Whale

p. 121 **This, My Son, Is How You Kill a Whale...** A segment about Lamalera in the BBC's *Human Planet* documentary (season 1, episode 2, "Oceans: Into the Blue," BBC, 2011) purports to tell the story of how Ben spears his first whale. However, it is fabricated, with filmed footage of Ben intercut with footage of a different hunt so that it appears he is the one who spears it, when actually he did no such thing. Ben explained to me that the documentary team had asked him to stage certain scenes, but that he had had no knowledge of how they had cut the film together afterwards. When I contacted the BBC, the company issued the following statement, "On review, the BBC does not consider that the portrayal of a Lamaleran whale hunter named Benjamin [*sic*] Blikololong, shown supposedly harpooning a whale, is accurate." They subsequently withdrew the entire *Human Planet* series from distribution for a full editorial review, an event that was widely covered in the British press, as similar fabulations had previously been exposed in other segments of the show (Press Association, "BBC Shelves Human Planet over Whale Hunting Breach," *The Guardian,* April 26, 2018).

p. 136 **Oa has a simple repetitious structure...** This also applies to its modern refinement, the dolo dance.

p. 139 **he slowed *Kanibal* so that its pace was just a little faster than that of the hidden whale...** Across the centuries and the world, whalers from Nantucket to Lamalera have employed this trick and rule of thumb to track diving whales.

p. 148 **The average Indonesian male died at about sixty-seven...** World Bank, "Life Expectancy at Birth, Male (Years)," https://data.worldbank.org/indicator/SP.DYN.LE00.MA.IN.

p. 151 **the intellect of sperm whales...** The most definitive book on sperm whales is Hal Whitehead's *Sperm Whales: Social Evolution in the Ocean* (Chicago: University of Chicago Press, 2003). More concise, less academic explanations can be found in Shane Gero, "The Lost Culture of Whales," *New York Times,* Opinion, October 8, 2016; James Nestor, "A Conversation with Whales," *New York Times,* Opinion, April 16, 2016; and Brandon Keim, "Whales Might Be as Much Like People as Apes Are," *WIRED,* Science, June 25, 2009.

Chapter 6: The Laughter

p. 161 **the women of southern Lembata had been regularly meeting in the same palm grove to barter...** In telling the origin story of the Wulandoni Market, I have drawn from Jacobus Belida Blikololong's unpublished history *Sejarah Pasar Barter Wulandoni.* Blikololong was able not just to draw on the oral history

335

of his people but actually to travel to Pantar in 2013 to interview the residents there about their memories of the events, which corroborated the Lamaleran history. In addition, the people of Pantar are much better genealogists than the Lamalerans, and some village elders were able to recite all six of the intervening generations between the event and the present day, which led Blikololong to conclude the event likely happened around 1830, which is consistent with other stories of it occurring around the dawn of the nineteenth century. During his trip to Pantar, Jacobus was even able to locate the bones of the fallen Lamaleran warrior when he found a tomb of stacked stones in the distinctive Lamaleran style at the edge of the jungle where the stories said Dato had landed. Jacobus then returned the remains with great ceremony to their Spirit House. This incident is often talked about in the tribe as proof of how the stories of the Ancestors are true. Robert H. Barnes in *Sea Hunters of Indonesia* also provides a shorter version of this history.

p. 161 **challenged the Lamalerans to send forth a champion for a duel...** Whether the duel was fought over the ownership of the whale is unclear. It may have been just to establish the dominance of one tribe over the other. At the time, there was a widespread tradition in the Solor Archipelago that whenever two tribes met, a duel with machetes had to be fought to honor Lera Wulan.

The tradition of dueling also played an important role in Islam's entrance into the Solor Archipelago. Jacobus Belida Blikololong has recounted to me stories that Islam spread throughout the islands when Muslim champions forced losing tribes to convert.

p. 164 **the conversion rate had been stable for centuries...** This is a curious phenomenon, as one would think market forces would drive prices up or down. However, the Lamalerans I have spoken to are very insistent that the price of a munga has not changed in living memory, and the prices listed by Barnes and other anthropologists through the years have not changed as well. Lamaleran women will sometimes go to other parts of the island or even off-island to get a better exchange rate, but the rates in Wulandoni remain firmly fixed by tradition.

p. 165 **Animists have had to label themselves...** Indonesia's tribes have long clashed with the central government, from the forced relocations of the Mentawai islanders in the 1970s (Cain Nunns, "Life on the Mentawai Islands: Displaced, Robbed, and Washed Away," *The Guardian,* November 16, 2010) to the contemporary coerced conversions to Islam of peoples like the Orang Rimba (Rebecca Henschke, "Indonesia's Orang Rimba: Forced to Renounce Their Faith," *BBC News,* November 17, 2017).

p. 167 **the Luki lived in Pantai Harapan...** This village is today referred to as both Pantai Harapan, its Indonesian name, and Luki, its Lamaholot name.

p. 167 **Enmity was not new between the Nualela and Luki tribes…** A full history of the tribes' complicated, centuries-long relationship can be found in Barnes's "Construction Sacrifice, Kidnapping, and Head-Hunting Rumors on Flores and Elsewhere in Indonesia" and *Sea Hunters of Indonesia*, especially pages 8, 378, and 384. Jacobus Belida Blikololong also gives a version of this history in his unpublished history of Wulandoni, *Sejarah Pasar Barter Wulandoni.*

p. 170 **those few policemen were not enough to control the scores of Lamalerans…** Ironically, the only police station in southern Lembata is in Wulandoni, but its three staff were conspicuously absent during the riot. Some people would later whisper that the Muslim policemen had abetted it.

Chapter 7: The Way of the Lamafa

p. 176 **The Lamalerans rejected some proposed modernizations…** Robert H. Barnes provides an overview of these events in his report for the International Work Group for Indigenous Affairs in *Whaling off Lembata: The Effects of a Development Project on an Indonesian Community* (Copenhagen, 1984).

p. 177 **with massive drift nets whose five-inch weave…** Drift-net inch sizes refer to the width of the weave of their netting; larger weaves are able to handle bigger fish but let smaller fish through.

p. 180 **an improved ability to hold their breath while spearfishing…** Erika Schagatay, Angelica Lodin-Sundström, and Erik Abrahamsson, "Underwater Working Times in Two Groups of Traditional Apnea Divers in Asia: The Ama and the Bajau," *Journal of the South Pacific Underwater Medicine Society* 41, no. 1 (2011): 27–30; Megan Lane, "What Freediving Does to the Body," *BBC*, Science and Environment, January 12, 2011; and Carl Zimmer, "Bodies Remolded for a Life at Sea," *New York Times,* April 19, 2018.

p. 181 **the most lucrative fishing industry in the world…** Valuations are from the PEW Charitable Trust's 2016 report "Netting Billions: A Global Valuation of Tuna," http://www.pewtrusts.org/en/research-and-analysis/reports/2016/05/netting-billions-a-global-valuation-of-tuna.

p. 181 **But as ocean resources closer to home have become depleted…** For an overview of the embattled health of global marine ecosystems and fisheries, see Callum Roberts's *The Ocean of Life* (New York: Viking, 2012). Also see *Four Fish: The Future of the Last Wild Food* by Paul Greenberg (New York: Penguin, 2010).

p. 181 **the earth's most valuable remaining tuna fishery…** PEW Charitable Trust, "Netting Billions: A Global Valuation of Tuna."

p. 181 **having already destroyed the atolls between their home and Lembata en route…** In 2011, I spent nine months living on the Indonesian island of

Sumbawa, during which I became friendly with a number of these fishermen and heard their stories of raiding Flores and the Solor Archipelago. I even spent a week at sea with a crew of spearfishermen, who used scuba equipment improvised out of industrial tire pumps to clean out coral beds. Though the men I accompanied did not use dynamite, while with them I saw several dynamite fishers at work.

p. 182 **by as much as 87 percent, according to some estimates...** The Lamalerans do not keep as careful catch records for rays as they do for sperm whales, so determining an exact count is impossible. However, the hunting results of the Lamakerans, another harpoon-hunting tribe that shares a fishery with the Lamalerans, has been catalogued. In 2001, the Lamakerans caught 1,500 rays of all types. In 2014, they landed 200, a decline of 87 percent. Elsewhere in Indonesia, manta ray populations had declined by as much as 94 percent, and worldwide their population has been crashing, as their gills are sought for use in Chinese medicine and longlines snag them as tuna bycatch. Sarah A. Lewis et al., "Assessing Indonesian Manta and Devil Ray Populations Through Historical Landings and Fishing Community Interviews," *PeerJ Preprints* 6 (2015): e1334v1. Also see Claire Maldarelli, "In Indonesia, Authorities Stop Sale of Endangered Manta Rays," *New York Times,* September 30, 2014.

p. 183 **high-grade sushi meat could sell for thousands of dollars a pound...** Associated Press, "A Bluefin Tuna Sells for Record $1.76M in Tokyo," *USA Today,* January 4, 2013, https://www.usatoday.com/story/news/world/2013/01/04/bluefin-tuna-tokyo-sushi/1810557/.

p. 188 **In Lamaleran, there are specific words for describing everything...** See the glossary for further notes on Lamaleran spellings.

p. 189 **These ultra-specific words allowed Jon...** Indigenous peoples around the world have developed similarly unique language to describe their singular circumstances. Sami reindeer herders have more than a thousand words for different types of deer, including a word that signifies a bull reindeer with a single testicle. David Robson, "There Really Are 50 Eskimo Words for 'Snow,'" *Washington Post,* January 14, 2013. Just miles away from Lembata, a mountain tribe has separate verbs for each type of fruit they pick, saying not "I pick the apple" but "I apple" (interview with Hanna Fricke, May 9, 2016).

Chapter 8: A New Year

p. 195 **For the Lamalerans, time is a spiral...** The fluid nature of time in Lamalera is the subject of much of Anita Lundberg's work with the tribe, especially "Time Travels in Whaling Boats," *Journal of Social Archaeology* 3, no. 3 (2003): 312–33; and "Being Lost at Sea: Ontology, Epistemology, and a Whale Hunt," *Ethnography* 2, no. 4 (2001): 533–56.

Notes

Chapter 9: *Nekat*

p. 217 **drawn first by a documentary...** Most notably: a documentary was made with Robert Barnes's help in the late 1980s, the tribe was featured in a short segment in the BBC's *Human Planet* series in 2011, and then it starred again in an hour-long BBC documentary, *Hunters of the South Seas,* in 2015.

p. 217 **around two hundred foreign backpackers a year...** My estimate of around two hundred independent tourists a year is drawn from records kept by the homestays, data provided me by the Ministry of Tourism, a log I kept of each tourist I saw while in Lamalera, and interviews with officials from the Ministry of Tourism, including Lembata's head of the Office of Tourism, Antonius Lianurat (May 9, 2016). However, determining the exact number of independent tourists who visit Lamalera annually is tricky, as the records kept by the Indonesian government and homestay owners are incomplete—one homestay owner even burned some of his records during a dispute with the Ministry of Tourism—and the government, by its own admission, is not able to track everyone who arrives in the remote region.

p. 217 **a much larger number of Indonesian visitors...** It is difficult to determine how many Indonesian visitors arrive in Lamalera on tours because the government keeps data only of domestic tourists to all of Lembata, not individual locations on the island. In 2014, the Ministry of Tourism recorded 3,928 Indonesian tourists to Lembata, about half of whom were probably going to a popular harvest festival held by another tribe and the other half of whom may have visited Lamalera or other destinations.

Chapter 11: In the Middle of the Typhoon of Life

p. 250 **the Indonesian branch of the World Wildlife Fund (WWF)...** Julien Fudge, *The Solor and Alor Islands—Survey Results: 26 July to 11 August 2007,* report for WWF Indonesia, September 2007.

p. 251 **to have the entire region designated a marine national park...** In September 2001 and May 2002 the World Wildlife Fund (WWF) and the Nature Conservancy (TNC) funded expeditions to the Savu Sea to chart the biodiversity in the area for the first time, especially its cetacean populations. Over annual expeditions during the next three years, WWF and TNC collected the scientific data needed to argue for such a reserve and recruited several other international NGOs to aid their efforts, including Photovoices International, an organization that helps indigenous peoples tell their own stories by providing them with cameras and photography training. These efforts resulted in a number of reports, including *The Solor and Alor Islands—Expedition Results and Data Collected During 2 Reconnaissance Trips: 9–12 September, 2001, and*

7–19 May, 2002, compiled by Lida Pet-Soede, WWF Wallacea Bioregional Program, for WWF Indonesia and the Nature Conservancy; and *Alo Rapid Ecological Assessment—Cetacean Component: Visual and Acoustic Cetecean Surveys and Evaluation of Traditional Whaling Practices, Fisheries Interactions, and Nature-Based Tourism Potential, October 2001 and May 2002 Survey Periods* by Benjamin Kahn, for WWF Indonesia and the Nature Conservancy. Also see Benjamin Kahn's *Indonesia Oceanic Cetacean Program Activity Report,* the Nature Conservancy, May 2004; *Indonesia Oceanic Cetacean Program Activity Report: April–June 2005* (Cairns: Apex Environmental, 2005); and *Solor-Alor Visual and Acoustic Cetacean Surveys,* the Nature Conservancy SE Asia Center for Marine Protected Areas (Cairns: Apex Environmental, 2003).

p. 251 **the tribe feared that WWF also sought to end the hunt...** Extensive interviews with Lamalerans. Also, Eugenis Moa, "Tanpa Kotekelema, Lamalera Akan Mati," *Pos Kupang,* May 26, 2007.

p. 251 **it wanted only to help the Lamalerans establish tuna fishing and ecotourism businesses...** Interview with Zakarias Atapada, WWF representative to Lamalera during this time period, August 29, 2017, and correspondence with WWF representatives, January 2018.

p. 251 **WWF held a meeting with the Lamalerans...** The conflict between WWF and Lamalera was widely covered in the Indonesian newsmedia: Lorensius Molan, "Konservasi Laut Sawu Dan Kegusaran Nelyan Lamalera," *Antara Sumber,* March 26, 2009; "Masyarakat Lamalera Tolak Konservasi Paus," *Kompas,* March 23, 2009; "Laut Sawu Sebagai Kawasan Konservasi," *Pos Kupang,* May 3, 2009; Pewarta, "Tiap Tahun, Nelayan Lamalera Tangkap 20 Ikan Paus," *Antara,* March 23, 2009; and "Nelayan Lamalera Tidak Dilarang Tangkap Paos," *Antara,* June 29, 2009. (Many Indonesian newspaper articles are not credited to their writers, and some Indonesians only have single names, which accounts for the unusual formatting of some citations.)

The report put out by the Working Group Conservation for People, an indigenous rights activist group, was highly critical of the international NGOs and Indonesian government, accusing them of discrimination and even violating the human right to self-determination: Ruddy Gustave and Ahfi Wahyu Hidayat, *Politik Konservasi Laut Sawu: Antara Menyelamatkan Ekologi Laut dan Harapan Orang Kalah* (Denpasar, Indonesia: Working Group Conservation for People, 2009). I had the opportunity to interview Ruddy Gustave several times. I was also able to interview Benjamin Kahn on several occasions.

p. 251 **the marine reserve would not limit the Lamalerans' hunting...** WWF also released a statement to this effect: *WWF Position Statement, 63rd International Whaling Commission (IWC) Meeting, Jersey, 11–14 July, 2011.*

p. 251 **WWF dispatched a PR team to Lamalera...** "Nelayan Lamalera Hadang Tim WWF," *Aktualita NTT,* April 2, 2009.

p. 251 **its boundaries detoured around Lamalera...** "Lembata Tak Masuk Konservasi Laut Sawu," *Spirit NTT,* August 22, 2009. Also see Kunto Wibisono, "Lamalera Tidak Masuk Kawasan Konservasi TNLS," *Antara,* May 24, 2009.

p. 252 **"This is what WWF is doing in the region!"...** For years, WWF officials played down the clash as a tragic misunderstanding and argued that it had been caused by a small British NGO that had pushed a plan for whale watching to replace whaling, which the Lamalerans had mistakenly attributed to WWF. However, reports commissioned by WWF years earlier had explored this possibility; as one 2002 report concluded, "A shift from traditional whale hunting to community-based whale watching should be seriously considered" (*The Solor and Alor Islands—Expedition Results and Data Collected During 2 Reconnaissance Trips: 9–12 September, 2001, and 7–19 May, 2002,* compiled by Lida Pet-Soede, 18–20). When I confronted WWF Indonesia with its internal reports and communications, a spokeswoman acknowledged that the NGO had not been forthright with the Lamalerans and that in offering to help them set up ecotourism and tuna fishing businesses, it was trying to get the tribe to harpoon hunt less (correspondence with Dewi Satriani, communications manager, WWF Indonesia, January 23, 2018).

p. 253 **It would have been to everyone's profit...** David Nolin, an anthropologist who was living with the tribe at the time and watched the conflict unfold, felt similarly. He wrote to me, "If [WWF] had approached [the Lamalerans] with a message of 'Lamaleran waters for Lamaleran fishermen,' then they would have had much greater success. Instead their 'socialization' approach involved showing up and telling people about what was essentially considered a done-deal, rather than listening and incorporating local concerns."

p. 253 **"The world's most vulnerable people are paying the price for today's conservation"...** John Vidal, "The Tribes Paying the Brutal Price for Conservation," *The Guardian,* August 28, 2016.

p. 253 **For the Lamalerans, the very idea of conservation is foreign...** An example of this belief can be found in an interview with Bona Beding in "In Lamalera, an Ancient Whale Hunting Tradition Continues" by Anastasia Ika, *Wall Street Journal,* November 5, 2014.

While helping a producer for the BBC documentary series *Hunters of the South Seas* in 2014, I translated a conversation that consisted of the Englishman trying to get the whaler to admit the merits of conservation by posing an escalating series of situations in which it would be wrong to take a whale: first, starting with a pregnant whale, then continuing to if the tribe had already taken dozens of whales that year, and then supposing if the whale was the last one on earth. The lamafa confidently answered that he would always take the whale because they were the Gifts of the Ancestors and could never disappear from the earth—unless the Ancestors were displeased. This conversation highlighted for me the fundamental disconnect between the viewpoint of most conservationists and many older Lamalerans.

Some younger Lamalerans, however, have a more scientific view of conservation and agree about the dangers of overfishing.

p. 254 **analyses by the World Bank and others...** Claudia Sobrevila, *The Role of Indigenous Peoples in Biodiversity Conservation: The Natural but Often Forgotten Partners* (Washington, DC: World Bank, 2008). Also see Jason Clay, Janis Alcorn, and John Butler, *An Analytical Study for the World Bank's Forestry Policy Implementation Review and Strategy Development Framework* (Washington, DC: World Bank, 2000).

p. 262 **traditional people feel more fulfilled than citizens of industrialized nations...** For centuries, Western societies mostly viewed life in foraging societies as Thomas Hobbes described it: "poor, nasty, brutish, and short." But by the mid-1960s, an abundance of anthropological fieldwork was beginning to show that life was better among such people than expected—in fact, it was so good that some anthropologists even declared them "the original affluent society," saying they led more spiritually fulfilling lives while only working four or five hours a day. Marshall Sahlins, "Notes on the Original Affluent Society," in *Man the Hunter,* ed. R. Lee and I. DeVore (Chicago: Aldine Publishing, 1968); and Marshall Sahlins, *Stone Age Economics* (Chicago: Aldine Publishing, 1972). Since then, scholars have nuanced their enthusiasm, suggesting that hunter-gatherers may work harder than original reports suggested, though still much less than citizens of advanced nations. David Kaplan, "The Darker Side of the 'Original Affluent Society,'" *Journal of Anthropological Research* 56, no. 3 (2000): 301–24. But the assertion that humans have in many ways had more difficult lives ever since abandoning their hunter-gatherer lifestyles is, among scholars, no longer very controversial. John Lanchester, "How Civilization Started: Was It Even a Good Idea?," *New Yorker* (print edition), September 18, 2017.

Drawing on decades of research from a variety of disciplines, Jared Diamond offers a comprehensive overview of the differences between traditional and advanced societies in *The World Until Yesterday: What Can We Learn from Traditional Societies?* (New York: Viking, 2012). He also offers a list of lessons that advanced societies could learn from traditional societies, such as emulating the tighter social bonds that people from traditional societies usually enjoy, while reminding citizens of industrial nations that there are many material advantages to a modern lifestyle. Sebastian Junger examines the mental-health benefits that tribal life conveys to its participants, especially veterans returning from war, in *Tribe: On Homecoming and Belonging* (New York: Twelve, 2016).

p. 262 **hunter-gatherers work about twenty hours a week...** This estimate is low for the Lamalerans during the hunting season, but correct for other months, when a man might fish three days a week and then spend the remaining days in light labor, like mending nets.

Chapter 12: The New *Kéna Pukā*

p. 274 **the Lamalerans are the last known people to use [lashed-lug boatbuilding techniques] on a large scale...** I had the good fortune of interviewing anthropologist Daniel Dwyer in Lamalera (May 1, 2015), where he showed me the principles of téna construction in person and informed me that these were the last regularly made lashed-lug boats of their type in the world. *The Lashed-Lug Boats of the Eastern Archipelagos* by G. Adrian Horridge remains the definitive resource on these types of boats (Greenwich, UK: National Maritime Museum, 1982). Also see Adrian Horridge, *The Prahu: Traditional Sailing Boats of Indonesia* (Oxford: Oxford University Press, 1986). Robert Barnes in *Sea Hunters of Indonesia* provides a cogent overview as well (page 204).

p. 281 **their brains had come to work differently than his own...** Such a gargantuan question is obviously impossible to tackle in this short space. However, researchers have found that sustained exposure to computer, TV, and cell phone screens does affect the brains of young people (Jon Hamilton, "Heavy Screen Time Rewires Young Brains, for Better and Worse," NPR.com, November 19, 2016), that citizens of wealthy advanced nations are more likely to suffer from PTSD and depression (Sarah Boseley, "PTSD More Likely to Afflict People in Affluent Societies, Scientists Say," *The Guardian*, July 27, 2016), and that hunter-gatherers are much more attuned to aspects of the natural world, both physiologically, perhaps because they have evolved more sensitive noses and other organs in the forest, and culturally, with advantages like specialized languages (Joanna Klein, "They Hunt. They Gather. They're Very Good at Talking About Smells," *New York Times*, January 19, 2018). Ultimately, a growing body of evidence suggests that there are fundamental differences between people who live as humanity's ancestors did and those who live under the pressures of an industrialized society.

Chapter 13: Against the Leviathan

p. 291 **The governor... was set to announce a drive to bring more tourists to Lamalera...** "East Nusa Tenggara to Promote Traditional Whaling," *Tempo*, May 5, 2016. Though in 2016, the number of tourists visiting Lamalera would actually slightly decline.

p. 298 **all of which are well documented in scientific literature…**See the note for chapter 11 discussing the comparative advantages and disadvantages of modern and foraging life.

p. 303 **swaths of the 370 million indigenous people worldwide have emerged worse off…**UN Department of Economic and Social Affairs, *The State of the World's Indigenous Peoples.*

p. 304 **must empower them to make their own choices…**In practice, this means that governments should recognize indigenous peoples as a special class of citizens and offer them extra support. Corporations should not exploit indigenous groups or their environments. NGOs, like conservation groups, should balance their goals with respecting locals' rights to continue their traditions. And individuals the world over can help by pressuring the offending governments or organizations and supporting NGOs that fight for indigenous rights.

Epilogue

p. 313 **several readings of the relevant Indonesian laws…**A good summary of the legal complications can be found in "Marine Mammals in the Savu Sea (Indonesia): Indigenous Knowledge, Threat Analysis, and Management Options" by Putu Liza Kusuma Mustika (master's thesis, School of Tropical Environment Studies and Geography, James Cook University, August 2006). Mustika finds that Lamaleran whaling is "subsistence whaling according to the IWC (International Whaling Commission) definition" (page 183) and that under Indonesian law "traditional hunting is allowed as long as it" is "conducted sustainably" (page 175), though he is equivocal about the legality of the Lamalerans hunting dolphins. Also see Ruddy Gustave and Ahfi Wahyu Hidayat, *Politik Konservasi Laut Sawu: Antara Menyelamatkan Ekologi Laut dan Harapan Orang Kalah;* and Polite Dyspriani, *Traditional Fishing Rights: Analysis of State Practice* (New York: Division for Ocean Affairs and the Law of the Sea, Office of Legal Affairs, United Nations, 2011).

p. 313 **the Lamalerans' poaching of manta rays was not…**Claire Maldarelli, "In Indonesia, Authorities Stop Sale of Endangered Manta Ray Parts," *New York Times,* September 30, 2014.

p. 313 **The goal of the arrest…**"Orang Lamalera Diminta Berhenti Tangkap Paus dan Pari," *Bali News Network,* November 24, 2016.

p. 313 **the Nature Conservancy was publicly arguing…**Jon Emont, "A Whaling Way of Life Under Threat," *New York Times,* August 3, 2017; and interviews and correspondence with Glaudy Perdanahardja and Yusuf Fajariyanto of the Nature Conservancy, fall 2017 and summer 2018.

GLOSSARY

Spelling Lamaleran words is a complicated task as there is no standard dictionary of the language. When rendering Lamaleran words, I relied on Gregorious Keraf's *Morfologi Dialek Lamalera* (Jakarta: University of Indonesia dissertation, 1978), Peter D. Bataona's *Kamus Istilah Lamalera — Inggris* (Jakarta: PT. Ikrar Mandiriabadi, 2008), and Robert H. Barnes's *Sea Hunters of Indonesia* (Oxford: Oxford University Press, 1996). But spellings differ across these sources: for example, the three works render "téna" at different points "tena," "téna," and "ténā." And Lamalerans themselves are loose with spelling: Jon, for one, freely writes his name as "Yohanez" and "Yohanes."

Accordingly, I have most often followed Barnes's spellings as the best representation of how a native English speaker and professional anthropologist would portray a word, turning next to Keraf's and Bataona's grammars. But there are many exceptions to this rule. The Lamalerans do not spell their own names with accents, and so I have mostly adopted their spellings rather than the formally accented ones used by Barnes for clan and personal names. Barnes worked in Lamalera almost three decades before me, and his spellings and phrasing have occasionally struck me as old-fashioned, so in several cases I have updated them. For words that had not previously been recorded, I tried to render them according to Barnes's system of accents, while acknowledging I am not a professional linguist.

Ata mola: A Lamaleran shipwright.

Auto: The buses that transport Lamalerans between the village and Lewoleba, often converted dump trucks.

Baleo: The call that summons Lamalerans onshore to hunt sperm whales.

Běfānā: Gifts of whale meat, drawn from an individual's umā portion, and the physical embodiment of the Ancestors' directive for the Lamalerans to share their good fortune with each other.

Bělelā: Oceanic manta ray, *Mantis birostris.*

Bereung alep: The secondary harpooner of a téna or jonson, literally translated as "the lamafa's friend."

Boli Sapang: The téna of the Hariona clan, which Jon usually serves on.

Bōu: Golden-brown ray, *Mobula kuhlii.*

Demo Sapang: The téna of Ignatius's branch of the Blikololong clan.

Dolo: A traditional Lamaleran dance, still performed at festivals and parties.

Dpa: A Lamaleran unit of measurement, from the center of a person's chest to the tip of his outstretched arm, used before metric measurements were introduced and still sometimes employed.

Duri: A Lamaleran flensing knife, forged by blacksmiths in the tribe and measuring about two feet long.

Hâmmâlollo: The harpooner's platform, a bamboo platform that juts out over the prow of a téna.

Ige Gerek: The animist Calling of the Whales ceremony performed by the Lords of the Land at the end of April every year to summon the whales.

Jonson: A new type of small Lamaleran boat powered by an outboard engine.

Kāfé kotekĕlema: The great harpoon, used for spearing sperm whales.

Kebako Pukā: The original téna in which the Lamalerans fled their ancestral home after it was destroyed by a tsunami. All modern téna are still made according to its blueprint.

Kefela: The Lamaleran term for mountain dwellers, sometimes used as an insult among the tribe.

Kélik: The lamafa's portion of a catch that he cannot eat but must give away or be cursed.

Kéna Pukā: The téna of the Mikulangu Bediona clan, Frans's clan.

Kotekĕlema: A sperm whale, also known as the Gift of the Ancestors or to science as *Physeter macrocephalus.*

Labalekang: The name of the volcano behind Lamalera. Also known by the more formal name of Ile Labalekang.

Lamafa: The lead harpooner of a téna or jonson.

Glossary

Léfa: The Season of the Open Sea, May through September, when the monsoon has ended, sperm whales congregate near Lamalera, and the good weather encourages hunting. Much of the Lamalerans' annual take of sperm whales occurs then, though they also opportunistically hunt at other times.

Leka: The lifetime right for a lamafa to lead a ship, formalized by him storing his harpoons on it.

Lika Telo: The "Big Three" clans, the direct descendants of Korohama's sons. They are the aristocrats of Lamaleran society, and their chiefs perform many important civil and traditional functions.

Lords of the Land: Leaders of the Wujon clan, the indigenous inhabitants of Lamalera who still reputedly possess shamanistic powers, including the ability to summon the sperm whales.

Materos: General crewmen on a whaling ship, from rowers to bailers.

Misa Arwah: The Catholic mass that follows Ige Gerek.

Mōku: Whiptail devil ray, *Mobula diabolus.*

Munga: A unit of six that is the foundation of Lamaleran counting and the basic unit of the barter economy.

Nuba Nara: The sacred stones that are the locus of the power of the Lords of the Land.

Oa: A now extinct Lamaleran dance that was once performed by courting youth every Saturday night in the village square.

Sirih pinang: A combination of sirih peppers, pinang nuts, a type of areca (a.k.a. betel) nut, and powdered coral, which when chewed produces a mild tobacco-like high, and which is ubiquitous among Lamaleran women. Proferring it to guests is also a sign of traditional hospitality in eastern Indonesia, and during these occasions it may also be chewed by men.

Talé tou, kemui tou, onā tou, mata tou: A saying of the Ancestors, meaning "One family, one heart, one action, one goal." It reminds the Lamalerans that the unity of the tribe is paramount.

Téna: A traditional large Lamaleran whaling ship.

Tobo Nama Fata: The Council on the Beach, held annually in advance of Ige Gerek, in which the Lamalerans set the rules for the coming year of hunting.

Tuak: Palm wine.

Umā: An individual's share of whale meat, granted for their work on a téna or membership in a clan. The foundational unit of ownership in Lamaleran society.

VJO: The jonson that Jon managed for Salés.

ABOUT THE AUTHOR

Doug Bock Clark is a writer whose articles have appeared or are forthcoming in the *New York Times Magazine, The Atlantic, National Geographic, GQ, WIRED, Rolling Stone, The New Republic,* the website of *The New Yorker,* and elsewhere. He won the 2017 Arthur L. Carter Journalism Institute Reporting Award, was a finalist for the 2016 Mirror Award, and has been awarded two Fulbright Fellowships, a grant from the Pulitzer Center on Crisis Reporting, and an 11th Hour Food and Farming Fellowship. Clark has been interviewed about his work on CNN, BBC, NPR, and ABC's *20/20.* He is a visiting scholar at New York University. His pictures are featured in this book and have also appeared in the *New York Times, The New Republic, WIRED, Men's Journal, ELLE, BuzzFeed,* and others.